Mothers OF THE REVOLUTION

The War Experiences of
Thirty Zimbabwean Women

Compiled and edited by
Irene Staunton

James Currey
London

Indiana University Press
Bloomington and Indianapolis

First published in Zimbabwe by Baobab Books 1990
This edition published 1991 in North America by
Indiana University Press, 601 North Morton Street,
Bloomington, Indiana 47404
and in Great Britain by
James Currey Ltd, 54B Thornhill Square, Islington, London N1 1BE

The paper used in this publication meets the minimum requirements
of American National Standard for Information Sciences--Permanence of Paper
for Printed Library Materials, ANSI Z39.48-1984.

Manufactured in the United States of America

British Library Cataloguing in Publication Data
Mothers of the revolution.
  1. Zimbabwe 2. Wars
  I. Staunton, Irene
  355.0218
  ISBN 0-85255-210-6

Library of Congress Cataloging-in-Publication Data
 Mothers of the revolution / compiled and edited by Irene Staunton.
        p.   cm.
  ISBN 0-253-35450-1. -- ISBN 0-253-28797-9 (paper)
  1. Zimbabwe--History--Chimurenga War, 1966-1980--Personal
  narratives. 2. Zimbabwe--history--Chimurenga War, 1966-1980--Women.
  3. Women--Zimbabwe--Biography. I. Staunton, Irene.
  DT2990.M69   1990
  968.91'04--dc20   91-9980

1 2 3 4 5 95 94 93 92 91

Cover design: Maviyane Pike
Mapwork: Judit Hargitai and Steve Murray

Contents

Acknowledgements

WE would like to thank all the women who participated in the project for receiving us with such warmth and for giving so generously of their time and their stories. We would particularly like to thank all those women who, for one reason or another, we were not able to include in this book: Mama Dube, Esther Khumalo, Mikirina Makanha, Linah Makiwa, Bertha Moyo, Jane Mpala, Fenny Mtongana, Kresenzia Muzenda, Molly Ncube, Mcondo Ngwenya, Melitha Nyathi, Emilia Ndlovu, Alice Sangarwe, Roni Sangarwe, Gremerina Zembiti.

We would also like to offer our thanks to the translators and co-ordinators on the project, without whom there would have been no book: Elizabeth Ndebele, Margaret Zingani, Rose Mazena, Mary Nyamangara, Betty Biri and Eileen Mutwira. Very special thanks is due to Margaret Zingani who tirelessly translated and transcribed the majority of the tapes from both Shona and Ndebele and who was a wonderfully supportive companion on many journeys.

We would also like to thank everyone who has shown their support and encouragement: in particular, Thandi Henson, Amos Kanyonga, Jeremiah Khabo, Mia Lewis, Mette Maast, Margaret Manyau, Eugenia Matthews, Langton Mavudzi, Joshua Mpofu, Revd Menson Mpofu, Ruvimbo Mujene, Edward Mutema, Connie Ndebele, Joshua Nyoni, Sethembiso Nyoni, William Nyamangara, Sita Ranchod, Elizabeth Rider, Silas Tarivingana; and Margaret Waller and June Webber who processed the photographs.

We would also like to acknowledge with gratitude the support of NORAD, whose initial support by way of funding the research component of the book made the whole project possible.

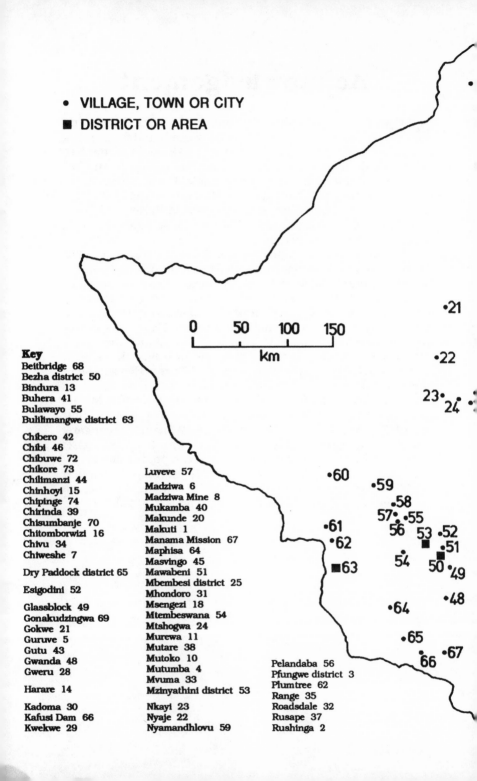

- VILLAGE, TOWN OR CITY
■ DISTRICT OR AREA

Key
Beitbridge 68
Bezha district 50
Bindura 13
Buhera 41
Bulawayo 55
Bulilimangwe district 63

Chibero 42
Chibi 46
Chibuwe 72
Chikore 73
Chilimanzi 44
Chinhoyi 15
Chipinge 74
Chirinda 39
Chisumbanje 70
Chitomborwizi 16
Chivu 34
Chiweshe 7

Dry Paddock district 65

Esigodini 52

Glassblock 49
Gonakudzingwa 69
Gokwe 21
Guruve 5
Gutu 43
Gwanda 48
Gweru 28

Harare 14

Kadoma 30
Kafusi Dam 66
Kwekwe 29

Luveve 57
Madziwa 6
Madziwa Mine 8
Mukamba 40
Makunde 20
Makuti 1
Manama Mission 67
Maphisa 64
Masvingo 45
Mawabeni 51
Mbembesi district 25
Mhondoro 31
Msengezi 18
Mtembeswana 54
Mtshogwa 24
Murewa 11
Mutare 38
Mutoko 10
Mutumba 4
Mvuma 33
Mzinyathini district 53

Nkayi 23
Nyaje 22
Nyamandhlovu 59

Pelandaba 56
Pfungwe district 3
Plumtree 62
Range 35
Roadsdale 32
Rusape 37
Rushinga 2

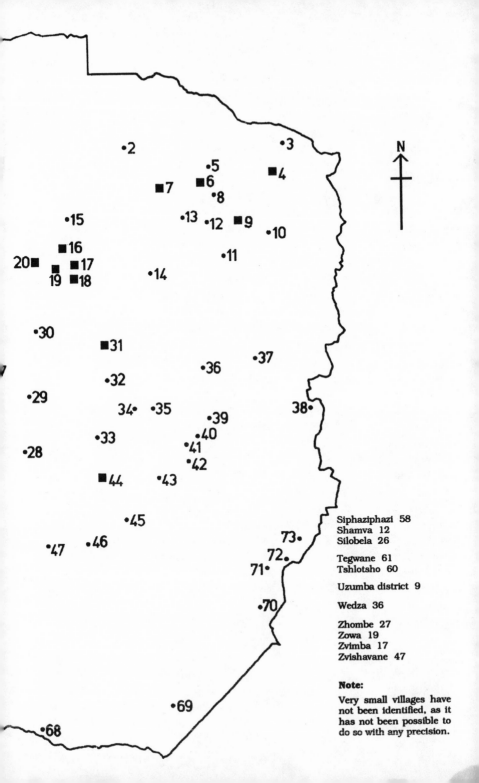

Siphaziphazi 58
Shamva 12
Silobela 26

Tegwane 61
Tshlotsho 60

Uzumba district 9

Wedza 36

Zhombe 27
Zowa 19
Zvimba 17
Zvishavane 47

Note:

Very small villages have
not been identified, as it
has not been possible to
do so with any precision.

Introduction

Mothers of the Revolution tells of the war experiences of thirty Zimbabwean women. Many people suffered and died during Zimbabwe's war of liberation and many accounts of that struggle have already been written. But the story of the women, the wives and the mothers who remained behind, has not yet been told.

These are their stories: stories that reveal courage, endurance, humour and wisdom. They are stories that celebrate the fortitude and strength of the mothers of the struggle.

The war visited different areas of the country at different times and with varying degrees of intensity. For some women, the war was with them for a year or two; for others it lasted much longer. Time was not something measured in weeks or months, but by the impact of violence or grief or need; and by the rhythms of the seasons or of motherhood.

Mothers of the Revolution, therefore, contains few dates. It is not a conventional history in which the women's words have been analysed, sifted or put into some other framework. Rather the book provides, in their own words, a context, a new perspective on the war, as it is remembered by women ten years after independence.

As Elizabeth Ndebele put it: "Time elapses, the mind accepts some terrible things and forgets others. Now we can talk and sometimes cry over what we went through . . . then, we could hardly, if ever, talk about such things."

Not unnaturally, several common preoccupations and themes emerge from these stories, such as fear. Fear for the lives of their children who had gone to join the struggle; fear for the survival of their homes and their children who had remained behind; fear of 'contacts' between the freedom fighters and the Rhodesian security forces; fear of the soldiers, fear of sell-outs. There is also, again and again, a remarkable sense of persistence and acceptance: acceptance of war, and the consequences of war, of situations over which they had little or no control, but which they continued to believe would, ultimately, bring a better life – freedom and independence for everyone.

These women, the mothers, were both victims and actors. Throughout the war, over and over again, they fed and protected the freedom fighters and they risked their lives to do so. This they know and it is a fact of which they are proud. "The men were around, but they only used to say, 'Hurry up [with the food] before the soldiers come and beat you up!' " They regarded the *vakomana* as their children, everybody's children, with needs which they as women, as mothers, had a responsibility to meet.

This is the underlying theme which emerges strongly from these interviews and which now needs to be asserted: "Without the women, the war could not have been won."

The idea for the book developed out of my belief that unless the stories of women, especially women in the rural areas, were recorded, they would not be heard within the larger context of Zimbabwe's history.

The women we spoke to were all contacted through people whom they knew and trusted, and who first asked them whether they would be willing to share their stories with us. We tried, in a comparatively short time, to cover as many different areas of the country as possible. We – Elizabeth Ndebele, Margaret Zingani and myself – singly or together, visited all the women in their own homes: journeys which sometimes became stories in themselves.

Wherever we went, everyone received us with great warmth and 'the mothers' showed an enormous willingness to share, even to unburden themselves, in order that the contribution made by women during the struggle for liberation might be heard.

The majority of the interviews were conducted in either Shona or Ndebele and then translated into English by Margaret Zingani. As far as possible we have tried to use the words the women themselves used.

We have included a little about the women's own backgrounds as these reflect their personalities, provide the context of their experiences and the beliefs which gave them so much strength and resilience. Their hopes for, and reflections on, the future deserve to be honoured by us all.

As one of the women put it:

"Now that you have come and I can say this to you, I am relieved and thankful. I hope when the book is published, my grandchildren will be able to read my life history and, at last, people everywhere will know what I think concerning my child and the war."

Irene Staunton
Harare, 1990

Glossary

amai – mother. It is polite to address a married woman as, for example: mother of Tsitsi/*amai vaTsitsi*.

ambuya – grandmother, paternal aunt.

ANC/SRANC – Southern Rhodesian African National Congress commonly referred to as the African National Congress. Nationalist movement formed in 1934.

assembly points – areas designated for the return of freedom fighters after the cease-fire in December 1979.

auxiliaries – District Assistants often used by the authorities to harass and arrest people suspected of sympathizing with the freedom fighters. Sometimes identified with Muzorewa supporters.

cease-fire – which began, following the Lancaster House agreement, on 28th December 1979 and enabled preparations for a free election to commence.

chimbwido – errand girl; also the name of a wild fruit and thus a term that can be used to suggest beauty, ripeness.

CID – Criminal Investigation Department of the police: CIDs, members of that department.

CIO – Central Intelligence Organization: CIOs, members of that organization.

DC – District Commissioner. The people who worked under the DC were called District Assistants.

dzakutsaku (s.) *madzakutsaku* (pl.) – literally many or multitude. Used in a prophetic sense by UANC supporters to mean that it was 'the party for everyone'; used with condescension by people who did not belong to the UANC to suggest people with no political direction.

gandanga (s.) *magandanga* (pl.) – a wild savage person, an ogre. This was a term used by the Rhodesian Front regime in much of their broadcast and printed material, the object being to denigrate the freedom fighters and suggest fear.

Gonakudzingwa – a 'restriction' camp on the Mozambique border, south of Chiredzi, adjacent to a game park and covering an area of approximately twenty square miles. Before 1965, detainees had a degree of freedom and were, for example, allowed to receive visitors and go hunting. After the Rhodesian government declared a state of emergency in 1965, it became a 'detention' camp covering a smaller area which was divided into six small camps, each surrounded by barbed wire. It was closed in 1974 after Mozambique achieved its independence.

keep – 'protected village' where, during the liberation war, people were moved into a fenced area protected by guards.

lobola – from the Shona *roora* – payment/gift given to the father of the bride by her prospective husband after negotiations have taken place between both families.

mai – mother/Mrs.

mbuya – grandmother, mother-in-law.

mujiba – scouts/messengers/look-outs. Young men and boys who acted for the freedom fighters. From *mujiba*, a dance requiring great physical strength.

muti – medicine.

mudzimu (s.) *vadzimu* (pl.) – spirit elder/s of family.

mukoma (s.) *vanamukoma* (pl.) – brother/s. A term used to refer to the freedom fighters, which would not be immediately recognized by outsiders or the security forces.

mukomana (s.) *vakomana* (pl.) – boys.

n'anga – healer, herbalist and sometimes a spirit medium.

NDP – National Democratic Party led by Michael Mawema. Other members included Robert Mugabe, Moton Malianga, George Silundika, Eddison Zvogbo, Ndabaningi Sithole, Leopold Takawira, Herbert Chitepo and Enos Nkala.

ngozi – a spirit of the dead which returns to avenge the family.

njuzu – a water spirit.

pamberi – forward.

poshito – from the Portuguese *poshto* meaning a hut.

pungwe – a meeting that lasts through the night.

roora – a marriage transaction. (*See* lobola.)

sadza – thick porridge made of maize meal.

Selous Scouts – notorious special unit of the Rhodesian army formed in November 1973.

UANC – United African National Congress, political party formed ⟩ by Bishop Abel Muzorewa in 1973.

vakomana (s. *mukomana*) – the boys, i.e., the freedom fighters.

vanamukoma (s. *mukoma*) – brothers, i.e., the freedom fighters.

ZANU – Zimbabwe African National Union formed in 1963 following a split in ZAPU.

Zanla – military wing of ZANU.

ZAPU – Zimbabwe African People's Union formed in 1961 following the banning of the NDP.

Zipra – military wing of ZAPU.

Wha Wha – prison/detention centre outside Gweru.

1 **Seri Jeni**

Madziwa, Mount Darwin

I WAS BORN in Guruve. I was the eldest of seven children but all of them except my brother died at birth or shortly afterwards. My mother also died when I was still a very small child and my grandmother, my father's mother, looked after me. My father's second wife, whom he had married after my mother's death, then died too. This meant that *all* the children (that is, my mother's children and my aunt's* children) went to live with my grandmother. It was very difficult for her to look after such a large family.

We were such a big family that we could not even ask our father to send us to school. I managed to go as far as standard one by working in other people's fields. Sometimes the teachers sympathized with me and even if I did not have enough money, they allowed me to attend school. Most times I was also late for classes, but the teachers did not punish me because they knew I had to prepare food for my three younger sisters and two brothers before I left for school. After class the teachers always let me go home

---

* Aunt – *mainini* – literally 'little mother', i.e., in this case, second wife.

earlier than the rest of the school children and they excused me from doing homework because I had to take care of my younger brothers and sisters.

I stopped going to school to give a chance to the younger ones. It was, after all, very difficult to go to school and, at the same time, think about and organize all the cooking for the rest of the family. When I had finished standard one, I was able to write my name and a letter, which was the important thing.

I then stayed at home for a long time before I met my husband. He had been working as a driver in the Chidavaenzi* store in Guruve. After my marriage things seemed to change a bit for the better. My two younger sisters were by then old enough to look after the rest of the children. When they eventually married, they left my brothers to cook for themselves because my grandmother was by then very old and depended on us.

After I had got married I moved to my husband's home in Madziwa. He was still working as a driver but he had been transferred to Harare. About five months later he resigned and joined me at home.

During those years in Guruve there was plenty of politics. Those were the years when ZAPU started. Everyone, men and women were involved in the party. The police would come to arrest them. They would tie their hands together and their feet together and throw them into trucks. Then those who had not been arrested lay in the road to prevent the trucks from moving.

The police could do nothing but neither could they release those they had arrested. The police would plead with people to get up off the road and because the police usually came in large numbers, they managed to convince people to move away. If they refused and it was impossible for the car or the lorry to move, the police had to wait until people chose to leave the road. Obviously they could not lie there forever. There always came a time when they gave in, saying, "Let them go and kill those people but we also want to go, and if it means being killed, then let them kill all of us," and they would challenge the police to run them over. Seeing people being arrested and thrown into trucks was disturbing. Everyone was concerned, especially the children who had parents who were actively involved in politics.

* The name given to a chain of stores in the rural areas.

I was worried. We children wondered why it was happening that old people were being arrested and thrown into trucks. We thought it was better for the old people to give in. But if ever the ZAPU people heard you say such a thing, they threatened to kill you.

I realized that people were not free and that is what they were trying to do, free themselves from colonialism. That is what the police were against and what they were arresting them for. People were trying to resist a bad type of government. People were arrested and put in Gonakudzingwa. They left their families with no one to look after them for many years. The arrested men would write from prison asking for assistance and then a few clothes were given to the family. When the wives went to visit their husbands they only went as far as the gate: that is where one spoke with one's husband through a small window. The men did not have any privileges. They were not even allowed to hold their own baby, if the wife had a baby: they just had to look at each other in the presence of a policeman.

But this all happened before I married. My husband never joined ZAPU and, when we came here, it was quite different: there was no party in this area.

I came and stayed with my in-laws for a year. When it was time to plough the fields, we ploughed those belonging to my father-in-law, but when it was our turn to plough, they gave us an ox and a plough but did not help us. So we had to plough alone, just the two of us, me and my husband. One of the cattle was difficult to control and once, when we were ploughing, we did not realize that my child was following us. By the time we turned to plough in the opposite direction, the child had lain down in the furrow. The cattle were moving ahead on their own, without anyone to lead them. I was behind them and my husband was holding the plough. Suddenly the cattle started with fright and left the furrow. I ran to control them and realized that my child was asleep in the furrow and that is what had frightened the cattle.

My husband stopped the cattle and we both sat down, with our child, considering how it had almost died. It was very distressing to realize that the child might have been killed by those cattle and all because we had no help. We always helped my in-laws but they were not willing to help us. We felt used and rejected. That was our main problem when we first came to live at Madziwa.

You see, we had only one ox and a plough. My husband's relatives refused to work with him because they said he was poor. In the end we ploughed with another family for, as we say, 'one thumb cannot squeeze a louse'. On another occasion, my in-laws took everything from us and we had nothing to use in the fields. We had to borrow from other friends and as a result, we ploughed very late and only harvested eleven bags of maize. I obtained six and my husband's second wife harvested five.

After that my husband found a job as a driver in Mount Darwin. That year he bought two oxen and three cows. Then life began to change for the better. From that time we managed to plough as much as we wanted to and we managed to send our three children to school without any problem.

My husband's relatives started coming to see us; they began to be friendly because we were no longer poor. Soon I realized that my husband had a lot of relatives. In the end things turned out well for us.

My first three children are the ones who suffered during those years, but it was really only for a short period. By the time I had the rest of my children, life was easy: I had no problems at all. We planted potatoes, maize and cotton and we made money. I was working in the fields while my husband was employed. After several years, and before the war, my husband left his job to concentrate on ploughing. He worked on the land with us for three years before we were moved into the keep*.

During that time, I heard that there was war in Mozambique but I did not know it would come to our country. I felt that this district should do some of the things that people in Guruve had been doing, but it was always very quiet here. ZAPU was the first political party that came into this area. There were very few members and they did not come out into the open. They had small books [membership cards]. It was only after a police search, when those books were found, that you knew who the members were. The police were told by informers and then they went and searched the person's whole house, throwing out everything as they looked for evidence. Even my home was searched once. If

* Keep – 'protected village' where, during the liberation war, people were moved into a fenced area 'protected' by guards.

they discovered that you were a member of the party, they arrested you.

It was quite a long time after that that the guerillas came. At the beginning, there were only a few at a time. It was only later that they came in full force. They even came to my house.

That was the first time I saw them. There were three boys and I prepared them a meal. In the evening, some other guerillas came and again I gave them food. The guerillas then called all my children together and told them that if they ever told anyone that I had given them food, it would be the end of us all. My children never talked about it to anyone; they were very disciplined.

The comrades talked to us a bit. They said that they were our children and that they were fighting for our country. They said they were not fighting for their own freedom, but for the freedom of everyone in the country. Then they said, "Please make us some food; we, your children, are very hungry," and they left and went into the bush. I prepared the food and carried it into the bush. We did this for a number of days.

Because my husband had a car, the comrades used to send him to purchase whatever they wanted from Harare or Bindura. He bought clothes and food for them and he would deliver them to an agreed point. The soldiers did not know that my husband was involved; they did not have a clue, although once they did become suspicious and came to look for him at our home. They asked where he was and I said he had gone to Bindura. They did not believe me so they asked my neighbour, my sister-in-law, who confirmed my statement. I do not know what they had heard to make them so very suspicious.

Then the Smith government told us that we would be moved into the keep. We were told to build our own huts within the protected village. Some people hesitated to do so because they were afraid to be the first to build their home there. The problem was that people who had not built their houses, had no time to do so, as we were all moved into the keep before the stipulated date. You were supposed to move all your property into the area on one single day and the authorities said that if we did not do so, we would not be allowed to bring anything in afterwards. There had been a contact* and that is why we were moved so suddenly.

* 'Contact' between security forces and guerillas.

The authorities said that we had fed the guerillas and that was why they had the energy to fight.

My husband spent the day carrying maize into the keep for other people and, by about four o'clock in the afternoon, he had still not begun to carry our own belongings. We started to mourn lest we had no food for the children. You see, my husband had a car and was being hired by others to carry their maize to the keep. But at last, in the evening, he delivered our maize. We had nowhere to put it so we just poured the cobs on the ground outside.

Once we were in the keep, the children stopped going to school but, finally, a year later, they were allowed to attend school again. The school was outside the keep but everyone, teachers, and school children, all stayed in the keep. The grocery shops remained open.

It was after this that one of my children joined the struggle. What happened was that she woke up early in the morning and got ready the various things she used to sell. Then she changed into a denim dress, underneath which she wore a jersey and she put her brother's baby on her back, saying that she was going to the township. She left the keep and then gave her little brother the baby. She said, "Bye-bye, we shall meet again some day."

At the end of the day, as it grew dark, I asked my other children where she was. The little boy said she had told him that she was going to the shopping centre but that, as she left, she had said, "Bye-bye, we shall meet some day." She never returned.

I did not sleep that night. I felt very worried and powerless. The following morning I told my husband that our child had disappeared and he said that I should have told him before, so that he could have reported it. After a week some men arrived to say that their son wanted to marry my daughter. My husband was very annoyed because he thought that meant that they knew where my daughter was. He wanted to beat them but my brother-in-law stopped him.

After that the police regularly came to my house to ask about my daughter. They said that we were looking for a child who was long dead. They said that they had seen her go and that she had been killed immediately.

This was untrue. She went and fought in the war. It was a painful thing to think about. When a person was killed, the security forces hung the dead body on a chopper and every time this happened, I thought it could be my daughter. I had no happiness for thinking about my child. Each time

I heard that comrades had been killed in such and a place, I thought she could be one of them. I was worried. She was my fourth born child and she had been very interested in the war and had often gone to the base: many children did. They simply told the guards on the keep gate that they were going to the township. It was three years before I heard about my daughter again.

We had lots of problems living in the keep. Every time we returned from fetching water, the DAs* stirred the pots to make sure there was nothing hidden inside. Each time we left the keep the guards required us to jump up and down. One lady was forced to jump so hard that the cloth she was wearing fell off and, as she had nothing underneath it, she stood there naked.

My field was very near the keep and once, when we were not allowed out of the keep for three whole days, cattle entered the field and ate all my crops. I could see them doing so, but I could do nothing at all about it. Sometimes we spent days without water because we were not allowed out of the keep. Sometimes the cattle entered the keep and ate the thatching from off the huts because they were so hungry. Life was very difficult in the keep because we were watched all the time. But in spite of this people did everything they could to help the comrades. My husband continued to buy things for them. Sometimes he filled a car tube with mealie-meal and other things. Then he fitted the tube into a tyre and put the tyre on the car so that one wheel was inflated not by air but by his purchases for the comrades. Then he drove outside. He went to an agreed point where he emptied the contents of the tube out for the comrades.

My husband always helped the comrades willingly. He often said that if the war had started when he had been younger, he would have gone to join them. So he was glad of anything he could do to help them.

Nonetheless, I was very worried. My husband was fighting a war. My home was always being watched and the authorities said that we were for the guerillas. My husband never liked attending the meetings that were called in the keep by the authorities. I had to force him to go because if he hadn't, we would have had trouble. Actually he was afraid that he might be forced to answer negatively to whatever was said by the authorities.

* District Assistants.

Usually when people went to the base, a few *mujibas* remained at the keep to watch and listen to what happened in the keep. If the authorities got to hear that we had all gone to the base, they would call the security forces to say that everyone in Keep Five had gone to the base. Soon afterwards, helicopters would fly above it. People would flee, some would fall into pools, and some would run so far away that they would only return the following day. The authorities always got their information from sell-outs but, fortunately, no one in our keep was killed because of their activities. Still, at that time, you could never tell anyone about anything because you could be sold out.

When the war was over, I heard that the comrades were in the Rushinga area and so I went to their base – I was the first one to go there in search of my child. I asked my son to accompany me and he drove me in his father's car. My husband had died while we were in the keep after being sick for a while.

When we arrived, I started to ask for my child and I, in turn, was asked a lot of questions: why I was looking for her there, how did I know that she had returned, and so on. I told them that all I was doing was looking for my daughter. I explained that I had heard that they, the comrades, were returning and I could not just sit and wait.

All the children who had left the country to fight had changed their names and so if you mentioned someone by their real name you would never find them. I was fortunate I had been told my daughter's new name by someone who had been with her, but I was afraid to mention it to them. I just sat there while they questioned me about this and that.

There were a lot of comrades all wearing similar clothes and you could hardly tell boy from girl. They were all carrying guns. In one group I saw someone who looked like my daughter and I told my son. This girl had also noticed the car – my child knew her father's car. She wanted to come across to me but her friends told her she must first tell their superiors. She did this and they allowed her to come and see us. She came and we embraced each other. She fell down and began to cry, crying for her father who had died.

Then the other comrades came to see what had happened. They asked what we had done to her. They said that this was why they did not allow people into their base because we caused a lot of problems. I said I had done nothing and her brother suggested that she was crying because her father had died. The comrades told her that she should not cry for her father as he had died a natural death and had a proper burial while she had seen many comrades die brutally who had never been properly buried. Then she was taken away from us.

We spent the night there and she came and joined us and we talked through the night. The following day she was again given time to come and talk to me and I told her everything about her father's death. She then asked me to buy her some clothes. Afterwards, we returned home and I sent her brother to buy her clothes. He did this and then took them to her at Rushinga by bus.

My daughter had been away for three years and when she returned she had learned to type and she is now working in Masvingo as a typist.

Those years were very hard years. The war was serious. The problem now is that we are still behind, even after all that suffering. We have no strong representative in our area. We have heard that in other districts, dams have been built and many development projects have begun, but we have seen nothing of this here. The people who were strong and could have been good leaders were killed during the war, often because of sell-outs.

Our lives have improved in that we can sell our crops at reasonable prices but, on the other hand, everything else is now so very expensive. We get enough food from the fields; it is only that the cost of everything else is now so high. But things are generally better and we are once again living in our own homes.

I have been very lucky in my oldest son who carried a heavy load as he had to look after the whole family when my husband died. He sent nine boys to school and all of them are well educated. He really worked hard.

That is all.

2 Sosana Marange

Mutumba, Mount Darwin

I WAS BORN in Musana in Gwashavanhu village. Life was not easy during those years because my parents were poor. I was the oldest girl and the first born of nine children: eight girls and one boy. We had to work for money to go to school and I only went as far as standard two. I got married in 1954 and came to live in Mutumba.

Here I found that my life was even worse than it had been before because my husband had no parents. His uncle, his father's brother, was responsible for him. All the children in his family had been given to other relatives when his father died and, because his mother had refused to become the wife of one of her husband's brothers, she was sent away. As you know, once a child has no parents, life is very difficult.

My first child, a girl, was born in 1956. However my mother-in-law did not like me because my husband was not her child. So finally I decided that I wanted to go back to my people, but my husband refused me permission to go. He told me not to bother about other people, because I was married to him, not to them. I took his advice and I stayed with him and we had a second child in 1958. Then we were given our own house.

11

So we had a house but we had nothing else – except one pot and one plate. I ate from the pot and my husband ate from the plate. Sometimes my mother-in-law took them both away from me and then I had to beg her to let me have them back. This went on for some time until my husband agreed that the situation was very bad and so he looked for a job. He found employment at Chidavaenzi store as a cleaner.

At the time I was one of two daughters-in-law, the other one being her son's wife whom she loved more than me. She always considered her first – some people are just very discriminatory. But fortunately we were not short of food because I had my own maize and my husband received rations of mealie-meal from his employer.

When my husband began to work, life for our family began to improve. My husband was earning one pound ten shillings a week which at that time was a lot of money. So we managed to send our first child to school. I also worked on the land but I always had to plough last, because the cattle owners wanted their fields ploughed first. Nonetheless, the Lord blessed me and I grew enough food, although I was always the last one to plant crops.

By the time I had had my third child, my husband had been promoted from cleaner to storekeeper and so he earned more money and we were very happy. I had no problems, I got everything I wanted easily. Between 1956 and 1981 we had eleven children, but three of them died so now I have eight.

I don't quite remember when the war started here. I think it was in 1974. Before then, we had heard of the war in Mozambique but we did not understand what it meant until it actually came into this area. We had also heard that people were being arrested, that their maize was being cut down, and that dip tanks were being closed. We heard that people in Harare held ZAPU meetings but we were not concerned. We really only understood what political meetings were after the war came here.

Then, in 1974, a group of eight comrades came into our area. I still remember some of their names: Mabonzo, Maware, Bhiriadhi and Mudengumunei. They came to our village which is a very big one. We cooked sadza every day for them and they spent a whole month in the village.

When they first came they called a meeting, a *pungwe*,

at night and they introduced themselves as guerillas. They said they had come to free parents from oppression. They said that we were very oppressed, meaning that all employees were paid very little and that we were being forced to dig contour ridges. One could be arrested and sent to prison if one did not dig them. There were a lot of things the comrades were going to free us from. But after they had been with us for a month, the sell-outs reported them to the DC and told him that the guerillas were being harboured in Musiwa's village.

Then, one afternoon, two CIDs were sent to our village. They came like ordinary people and they were given a meal in the evening and treated like any ordinary village person. In the meantime, the villagers sent a message about their presence to the comrades and, a bit later, they came and took the CIDs away. A few days afterwards, some village elders were taken from their homes to the camp by the soldiers.

Then the security forces came and asked us where the CIDs, their colleagues, had gone and we told them we had no idea. The security forces said that they had heard that the villagers had been harbouring guerillas but we denied it. Then they burnt down the whole village.

It happened like this. I woke up early one morning as I heard the dogs barking. I went outside and saw that the headman's home was on fire. I went back into our house and woke my son up. I told him to leave because I knew that the soldiers were after the young men. The very day before they had taken some people from the village and I was afraid they might take him as well. He then left.

I waited for a little while longer and then I went outside again and saw that the fire was much nearer our home. They were burning my in-laws' houses. I quickly woke up my husband thinking we might be burnt alive inside the house. Then I looked for a tin in which I had put some money and hid it outside in the contour ridge under the grass. I put my baby on my back and my other two small children on my shoulders and began to run away. My eldest daughter and my husband's second wife were washing dishes in the river and my husband went to tell them that the soldiers were firing the village. My husband's second wife was so frightened that she forgot she had left her baby sleeping in the kitchen. So when my husband asked her where the baby was, she said she thought I had taken it with me. My husband told her this was not possible as I was already carrying three children. So she ran back to collect her baby with an empty bag to carry the child's nappies but she couldn't think at all and so brought nothing with her for the baby. We all ran to a certain person's home that was a little way from the village.

Next jet planes flew overhead. It was serious, houses were being burnt down while the jets were firing guns at us. The owner of the house was worried as there were so many people there. He knew that if the soldiers came he would not be able to explain us to them. He suggested that we should go away.

I advised my husband's second wife to return to her home. Then I took two of my children – the two that were at school – to my brother-in-law who was teaching there. I took the other two small ones to another brother-in-law in another village. I did all this on the same day. Then, having put all the children in relatively safe places, my husband, I and the baby returned home. We wanted to see what had happened although what I actually wanted was to collect the tin of money I had hidden. We found that there was nothing left except for my money tin which I collected and hid under my dress.

It was almost sunset. There was nothing left. The cattle had got out of the kraal and the calves were suffering from hunger. We then met people who told us that everyone had been told to gather at the Bradley Institute and where they were being taken to Bindura. We went to Bradley.

As we arrived, one soldier pointed his gun at my husband but another soldier stopped him from shooting. They wanted to know where we had been and why we had taken so long to get there. My husband told them that our field was a long way from our home and that we had left very early for the fields before the village had been fired. He explained that it was only much later that we had heard that we were supposed to gather at Bradley. The soldiers accepted his explanation and told us to join the others.

In Bindura, the following day, we were all told to form a queue. Then a white soldier and one of the CIDs who had been in our village, went down the line picking out people, those he had seen when he was in the village who had had meetings with the comrades and so forth.

You see what had happened was that one of the CIDs

had been killed by the comrades and this one had been left for dead. When he recovered, he had reported the matter and that was what had caused the authorities to burn down our homes.

But many of the people who were being picked out had never been to the comrades' base or attended any *pungwes*. Those people whose names were being called out went to one side and they were beaten. The security forces beat them so hard that some women had miscarriages, some fainted and some became unconscious and only came round after water had been poured over them.

There were 383 people from two villages. We were kept at Bindura and we were given a big tent to sleep in. It was the rainy season and water leaked into the tent. There was nothing on the ground, so we slept on the wet soil. We were given mealie-meal and relish and we cooked for ourselves. But it was very difficult to start a fire in the mud. We had to put a lot of logs at the bottom and start the fire on the top so that many logs could burn before the fire reached down to the wet ground.

Each morning we were ordered to clean the toilets but we were not supplied any cleaning materials. You won't believe it when I say we had even to touch human faeces with our own hands and then we had to use those same hands to eat. It was terrible.

At first both men and women had to sleep in the tent together. But then one of the men got hold of his own tent and so some men moved out into it. This made things a lot better. We did not have any blankets or clothes except those we'd been wearing when we arrived. If you were lucky a relative might lend you a blanket or something to wear and that made life a bit more comfortable.

There was one kind guard who used to lend his room to expecting mothers when he was on duty. He consoled us and said that we should be patient because everything had an end and that some day all our problems would be over. At first we did not believe him but his words encouraged and helped us to live through those difficult times.

Two women were expecting and when their babies were due we divided the tent with blankets into two sections so they could have some privacy. Both women had baby boys within a few days of each other. This gave us some kind of hope. We thanked the Lord for giving us babies that lived despite the unbearable conditions. It was a relief to see something living like a baby, a new life arising from people who had lost hope. We called the two children *Gorerehondo*, the year of the war, and *Gorerenhamo*, the year of troubles.

It was a painful situation. We could not even discuss anything with the relatives and friends who visited us because we were guarded by policemen. We could only cry quietly within our own hearts. It was very painful. We did not know whether life would ever get any better or whether this was the beginning of the end.

We spent a month in that tent in Bindura. Some people were imprisoned and sent to jail. Then we were put into lorries which were to drive us back to our homes. But before we got there, we met a policeman waiting at the turn-off to the main road, and he told us that we were not to return home but that we had to gather at Nyarukunda school.

At the school each family was given a bowl of mealie-meal daily which was donated by women from the neighbouring villages. We received the meal for two weeks and then the grinding mill was closed down and there was nothing. Church people then had collections and gave us some money which we used to buy mealie-meal. When this was finished, we had nothing again. We then sent word to the chief that we had no food and he managed to get us two bags of mealie-meal and a bag of beans. We made this last for some days.

Then the chief told the DC that we had no food and he sent us a bag of mealie-meal and a bag of beans. That did not last for many days although each family cooked very little sadza – just enough for the parents to smell it while the children scraped the plates. It wasn't much at all. The DC then told all of us who had given our children to others to look after that we should collect them and bring them to the school.

Then the DC arrived. It was just at a time when we were eating but he made us stop immediately so that we could have our finger-prints taken. He did not allow us to finish our food or time to collect the plates and bowls which had been lent to us by the villagers. Even clothes that had been washed and put on the line to dry had to remain there. After taking everyone's finger-prints, five trucks arrived from Bindura to pick us up. We wondered what was going on. We were instructed to get on to the lorries without saying anything. The DC also got on to one of the lorries and announced that he was going to throw us away. He said he did not want us. We could not return to Madziwa again. We were all very sad and began to cry. The DC then said that we were crying for nothing. He said we should not cry because we had killed his 'dog' – by this he meant the man from the CID.

The DC drove in front and the trucks followed. We cried. Even the dogs that were around tried to follow us, barking and whining, but they got nowhere. Some of them were even run over by the lorries. When we reached the main road we shouted out to friends and relatives that we were going to be thrown away. Everyone cried. We spent the night in Bindura.

The next morning another truck was sent back to the school to collect what little property we had left behind, but most of the things had already been stolen. A few utensils were brought along. Then we were loaded on to the lorries again and, with the DC in the lead, we set off. He turned off at his office but we continued down the main road. Before we reached Harare one lorry had had a breakdown and it was sent back to Bindura and another one was sent on to us while we waited on the road.

We continued on towards Harare. We did not go through the centre but through the outskirts of the city. There we took the road to Enkeldoorn*. We spent the night at the DC's offices there but, in the middle of the night, we were told to wake up and cook sadza for the children because we still had a long way to go. So we did that. The DC's office gave us the mealie-meal.

Then we set off again, and again a lorry broke down and we had to wait for it to be repaired. We reached Fort Victoria† in the dark. The DC there was waiting for us. All the District Commissioners' offices on our way down and all the people in those towns had been told about us. They heard that we were going to be thrown away in Beitbridge. The people in Masvingo lined the road as we went by to see if it was true and to see what kind of people were being thrown away. Some people who worked on the road asked where we were going and we told them we were going to be thrown away. "Ah," they said, "these are the people that are going to be thrown

* Enkeldoorn is now called Chivu.
† Fort Victoria is now called Masvingo.

away in Beitbridge." They commented that as the lorries were so full of women it must mean that the men had been killed. In fact, most men had been imprisoned but my husband was with me.

We had been told that we would spend the night at the DC's office in Masvingo but he refused to allow this. So we spent the whole night travelling. The DC at Beitbridge had also been waiting for us but when we arrived it was late and he had left. Instead a policeman was waiting at the turn-off. He stopped the lorries and asked if we were the people from Shamva and told us to take the road to Chikwarakwara. So, finally, we arrived at the place where we heard we were going to stay. There was an enclosure with one big tent and many little tents inside it. We had spent such a long time sitting in the lorries that we fell down when we tried to get up. We were told that as soon as we had got off the trucks we should sit down immediately. We did this and the feeling returned to our legs.

After we had unloaded, we were allocated tents, one to each family regardless of its size. Because we could not live in such a way, we divided the tent with a blanket so that the parents slept close to the door and the children slept within, with a blanket to divide the boys from the girls.

In the morning the DC called us together. He asked us to tell him our story about why and how we had come to be there. We explained that it was because our DC said that we harboured guerillas. The DC said that everyone everywhere was doing that. He asked us what provisions we had and we explained that we had nothing, no blankets, no food, no pots and no clothes. The DC said that he would look after us, even though we had been thrown away, but that we should behave ourselves otherwise he would send us back. He sent lorries with mealie-meal and beans and we were given a lot of goats to kill twice a week.

We discovered that, before our arrival, the DC had held a meeting with his local people. He had told them that people with tails, who ate other people, were coming into their district. He said that if his people did not give us what we wanted, we would eat them.

We were sharing the same well with the locals and at first we were surprised to notice that, when we fetched water from the well, the local people kept far away and, if we approached them there, they ran away and only returned to collect their containers after we had gone. When we went to bathe and wash our things at the river they hid themselves in the trees, watching to see our tails. But our women were just like their women and our men just like their men. There were no tails to be seen. Sometimes we went to their gardens and they gave us vegetables but they went away immediately after doing so. They did not want to communicate with us for any length of time.

As I said before, we used the same borehole for drinking water as they did for watering their cattle. At first they did not want us to get water before the cattle did. But when we explained to them that we were just like them and that we had come into the area because we had been forced to move and it was all a result of the war, a war that they would also experience some day, they became more sympathetic. In the end, we understood each other's language: we spoke in ours and they spoke in theirs but we could understand each other. So having satisfied themselves that we were just ordinary people who did not eat other people, they felt free to tell us what they had been told about us. Then we too understood their peculiar behaviour.

Three days after our arrival in Beitbridge, the comrades arrived, the very same ones that we had fed. They told the guard that they had come to see their relatives and they were allowed in. They said that they had come to see where and how we were. They told us that we should stay there and co-operate with the authorities because they could not help us. They said that all would be well some day.

For almost a month we just sat about doing nothing except household chores. But then the DC came and said that he wanted us to do some work. He said that he would pay us three dollars a month, regardless of our age, to cut down poles. So we did that and earned some money. After we had cut the poles, we were given a place to build our own houses and these were built by the men and the DC paid them to do this. The houses were thatched with millet because there was no grass. After that we moved from the tents into the new houses. Then the DC told us to clear a piece of land for ploughing. We cleared 703 acres and were given a plough, seven donkeys, and a bag of seed millet* because the area did not get much rain. He told us that we should plant the seed after the first rains.

* Millet is a grain crop that withstands drought.

The comrades used to visit us and we liked this because we could discuss our problems with them. They always encouraged us by saying that all would be well and that we should co-operate. Their visits usually passed without incident, but one day they went into the camp office and demanded money. This was worrying because we thought we might be killed, but nothing happened except that the guards no longer spent the night at the camp and went to stay elsewhere.

Later on the DC told us that anyone who had somewhere else to go should go and that he would give us travel passes to Harare or to relatives or to the farms. He advised us not to go to Madziwa because he said that we would get into trouble, just as we had done before. So, little by little, people left: some went to stay with relatives, some went on to farms to look for employment and some asked for permission to settle in other areas.

During the whole period we were in Beitbridge, our lives were quite peaceful and nothing very nasty happened except that one man disappeared and died. You see, our language was different from that of the locals, even though we could communicate. But one day this man went to drink beer and, on his way home, he got lost and walked in the wrong direction. I suppose he tried to ask the way but because of the communication problem, he got more and more lost. We looked for him for days but could not find him and then we reported the incident to the DC. The man was later found dead about fifty miles away on the road to Chikwarakwara. Some of our men went to identify him and, because his body had already decomposed, they just buried him there.

Generally people in Beitbridge were not aware of the war although there were a few people who had been arrested years before and had been detained in Gonakudzingwa. Those few understood politics. But the comrades who visited us did not go and talk to the villagers in the neighbourhood. Finally, after quite a long time, only a few people remained at the camp and life began to get difficult once again. The DC received news that friends of his had been killed in the war, and so he was no longer very kind to us. He no longer gave us food, except for beans and salt which we exchanged with the villagers for mealie-meal and millet. We had planted our own fields but the rains had been very poor and we hadn't grown any crops.

As things got worse, the policeman who guarded us, advised us to think of leaving as he did not think that things would improve. He advised us not to spend all the money we had earned because we were right at the border, and if things got worse and we had to leave suddenly without money, we would have to walk long distances and it would be very dangerous. We took his advice, obtained travel passes and went to Harare. We had spent a year at Beitbridge. We returned in May 1975.

From Harare, together with my husband's second wife and her children, we went to my own home area in Musana and stayed with my parents. After a while my husband got employed on a farm as a labourer and we moved to that farm.

Then the war came to Musana and we remembered what the first comrades had told us. They said, if you see fire coming to one place, you should run to the place where the fire began. So, when the comrades came to Musana, we moved to Matepatepa and my husband got another job as a farm labourer. We remained there until after the war.

But while we were on the farm we began to meet the comrades again and we explained what had happened to us. One day we went to visit the keep for a church service and afterwards we met the comrades in those homes which had been left empty, after people had moved into the keep. They used these homes as their base. They wanted to know about us and why we had gone to the keep. When they heard that we lived on a neighbouring farm, they exclaimed, "Don't you know that we want everyone to leave the farms and move into the keep because we want to destroy the farms?" I told them we did not know that. They then told us that we should go and live in the keep. So I explained that the DC had said that he did not ever want to see us again and that we were afraid that we would be identified if we went into the keep. Then they left us alone.

But after a bit my husband and I felt that it would be better and safer if we went and built ourselves little huts in the keep. So I and the second wife requested permission to do this. We pretended that we were widows. We were given a place on which to build and then we looked for someone to help us build our little hut and my husband gave us money to pay him.

In the keep there was a small area called Tangwena which had many very small huts inside and where every family had only one hut regardless of its size. Tangwena was a sort of punishment area, where all our food was taken away by the authorities, who would only return us a little at a time each day, just enough for one meal. But we still had to take food out to the comrades who got angry if we failed to do so and would say, "How do you expect us to live?" So we would put the mealie-meal into a small packet, tie it up tight, put the little bag between our thighs and then put on two pairs of pants. Every time we went through the gate of the keep the guards would make us jump, legs apart, but we could still take the mealie-meal out in this way, for when we jumped it was quite secure. When I reached my garden I dug a little hole and hid the bag and the comrades would come and collect it.

Sometimes we put bags of mealie-meal in a scotch cart and then poured manure on top and said we were going to the garden. The scotch cart was always searched but no one ever searched very deeply through manure. Again, when we got to the garden, we would hide the bags at an agreed point so that the comrades could fetch them.

If cattle were ever killed in the keep, I bought meat, wrapped it in a clean plastic bag and then covered the bag with very dirty paper and then more dirty plastic bags to make something like a football for the little boys. Then we asked the children to kick the ball outside, as if they were just playing. Later someone would pick it up and take it to the comrades. Women would also wrap dried meat around their chests, under their breasts. They never discovered this hiding place when they searched us.

In the keep we had to wear an identity card all the time. It hung round your neck like a necklace so that you could be easily identified. Even if the helicopters flew overhead one had to hold up one's ID so that they could see it reflected in the sun. One could be killed for not having an ID.

There was also always someone who was watching from the observatory in the keep. If this guard saw smoke, it would be reported and the security forces would immediately accuse you of cooking for the comrades.

When we left the keep and met the comrades they would always ask where whether we had seen the 'busumani'. That was a term they used for the soldiers. Or, if we met the soldiers they would ask us whether we had seen the 'braki', meaning the comrades. Both terms are usually names given to cattle – 'busumani' means brown cattle and'braki' means black cattle. If one did not know what the comrades or the soldiers were really referring to, one could think that they meant cattle and reply accordingly. If you were very unlucky, you would point to cattle which lay in the direction of the comrades' base and then, if there was a contact, you were held responsible. So the best thing was always to say, I never saw busumani or braki anywhere. That was the only way to be safe.

After the war, when we had left the keep and returned to our homes, there were many human bones to be found everywhere. Everyone was asked to contribute ten cents to buy material in which to wrap them. People went around picking up the human bones, wrapped them in the material and buried them. We were told that if we did this it would rain. But it was very hard to do this. A human is different from an animal and one can always tell that the bone is a human one, so picking up those dead people's bones was really something difficult to do, but we had to do it.

Life in the keeps was very difficult. If we had to return to them today we would see it as a heavy and painful punishment. But when we two wives started living there, we took it in turns to return to the farm to stay with my husband. When he visited us, he said that we were his relatives and he was allowed in. We then began to plant the fields we had left behind before we had been transported to Beitbridge.

A week later we went to attend another church service and, on our return, we again met the comrades at their base. They told us to go away because soldiers were patrolling the area on horseback. On that occasion my son was with us but he lingered behind after we had hurried home. He arrived later and my husband asked him why he was so late. He explained that he had been talking to the comrades. We did not suspect anything since we often met and talked to them. The following morning my son went to work. He returned at lunchtime and changed his clothes. He put on two pairs of trousers and two shirts, he put on his father's big hat and strung his towel round his neck. On his way out he met his aunt who was returning from the river. She thought that perhaps he had taken his towel so that he could have a bath after work.

So it was that he left. We worried that he had gone to join the struggle, while we knew we were not supposed to be in the area and if the soldiers became aware of our presence, that would be that.

My son had always been interested in joining the struggle. Occasionally he had written letters to the comrades overseas asking them to come and fetch him or asking them how he might join them somewhere. However, all letters were posted through the farmer's postal bag and so they first went to the farmer's house. There the farmer's cook read my son's letters and showed them to the driver: he suggested that they should burn them as my son was only a boy. All children are adventurous.

Anyway, my husband told the farm foreman that my son had told us he wanted to get married and that we had responded by saying that we did not think he had enough money for the lobola. My husband explained that we now thought he must have gone to look for employment in town, so that he could find this money. My son was old enough to marry as, at the time, children married early so that the soldiers would not give them so much hardship. Young men were being forced to go for call-up. The foreman believed my husband's story and he told it to the farmer which is what we had wanted him to do.

When my son did not return home I thought, if my son has left with the guerillas, this is not so bad. I could say that because we had already suffered so much. But we have never seen my son again. The war ended but he never came. We waited and hoped to see him but . . . nothing.

The farmer was not such a bad man but he was one who made compromises. He pleased both the comrades and the security forces. Whenever he left the farm, say, to go on holiday, he would leave a letter with some money in it for the comrades. He would tell them that he was going away, that he had left something for them and that he hoped nothing bad would happen to his home or his farm while he was gone. He would, however, also inform the security forces of his departure and, as a result, his farm was never destroyed. I don't think his fellows, the security forces, ever knew that he was such a two-way person.

He told his employees that if the comrades were ever seen on the farm he would kill them all. People were afraid but, on the other hand, they knew what kind of a person he really was. The comrades told us what he did for them and, as a result, they did not bother the people on the farm at all.

If they wanted anything from the workers, people took whatever it was – food, money or whatever – to the comrades outside the compound.

We stayed on that farm until after the war and then I decided to go back home. I returned to our old home and built a shelter. We had nothing, no chickens, no goats, nothing. We began again by building our houses. The government gave us mealie-meal, groundnuts and other rations for two years. My husband continued to work on the farm during that period and then he returned home to join me.

We heard that the children of war were returning to their homes. We waited for our child but he never came. Some people told us he had been seen somewhere; others said they'd heard of him somewhere, but it was all untrue. We never saw my son again.

My daughter, who had been very young when he left, had married. It was through this girl that my dead son's spirit appeared. It told us that he had died. It said that it knew that we, his parents, were hoping to see him but he had died a long time before. My son-in-law came and told us these things and we went to see our daughter. She began to cry and we brought her home. There she began to talk as if she was her brother: he told us that he had died in the bush at Rusito, and what he wanted us to do. He said that, had he returned home alive, his father would have killed a cow to celebrate his life and that therefore he wanted an animal killed. We killed a goat, cut off its head and then wrapped it in clothes. We put the wrapped head in the house, just as one would do with a dead person. Then everyone danced and cried until dawn. The rest of the goat was eaten by the mourners.

The following morning an ox was killed and a grave was dug. My sons-in-law made a *banda*, which is rather like a mat made of thin poles, used for carrying the dead. We put the goat's head on the *banda*. The girl through whom my son's spirit had revealed itself, danced outside because she was not allowed to come into the house where the dead 'body', the goat's head, lay. Then we buried the dead 'person'. During this ceremony the girl lay unconscious but immediately afterwards she recovered. The following day the boy reappeared through the girl and thanked his father for what he had done. He said that now he had a home and he would rest there peacefully. He bade farewell to all the relatives who were in the house at the time and then he left us.

It is very painful and worrying to think of your child having gone forever, and that he died for the country. But, after thinking long and hard, one concludes that each person has their own destiny on earth. When I also think of the many other boys and girls who died during the war, just as my child did, I feel a bit comforted. And, since the day we discovered how he died and we did what he asked us to do, I have felt relieved.

Life now is much better than it was before, except for the wound, the scar left by the death of my son. We have all the things we need and we have cattle, our own plough and clothes.

3 Elina Ndlovu

Mawabeni

I WAS VERY YOUNG, twenty, when I married. I already had two children and the second baby was a year old. But I was a good respectful child. At first I don't think my in-laws liked me, but in time their attitudes changed. I took my mother-in-law as my mother and my father-in-law as my father. I did not hesitate to do what they asked as quickly as I could.

Even now they say my obedience was outstanding – but this was the way I was brought up.

Between 1955 and 1965 I had five children, one girl and four boys. I managed to bring them up well. I told them never to hit one another. If someone had done something wrong, they were to tell me and I would decide what to do. So they learned to respect each other and this pleases me very much.

My father-in-law thinks my children are as kind as I am. He told them so, because every time he visits us, my children made sure that he is given tea: he likes tea very much, better than food. He is flattered by their attention.

My father-in-law had three wives and eight daughters-

27

in-law. Of the eight of us, my father-in-law declared at a family marriage that I was his favourite. After he had said so in front of everybody, that was the end of that because his statement did not please others. But I don't think my sisters-in-law were really so jealous because later they were all quite friendly again.

Here in Bezha the liberation war began in 1977; that's when the freedom fighters first came to our district. The first group were Zipras and they arrived at about two o'clock one afternoon when we had just returned from the fields. I was eating with a neighbour who had been helping me in my fields. They arrived carrying their guns.

We'd heard a lot about them but we'd never seen them. Everyone was frightened. The children trembled with fear, but I tried to be courageous. At that same time other freedom fighters had gone to my neighbour's and were eating and playing radio music in broad daylight. They should have been more careful because, on the previous day, Smith's soldiers had been camping at a nearby school.

The comrades asked us if we had voted for Muzorewa. I said I hadn't, but they still demanded to see my hands, because if I'd voted they would have seen the mark*. Fortunately I hadn't voted because I didn't like Smith's government. How could I like it as my children had gone to fight in the struggle? The freedom fighter who had asked us if we had voted for Muzorewa threatened to beat us and then left. He was Zipra.

Some days later the Zanlas arrived. There was no difference between those comrades and the Zipras, but when they came they introduced themselves. They asked us to cook them some food, which we did, and we gave it to them in the forest. That first group was kind: they talked to us and treated us well but the groups that came later were very rough. They went round knocking at people's doors at night and telling us to go to their base for meetings.

My house has an upstairs and a downstairs and one day when they came and knocked for me, they came right up into my bedroom to wake me up. Then they asked why I was sleeping and whether I had been to the base. I told them I had and they left me, but if they'd known that I hadn't

---

* Mark – a sign that is put on one's hand in indelible ink after one has voted so that a person cannot vote twice.

been, they would have beaten me. People who did not go to the base were often beaten.

The freedom fighters used to say '*pasi*' meaning 'down' to anyone or anything they didn't like, so we nicknamed them *Pasi*. There were also children who couldn't keep secrets, and sometimes even told lies, they were always being asked by the guerillas about families in the neighbourhood. The Zanlas liked to spend a lot of time with children in the area. They would ask them what happened in their homes, what their parents thought and talked about, who the chairman or the secretary of Zapu was, and so on. The children then told them whatever they knew without understanding the comrades' intentions. The Zanlas then wrote down all the names of people, like myself, with posts in ZAPU and we were put on a list of people to be killed.

No one was killed although some of us felt that we were in danger. Because we worked together with people and because we all sympathized with each other, there were no deaths as a result of someone saying something about somebody else. The comrades always told us to work together, because they knew there was a danger of people dying or being killed for the wrong reasons or because of false information.

Once I met the Zipra freedom fighters when I was visiting my cousin in another village. We were going to go to a party together and we were looking very smart. The comrades asked us who we were and they talked to us, but none of the people around would answer. I was the only one who did and then they started asking me lots of questions. They wanted to know if there was a women's section of ZAPU in our village. There wasn't: men and women met together, and I told them so. They said they wanted me to start a women's section and that they would be coming to my village the following week to check if I had done so. They said they would kill me if I hadn't. They were pointing a gun at me as they talked.

They then accused us of cooking for the Zanlas. They said that the Zanlas had told people they, the Zipras, were the Selous Scouts, but that they were all fighting for the same cause. I explained that we also thought both groups were fighting for the same cause. They said that, all the same, civilians unnecessarily spent nights at meetings with the

Zanlas. I told them we had no alternative because they knocked us up at night, and if we didn't go, they could break our doors down. Fortunately a certain man then supported what I was saying. Everyone else kept quiet, even the owners of the house were afraid to say anything. They were silent. It was as if no one but me was there. I kept talking to the comrades until I felt as easy and relaxed as if I was talking to my own children. They said they wanted us to respect one another and they wanted us to appease our ancestral spirits so that we could free our country. They sent me to go and tell the people in my village about their wishes. I did exactly that and everyone accepted me, so I became chair of our branch until independence. Then I was elected on to our provincial committee.

The boys were in the area for a while after that and sometimes they came to my home, if they wanted to see me about anything. We were a good community and I was pleased because my children never talked about anything they saw or heard.

It appeared as if the Zanlas only mistreated us because we were ZAPU. The groups were divided at that time, as both parties wanted to rule. It seemed that the groups no longer liked each other. But at first we did not realize this: we thought that the two groups were together and fighting for the same cause. What I began to notice, however, was that the Zanlas didn't trust us and they would use force when it wasn't necessary, because we were not resisting. I don't know why they didn't trust us or why they believed they had to be harsh with us. Not all the groups were the same: some of them treated us quite well.

The *vakomana* told us that they had principles which they learnt during their training. They used to say that if they did not follow their rules and principles things would not go well for them. Mostly they were very respectful and obedient. One could see, whatever else they had been taught, they had learnt to respect others.

One afternoon at around four o'clock, the freedom fighters had a contact with the soldiers at our school. The soldiers, who were both white and black, had camped at the school and the Zanlas had heard about this. So, using the children, they sent us messages telling us to lie down, take cover and hide. Then we saw them running with groups of two or three people carrying their big guns. They went up a large rock and shot from that position. There was fear and commotion as gun shots were fired: bullets shot through the trees, towards our homes, and set fire to our fields. People ran in all directions. It was a very tough battle but there seemed to be no casualties.

Then, as it was getting dark, we all returned to our homes and no one moved until the next day. But then a lot people left their homes and went to hide in the forests. We heard that four soldiers died. They were just rumours; I do not know whether they were true or not. We were not allowed to go and look. Civilians were not supposed to know about such things. It was very frightening. No one knew what might have happened to others. We were relieved when we saw each other alive.

Then there was another contact at Mhukula and during this battle some Zanla comrades died. Such things were never stated openly. If ever you got to hear something you had to be very careful not to repeat it to anyone else. The soldiers took away the bodies of dead freedom fighters and used them to show that they had killed guerillas. But if any of them were killed, they never said anything about it.

Although the Zipras had left our area while the Zanlas had remained, sometimes Zipras came into the area when we were at the Zanla base. They always just listened from a distance and when they next met us, perhaps on the following day, they would tell us that they had heard what was being said.

Once I remember the Zanlas wanted to kill a certain old man because they said he was not a good man. So the children went to report this to the Zipras. They then arrived and shot bullets into the air, because they didn't want to fight, they just wanted to frighten the Zanlas. It worked because when the Zanlas heard the shots, they ran away and left the old man behind. So he survived.

Zipras did not want to fight with Zanlas although the Zanlas said a lot of bad things about Zipra. Zipras did not want people to be killed because they said both Zipra and Zanla should fight the enemy, not the people. That is why they came and shot into the air and the Zanlas ran away, and the old man ran away. This man was already old: he had married children but he ran to town and left his family home. His family thought he had been killed until they heard from others that he had left for town.

The freedom fighters used to tell us that the country

belonged to us. When they sang and shouted this, the spirit mediums spoke out. When I was young the ancestral spirits were not very popular, but they regained their popularity during the war.

So, when my son, Washington, left the country to join the liberation war, I entrusted his return to both my God and my ancestors. I had this strong feeling, that my child would return. There was also a traditional practice that had died away during our youth, which meant throwing snuff on the ground as if you were giving it to the dead. During the war, we took the custom up again because we trusted that it would help us. One would throw snuff on the ground whilst making certain wishes. If you wished your child well and that child had discussed his intentions with you, usually things would turn out well. But if the child had left after some argument or because going provided a way for the child to leave his home, then the child would usually suffer misfortune. If the child left well, on good grounds, one would have reason to feel confident and not feel a great sense of loss. The hardships that children faced were always worse if all was not well between the parents and the children.

I told those neighbours I really trusted that I was sure we would gain independence in my lifetime. It was my strong belief. That is how I was created, when something is going to happen, I feel it in my body. For instance, if during the war, I felt that I should not go to a certain place, it was because I felt certain that something terrible would happen there. Sometimes children from my village met soldiers on their way to school who beat them thoroughly. But if I told my children to go to school, and then threw snuff on the ground and talked to my dead grandparents, they would not meet the soldiers or, if they did, at least they weren't harmed.

You see, I have the spirit of my grandmother within me. I am a spirit medium and I have had these feelings for a long time. Whenever I heard that someone was ill, I could not eat. I was also a member of the Apostolic church for a long time and, during that time, I went to pray for the sick until I was shown that the person would live. But, after I had prayed, I would tell fellow members of the faith what I had been shown. Sometimes prophets were amongst those who prayed and they would sometimes prophesy that a person was going to live. But if I saw it differently and explained what had been revealed to me, that is what would happen. In time, people realized that there must be something different about me. Occasionally I would give instructions, depending on what I had been shown: I might tell people to clean the sick person with milk, or dress the person in particular clothes, and then they would be healed. Once we went to pray for a sick child and I told the parents that I had been shown that they always quarrelled and that it was this that was causing the ill health of their child.

What I am really trying to explain is that this feeling has been with me for a long time. But it was only later, when I was thirty-five years old, that the spirits came out from me and my people brewed beer to appease our *mudzimu*.

Of course the Apostolics were very disappointed because I had been helping them to do great work in their church. Even before I had become a church member I felt something was happening to me. But it was only after I had joined that I began to get sick now and again, so my parents took me to the traditional healer. It was he who told me about the spirits and that is when beer was brewed and why I now am what I am. My father talked to my husband before he took me to the African doctors and my husband was very understanding, but my father-in-law did not like the idea because he was a church member. As I see it, what I was able to do when I was in the church was due to the power of both God and my ancestral spirits. But because these two powers fought between themselves, I was very often not well.

Since I have accepted my grandmother's spirits, I do even better than I did when I was in the church. Some time ago I helped a woman whose husband had died and there were two men who loved her. She seemed not to know who to choose between the two. I advised her not to marry one of them – the one she seemed to want more than the other – and now he has died but the one she married, on my advice, is still alive. They are leading a very good life and are happy together. The man still says that he trusts me because I gave him a wife.

You see, the day before this woman's first husband died he told me that I would be his soldier. At the time I did not understand what he meant but when this wife had problems because her dead husband's relatives accused her of killing him, I was able to comfort and reassure her. I recalled her late husband's words and advised her not to leave her home as she wanted to do. So she stayed and she has now married a man who is a good husband to her.

Even after independence, during the dissident menace, I had a dream in which I was told that I should be careful not to talk about anyone; and, if a death occurred because I had said something about a certain person, it would remain forever a burden on my life.

My son went away for three years. He was one of those who went out of the country towards the end of the war. He was influenced by my brother who had been one of the first people to leave the country for Zambia. They went to prepare for war – that was in 1964. But of the three friends who went with him he is the only survivor.

At first my brother used to write to me but when the war started he was one of the first ones to fight. At the time I had told my people that I thought my brother had joined the liberation struggle because he had suddenly stopped writing. So I told my father not to sell all his cattle because if he did, and my brother returned, and found all the cattle had gone, he would not help us in time of need. Instead, he would say that as he had never been given any of the cattle that the family had acquired from lobola, he wasn't considered part of the family.

I had to tell my father this because he had been selling the cattle and there was only one cow left. It was not very clever of him to dispense with his riches just like that. But he listened to me and the cow had calves so, by the time my brother returned, we had quite a few cattle.

When Washington returned from the war he became a builder. He had done a building course before he left. Now he is employed by DDF*. When he returned he did not act big at all and he still treats me with respect because I am his mother. My husband is also a builder and he is often away on contract work. He built me this beautiful house and I helped him. My daughter was a temporary teacher but they seem no longer to need them and so she is no longer working. My third child is at the University of Zimbabwe. I think he's doing medicine because he is earning quite good money while he is studying.

* District Development Fund.

The people round here like good things and prosperity and, since independence, many women have had training in development projects. We have also sometimes visited other projects in Mutare, Harare and the Midlands. I also went to the Hlekweni Training Centre to learn how to make asbestos sheets using sand, cement and roughage. When I returned, I taught other women how to do this and we are making and selling them here. In Mutare I learned how to make bricks and again I have taught others how to do this and so we are also making and selling bricks. We have banked about $600 but if we include the money owed to us, we have more than a thousand dollars. So, since independence, life has been good.

4 Flora Sibanda*

Mawabeni

I WAS BORN in Mzinyathini. My great-grandfather was called Msinahanya, which literally means 'I do not care or bother about anybody'. My late grandfather was called Ukwanda, which means, 'We are many' or, by extension, 'We are poor'. But we have plenty of hair, just like everyone else, so we are not looked down upon, despite our material status. My father was called Kahlamizi Sibanda. I married a Dube here at Mantsheza's home. Mantsheza is my father-in-law's name. In our custom I should not mention his name in this way† but, for your sake, I am doing so.

When I finished my schooling I came to teach at Bezha school and that is where I met my husband, Zephania Dube. He was working in Johannesburg and had come home on leave. After we'd met and fallen in love, he wanted to take me with him to South Africa but I refused. I was the only child in my family and I was not prepared to leave my parents alone. Nonetheless, Zephania continued to make

---

* Flora Sibanda's married name was Dube but she reverted to her family name after her husband's death.
† Traditionally a respectful daughter-in-law would not mention her father-in-law's name but refer to him as the son of so-and-so.

preparations to marry me. He told my father that, after paying lobola, he would return to Johannesburg and leave me with my parents until he came back. But my father refused to accept his lobola under these conditions, because he did not think it would be fair on me, as we could not be sure when or if Zephania would return. Then he decided to write to his employers telling them that he was unable to return and he married me. At one time he said he would go back for a short period, but he never did. I suppose life turned out to be very good for him and he forgot all about going back to Johannesburg.

We led a very happy life. I had eight children. My husband decided to build a new home for my parents just next to ours, so that he could look after them in their old age – my being the only child meant that there was no one else to take care of them. Dube cared for them just as if they had been his own parents and he buried them well.

I was very industrious and did a lot of sewing. I made a lot of nice things which always won prizes at shows. The first time I won an iron and the following year I won a portable radio. On that occasion, I had sent my children to the show and, when it began to get late and they were still not home, I began to worry. Then I heard the sound of a radio and wondered who could be passing by. To my astonishment, the sound drew nearer and the children, calling out congratulations, told me what I had won. I loved that radio and carried it with me most times, even when I went to the fields. It gave me company. When the war came and a lot of things were being taken from our homes, I told my children to take my radio. They still take turns to have it and call it 'our mother's power' because I won it with energy and hard work.

Then Dube himself died and I was left alone. I knew it would be difficult to send my children to school as I did not want to sell the cattle my husband had left for the children. So I decided to work hard, and with my children to help me, we continued to plough and plant and we developed this big orchard. I used to sell a lot of guavas. A truck came to fetch them. So I used these hands which the Lord gave me to work and provide for myself.

My children were well spaced I had no problems looking after them. I never needed to carry a child on my back when I was pregnant. When my husband died, I was still fit and could have had more children. But I refused to remarry. Had I done that I knew I would never be able to look after my children properly. So, when my husband's people suggested that I should marry his brother, I refused. My first born supported my views and told his uncles that they should leave me alone. Then my children knew that I would never leave them under any circumstances. Everyone is buried here, so why should I go? People have always been very kind to me. For example, a number of my children have married but I've never had to hire a bus for the guests, as most people do at their children's weddings. It is truly wonderful how people have helped me because they were good friends with my husband.

Dube was not interested in politics and we never discussed them. All we talked about was the Bible, and sometimes matters arising from school meetings with other parents. I was really surprised when my son went to join the struggle because we had never talked about politics in my family. Later I realized that he must have been influenced by others in Bulawayo. He had been working there for two years.

I first heard about the war after my son had left. Someone came and told me that my son was no longer in Bulawayo. I wanted to report him missing because I thought he might have been involved in an accident or some other harm might have befallen him. But I was advised by other villagers not to do this, as he, like other young people, might have left the country. I stayed at home hoping that I might hear from, or about, him but I never heard a word until he came back after the war at independence.

The first group which came into this area was Zanla. They wanted to know where the Zipras were. At about the same time the soldiers arrived and they wanted to know where the Zanlas were. Sometimes, if the soldiers were not satisfied with our answers, people were beaten.

The first time I saw Zipras they passed right by my home. I was going to town that day and so I had got up very early to prepare for my journey. Just as I was making a fire in the yard, I heard footsteps outside. I peeped out, thinking it might be donkeys, but it was the Zipras. The first thing I noticed were their guns. I went into the house because I was frightened. I almost missed the bus. On my return that evening I heard that a lot of people had been beaten and some had even been taken to hospital. We did not see those people, the comrades, again for a while. Later we heard that this group had gone to another area.

The comrades never told us anything. We only ever saw those boys, the *mujibas*, when the comrades sent them to tell us that they wanted food. We cooked and took the food to them. Before they shared it out, they made each one of us eat a small portion, because they were afraid of being poisoned. Anyone who did not do what they said was in trouble. The fact is they often beat us. Then we became confused, not knowing what was the right thing to do, which was the 'right' group, and what to say to which group.

Another thing that worried us was that sometimes you never saw your child for the whole night and you wondered what could have happened. I was fortunate because, as soon the war became serious, I sent my girls to stay with their brothers in town.

Children were born into the district as a result of the war but I've never heard of anyone whom a comrade returned to marry after the war. It was like a bad seed that was sown and now we have the fruits of that bad seed. I have never heard of either a comrade or a soldier who returned to claim their children. It is painful to have a child whose father is unknown.

The Zanlas would just arrive at any time. Our district is large and sometimes they spent days in other villages and we just heard about them. They would rotate from area to area. They always went in the opposite direction to the soldiers.

The soldiers in our area were both black and white, although some white soldiers painted themselves black. From a distance you could not tell the difference but, when they came closer, we could always tell who they were by their eyes.

The soldiers once became aware of a base somewhere quite nearby and they attacked it, and a lot of people died and a lot of homes were burnt down. A few days later, my daughter went to take the cattle from their pen early in the morning. I was on my way to the garden with my smaller children when I heard the sound of a radio. The soldiers had arrived at my house and, finding my daughter at the cattle pen, had told her to open the house. There they switched on the radio and turned the volume up very high.

Hearing the noise I made my way back and, on my arrival,

the soldiers called, "*Masalu**, come here." Then they asked me if I had heard gunshots the previous night. I said I had and they told me that they had killed all the Zanlas. Then they asked me where comrades were likely to be seen and I replied that we only saw them when they came and they could come any time. Then the soldiers just picked up their guns and ran away. They never even said goodbye.

They did well to run away because, just after that, I heard that the Zanlas were on the nearest mountain. The Zanlas also knew the soldiers were around: either they were both looking for or running away from each other.

It did not do to be too inquisitive in those days: things were serious and one had to mind one's own business.

After I had sent my children to town, I hired a boy to work for and help me. I continued to cultivate my garden and grew a lot of tomatoes. These I had no difficulty in selling because my house is not far from the road. I could not go anywhere and leave my home because I was looking after my children's possessions. I was very lucky because nothing unpleasant happened to our family.

There were many rules that we had to abide by before independence. Many were not good but we accepted them as a way of life because that was the way it was. Now, people, especially church-going people, are doing their best to keep their children through the churches. I don't think there are as many *tsotsis*† as there were before because children are attending clubs. Young boys no longer go from village to village in search of beer, they would rather spend their time in church. This seems very good to me because it is controlling and taming our children. This is not the only good thing brought about by independence. For instance, women are involved in development projects. Most women are making things – sewing, for example – and men are also engaged in carpentry and are managing to sell quite a lot of things.

At first, I did not understand about the liberation struggle but now that my son is back and I see good things happening, I realize the liberation struggle did us good. It brought peace and opened our minds. Now we are at peace and we talk and chat with whites. Our sons are marrying white girls and it is quite accepted. Before, it was frightening to learn

* *Masalu* – old lady (Ndebele).
† *Tsotsi* – person up to no good.

that someone's son had married a white girl: we did not think that we could go near them. Now, we are all one people. I urge you, my children, to remain united in this way. I am very happy.

Women did a great job during the war. They cooked and washed clothes for the comrades. Even when we had no soap, we had to find it and see that we washed their clothes properly. We did all this because we felt sorry for them and because our children were in the same situation and would need help wherever they were.

5   Juliet Makande

Chilimanzi

I WAS BORN in Kadoma. My father was a land development
organizer and my mother was just an ordinary person
with a little bit of education. She was not married to my
father who already had a wife and she already had a little
boy by another man. Later she had another three children
by different fathers.

It was my mother's responsibility to support her children. When she had my elder brother she was working as
a housemaid, but when she met my father she stopped work
and lived with him until my twin brother and I were four
months old. It was then that my father wanted to take us
from my mother and send us to a certain hospital to be
looked after as orphans.

You see my mother's parents wanted my father to pay
lobola. He, however, was not prepared to live with my mother
or take her as his second wife because he was already
married. He had a marriage certificate and he didn't want
his first wife to know that he had another woman. He just
felt that if he could remove the children, then he would not
have to pay lobola or maintenance or anything like that.

He had already made all the arrangements to send us away. My mother had no idea of his plans, until after they reached the hospital. Unfortunately for him, when they got there, he was told that they would not take us because my brother and I were Roman Catholic and not Anglican. This was because a sister at the hospital had asked my mother about the 'mother' of the twins and my mother had explained it was she. The hospital sister was surprised as our father had told them that the mother of the twins had died and that my mother was the sister of the dead woman. Hearing this, my mother began to cry because she realized that my father wanted to steal us from her.

So, then, it was all explained and the nursing sister told the matron. That is why my father was sent away by the matron. They said that they didn't want Roman Catholic children. They felt that if they told him the truth, my mother would have difficulties with my father. After that my mother decided to leave my father because she was afraid that he might take us away again.

So she went and stayed with her parents until we were in grade three and then my father came to take us away. He sent us to live with his brother in Chilimanzi. We stopped going to school for a year.

After that we were taken to live with our stepmother in Gutu and she was not very nice to us. So, at the end of the year, we asked if we could return to our own mother but my father wouldn't let us. We stayed there until I was in grade five. Then my mother sent her sister to fetch us. By that time I had almost forgotten what my mother looked like. My father agreed that we could go. As we had no money, my father said he would collect his salary in Mvuma and told us to meet him there. But, by then, he was in love with another woman and so we couldn't find him.

We went to the office where he was paid his salary. He was not there and we were told that he had not been in. We didn't know what to do, because we had no money. But luckily we met a man who worked with my father and, because he knew us, he gave us enough money to return to Gutu. My mother's sister did not want us to do this but there was nothing else to be done, we had no money. My father returned a week later and he said we couldn't go to see our mother because it was almost time for the schools to open again.

So I stayed with my father and I did grade seven. My father said I didn't do well enough, so he arranged for me to repeat, but I didn't finish the year because the war started in Chilimanzi and there were too many things for young girls and boys to do, other than go to school.

At the time, I didn't know much about the war. I had heard of the Zanla forces but I didn't know what kind of people they were. I only knew the soldiers.

People said that when the war comes, we are going to fight so that everyone will be rich and the schools will be free and we'll be able to go back to school and there'll be lots of jobs. So we were looking forward to the war, so that when it was over, we could go to school freely and get jobs very easily.

The school I went to was a long way from my father's place and you could meet either the Zanla forces or the soldiers on the way. If you were lucky, you reached school without difficulty, but what often happened was that the soldiers would come to the school to address us. We were afraid because the soldiers would expect us, especially the boys, to know about the Zanla forces. It was quite difficult because they always wanted you to make a statement – even if you knew nothing – about what the Zanla forces looked like, when you last saw them, what they were wearing and the direction they followed. Of course, the Zanla forces wouldn't let us tell the soldiers such things. So it was much easier not to go to school as you could then be on the watch for either of the groups.

If the soldiers came, you could run away and, if the Zanla forces came, we young girls would go and cook for them. The first time I saw the Zanlas was when I was waiting at a bus stop to send some things to my stepbrother who was at school in Gokomere. I saw men approaching. There were about six of them. At the bus stop there were no trees and nowhere to hide. I couldn't run away, I couldn't do anything. I just sat there. But I was shocked and afraid. I didn't know what to do, so I just sat still. They passed me and didn't talk to me.

They were wearing ordinary clothes, jeans. People said that the Selous Scouts were soldiers, mostly blacks, and that they didn't dress in uniform. They wore ordinary clothes but they carried guns. So, at the time, it was quite difficult to tell the difference between the Selous Scouts and Zanla forces.

At first I thought they were Selous Scouts – I had heard about them – or, perhaps, the Zanla forces. But I didn't know what I would say if they had asked me a question. Not knowing who they were, I was not sure whether I would give the right answer, the one they would expect.

Then three of them came up to me and said, "Do you know us?" I said "No." "Have you ever heard about *magandanga*?" they asked, and I again said, "No." They then said, "We are the *magandanga*," and they asked me why I was sitting at the bus stop and where I was going. I explained and then they told me to return home as they wanted food right away. They said that, if I knew of any other girls of my age or older, I should tell them to come to the base immediately.

I couldn't actually run because I was so afraid. I was trembling. But I hurried to tell my stepmother who was working in the maize fields. She said that I ought not to go in case they were Selous Scouts but rather wait at home to see what happened. Other people were also afraid. They too didn't know the difference between the Zanla forces and Selous Scouts. People said that Selous Scouts would often pretend to be Zanlas and when you went to cook for them, then they would bomb you. We knew we had to be careful of such people.

But this time everyone said the men were really the Zanla forces and that the young boys and girls had to go, although our parents were still very afraid.

My mother gave me a chicken because everyone was asked to bring some mealie-meal and a chicken. I took the food and went to the base. When I arrived, I saw a woman sitting there whom I knew. She was my *amainini* from our totem. I didn't know whether I was allowed to greet her so I just looked at her and saw that she had a very sad face. I felt badly about not greeting her because I knew she was somehow a relation. So I shook hands with her and saw that she felt like crying; but I didn't want to talk to her in front of everyone because I didn't know what to say.

Then I returned to the cooking place. One of the freedom fighters, a leader, came up to me and asked me if I knew the woman. I replied that I did and he asked me if I was related to her. So I told him that we shared a totem and that she was my *amainini*. Then he asked me if I knew her husband and I said, "Yes, very well."

The freedom fighter wanted to tell me that he was dead,

but he couldn't bring it out. I was confused because I didn't know the right way to talk to them and what they wanted or didn't want. So I tried to avoid speaking to him any further, because I didn't know what information he wanted from me. At about three o'clock, we had finished cooking. The freedom fighters had brought a lot of sweets, biscuits, jam and flour with them and after we had finished eating our sadza, they gave us some biscuits. Then one of the freedom fighters asked me to make a big pot of tea and told me to give some to my *amainini*. I did so and then she was asked to drink it all. She couldn't. She tried to do so but she couldn't – I think she was upset.

Then they told us that they were going on to another place and that we were all to go together. The boys were told to tell our parents that they had to attend a meeting that evening and that they shouldn't wear white or colourful clothes. At first we didn't even consider that if the soldiers came we would be in trouble. We just felt as if it was a good party. We enjoyed it because we didn't realize what danger was. There was a big crowd of people at the meeting. The freedom fighters told us that they had killed this woman's, my *amainini's*, husband the night before. Then, we realized that we shouldn't play around. They told us that they didn't want to hear of anyone saying they supported the party but doing all sorts of other things.

Later they said that parents could go but the girls had to stay. Everyone was afraid, after hearing that someone they knew had been killed. Even the freedom fighters were afraid. They had not been coming into Zimbabwe to fight the war for very long, and they didn't know whether people liked them or not. Sometimes, they told us, people would put poison in their blankets or in their food and they would die. At other times, parents might send their children to contact the soldiers who would come in the middle of the night and kill them all. They explained that that was why the *chimbwidos* and the *mujibas* had to spend nights with them – so that if anyone turned traitor, the children and the freedom fighters would die together.

At that time they believed my uncle was a sell-out. Before the war in our area, there was a white man who used to come out from Mvuma. They used to call him a district commissioner. He would tell the people to build contour ridges and do everything he told them to do. People didn't always do these things. I think the problem was that he didn't explain the reasons why they had to work hard and build contour ridges. So they didn't, because it was a lot of work. But my uncle would tell the DC where there were no contour ridges and where he should go. You had to pay a fine if you had land without contour ridges. So, if the DC came to this area, he would go to my uncle's house and then from there he would go to the villages. So people thought that he was responsible for both the contour ridges and the fines.

So, when the freedom fighters came, the first thing they asked was, "Do you know of anyone who has a son in the army?" or "Do you know anyone who works with government?" and so on. People told them. The Zanlas wanted to find out things from teachers, business people and people in the government like my father. The Zanlas wanted to meet them to find out what they were like.

My uncle had several stores and they found him at one of them. They took him and his wife away, and they left the little boy and the little girl in the house by themselves. Then they took everything from the store – mainly food because it was a grocery shop – and they gave it all away. They killed my uncle before they got to our village but they didn't shoot him. I don't know how they did it.

After that we knew they would kill, if they thought you were a sell-out.

Then we realized that we too were in danger. The freedom fighters could be happy when they wanted to be and they could be sour when they wanted to be. They could get angry very quickly and yet be happy at the same time. I think some of us felt it was nice to be with the freedom fighters – after we had got used to them. But our parents thought it was quite difficult because they understood that there would be trouble if the soldiers came.

When they arrived in a village, they would choose a girl to be a leader of the *chimbwidos*. It was quite hard to be a *chimbwido* but it was especially hard to be a leader. If you were an ordinary *chimbwido*, you knew that you were not alone. But if you were a leader, you were responsible and you had to see that there were enough blankets and enough food. You had to make sure that it was cooked nicely and that there was water for them to drink. If anything went wrong then you would be in trouble. And, when the soldiers came into an area, they looked first for the leaders because they thought they would have more information.

There was one group of freedom fighters who were very kind to me and were prepared to help me. They were not all like that. I think it was because they knew that I lived with my stepmother and, I think, some of them had grown up in similar circumstances. It is not easy to have a stepmother. For example, I did not go to school but my stepmother's children did. Her daughter, who was the same age as me, got the same pass in our grade seven exams but she was allowed to continue, and I had to repeat. My mother was not there to stand up for me and so things happened which were not fair. I also worked at the irrigation most of the time so, in many ways, I was just a worker and the freedom fighters in that group understood this.

It was unfortunate that we had to sleep with the comrades because sometimes we had sex with them. You couldn't even tell a friend about it because it might be said you were a prostitute or because the story would reach the freedom fighters and you would be in trouble. They always told us that we should never tell anyone. "We don't want sell-outs," they said. So if a group came today, you might have to 'go to the *poshito*' with one of them – that meant you had to sleep with him; and then if another group came the next day you might have to 'go to the *poshito*' with someone else. Some of the girls fell pregnant. The unfortunate thing was that we didn't know the real names of the freedom fighters. And, in our culture, you must have a totem for your child from its father. If you don't know the totem, you can't just pick one from your head. Your child has to know where it comes from. Many of the children who were born in the war still don't know their totems or even their fathers' real names.

Also, if you had to sleep with one freedom fighter today, and another the next day, it was hard to tell who might be the father of the child. In this case the girl would usually say it was a *mujiba* who had fathered the baby.

He would accept it, even if he knew it was not true. There was no chance for him to say otherwise.

Parents could not say anything either because they were afraid for their lives. The comrades didn't want parents to know that they were having sex with the girls but, of course, they did: there was really nothing that they could do.

One evening, around seven p.m. when people were eating, and we were serving sadza to the *poshitos* – the men who guarded the area – we heard something like a huge drum that went BOOM! It was a big blast.

Then we heard a freedom fighter shouting, "Shut up and lie down. Don't run, just lie down where you are." I just stood there holding a plate of sadza. Then one of the *mujibas* said, "Lie down!" I lay down and all I could hear were shots and babies crying and people screaming: the wounded screaming and shouting.

The battle lasted about an hour. Several people were killed, including one freedom fighter. Actually he was not killed but wounded by the soldiers. As we ran away, I saw him crawling along the ground. He was trying to get away too. Then he asked me to carry him. I tried but I couldn't do so, because he was quite a big man. So he said, "Go." I felt very bad about leaving him because he was hurt so badly. They had shot him in the thigh. Then he said, "Would you like to take my things and run away with them?" But it was still too difficult for me to carry the guns and run with them. I had not done this before. Then he said: "You can go." And I said I couldn't go and leave him like that and he replied, "No, you can go. You must run away, I will manage."

I went just a few metres and then I stood watching him. He gave his things to a man who was near him. Then he took something, I think it was a grenade and he opened it and it went shsh. Then I think he put it into his mouth and then . . . he was dead.

Then I ran away with the man to whom he had given his things and a bit farther on we met other freedom fighters. We told them what had happened and they went to see about it. Then we went on until we reached another village and we stayed there for a night. We slept outside without blankets as that incident had frightened us so much. The dogs barked throughout the night as people kept arriving, we couldn't tell whether they were soldiers or not.

The next morning I and my friends went to my aunt's home and stayed there. My stepmother had packed up all her things and gone to stay near a mission hospital. There were no buses. The Zanla forces had closed the bus routes. You had to get a permit from them to travel – just in case you met other Zanla forces on the way. Two days later, the freedom fighters came back and said that all the girls in the village had to return to their homes.

When I returned, my stepmother had gone. So it was quite difficult because the only other person at home was the man who was working for my father. He didn't know where my mother had gone.

The Zanlas wanted to know why my father was not at home and why my stepmother had run away. I told them I didn't know. Then they said that everyone must attend a meeting that evening. All parents had to go and register their children. If they were working, you had to say where they were and what they were doing. They asked me about my brother and my sister. I told them.

Then they sent me to Harare to tell my father that he must return home. I explained that I didn't have money to get there. So they told people in the village to contribute. When I got to Harare I gave my father the letter and we returned home together. My father told them that his job had required him to be in the city and he made excuses to the Zanla forces.

I don't think that they believed him. Then we had another contact with the soldiers, and the freedom fighters ran away. Luckily enough, no one was killed.

But then I felt it was all too much. I was very tired. I didn't know what to do. I thought that perhaps I should go to my mother in Mhondoro. I hoped there would be no war in that area. So I told the freedom fighters that my mother was very sick and asked if I could go and see her for a while. They said they would give me two weeks. But when I got to Mhondoro my mother was not there. So, instead, I went to stay with my brother in Harare. I didn't want to return to Chilimanzi.

Then the Zanlas went to see my father and told him that they would give him three days to fetch me back. Otherwise, they said, they would burn down his house. My father found me in Harare. It was a day when I was quite happy. My brother had told me that he would see if I could return to school to complete my grade seven and he had suggested that afterwards I should do a dressmaking course. I was quite happy and I had forgotten about the freedom fighters. My only worry was that I would meet a soldier. I felt that I would be ill, very ill and depressed if I saw them. I couldn't bear to think about it. Then my father arrived and told me

I had to return or they would destroy everything that belonged to us. He said, "There's nothing we can do about it. You have to go back." I didn't want to and I felt bad. But we went back to the village. Straight away the freedom fighters sent a *mujiba* with a letter saying I must go to them. I was so worried, I was crying. They said, "You were going to stay with your mother and we gave you two weeks, why did you stay for long?" I told them that my mother was so ill that I couldn't return. Then they were angry and said, "We have got mothers, just like you; fathers just like you. We can't attend to them when they are sick. We don't even know how they are. So, how is it that you think that you can stay with your mother? Why is it that other people can't stay with their parents? We are just like you."

I had no answer to give them. They told me it was their last warning and that no one was allowed to run away. They asked who would cook for them if all the young boys and girls ran away. They said that they needed the *chimbwidos* and *mujibas* to help them. I stayed with them all that day. But every day things got worse and worse. My stepmother had not come back. Somebody told the Zanla forces that my father was a sell-out. This person said that he had seen my father in Mvuma with the soldiers. So the Zanla forces sent for my father. I thought he would be killed. But he disappeared and went to Harare. I don't know how he managed it.

It's hard to know if my father really was a sell-out because, if you were working in government, you had to do what you had to do. That does not make you a sell-out because it's your job. But, at the same time, if you are told not to do something, either you have to resign or you have to go on. My father was working for government so he had to do his job. Also, if you were a government worker, and if you were a land development organizer, the soldiers would always come to you. So ordinary people might think that because you are working for a government they don't like, you must be a sell-out.

In some ways I think certain people were jealous of my father because he was a very good farmer and he still is a good farmer. And, sometimes, if people are jealous, they make up stories which are not true.

But, again, after my father had gone, I was alone – except for the worker, Felix. Then the Zanlas came for my father.

I was sleeping in one of the kitchens. They knocked on the door. I didn't know whether it was the freedom fighters or soldiers. They told me to open the door! They asked for my father. I said I didn't know where he was.

Others had already wakened Felix. They asked me why he was working for my father when he was not at home. "Who is going to pay him?" they said. I told them that he had been paid and that I didn't think my father could have gone far, because he hadn't said anything to me. But they had already heard the rumour that my father had run away. Then they told the worker to leave and said that they never wanted to see him at our place again. So then it was just me. They asked, "Did you know that your father is a sell-out?" I said I didn't know. Then they said, "We have told you before that your father is a sell-out. How can you say that you don't know?" So I said, "I'm not saying that my father is not a sell-out. He could be one or he could not be one. I have got nothing to prove that he is and nothing to prove that he's not."

Then they ordered me to tell them if I heard anything from my father. And I asked them if I could leave and stay with my mother. But they refused me permission. "Your father will come," they said. My father had a lot of cattle, irrigation and plenty of wheat.

So I explained how difficult it was for me to be by myself because I had to look after the cows and because I was frightened of the soldiers. I said, "I can't run away and leave the cows. They will go into people's fields and I will be in trouble." Then they said that they were going to share out the cows among the people of the village and they killed two for people to eat. I couldn't do anything.

Then two weeks before they went to the assembly points the auxiliaries arrived. They told us to go to the school for a meeting. But the Zanla forces had told us that no one was allowed to go to meetings called by the Muzorewas. They said that if we went there would be trouble. What could I do? The Muzorewas had already caught me.

I went to the meeting. It lasted all day. We waited for their chief to come and address us. But that same evening the Zanla forces were coming. Some of them had already gone to the assembly point. Some said that all the *chimbwidos* and *mujibas* must also go to the assembly points.

After the meeting I left with some other girls and we went

home, got ready and then went on to the Zanla forces.

When we got there someone had told the Zanlas that I was in love with one of the auxiliaries. They were very angry and they threatened to hit me. They said they would give me two sjamboks so I would tell them the truth. I said, "OK. Do whatever you like, but the truth is I'm not in love with any of the auxiliaries. If you think so, there's nothing I can do."

So they did nothing. Then we were called to go to a station from where they would be taken to the assembly points. Some went, some didn't go and those who didn't go hid their guns and walked about like ordinary people. But we knew that they were freedom fighters even though they were travelling without cards.

After about six months, my parents came home. About three days later, I went to the irrigation where my father had twenty-four plots. We often had to water and work in the irrigation. I worked there most of the time when there were no freedom fighters around. Also if you missed your turn for water, you wouldn't get it for another week.

I returned home quite late, about eight p.m., and the very moment I walked into the house, the freedom fighters arrived. Some came into the kitchen and some into the bedroom where my father was sleeping. When they arrived, my stepmother thought that I had come with them. This was not true. They asked my mother where my father was and she told them he was in the bedroom.

It was quite dark. There was was no moon. They went to the bedroom. My father was undressed and they asked him questions one after another. He couldn't answer. They started beating him and then they told him to go outside. I just stood there watching. I couldn't even shout because I knew that if I did, I could also be killed. I couldn't tell them not to do anything to my father because I couldn't tell them what to do.

Then, one of them said they had to go. They thought my mother, who had run out of the kitchen, had gone to tell the soldiers. One of them hit my father hard. I don't know what he used but my father fell down. I think they thought he was dying because they left him. He was screaming.

Then they ran away but they told me that I had to go with them. I thought that they were going to kill me as well. They could see that I was shivering with fear. So they told me they wouldn't do anything to me, but that if my stepmother had gone to fetch the soldiers, I would be in trouble.

So we went to another village which was a long way from my own. I had not eaten anything. I had no jersey, no shoes, nothing. They said, "You must stay here for a couple of days because we think the soldiers will be hunting for you." But the following day, I went back to my village. When I arrived I saw a big army truck at the house. My father was in the truck. My father had told the soldiers that I had come with the freedom fighters and it was I who had given them the information. This was not true. I hadn't seen them for a whole week. I don't know how they knew that my father had returned home. My father told the soldiers that if ever they saw me they should shoot to kill me straight away. When my sister-in-law saw me, she told me to leave quickly because my cousins had left with the soldiers and my father had given them permission to shoot me immediately.

At first I didn't know what to do but I thought I would go to my father's sister. When I explained everything to her, she understood because she knew what it meant to be at war. But there was nothing she could do, so she told me to go to her son in Zvishavane. But there was no transport and lifts were very expensive. I couldn't walk to the bus stop because it was far away and because I was afraid of the auxiliaries. At that time they were forcing people to attend rallies.

But one morning early, I left my aunt's house. I had on my old clothes but no shoes and no jersey. I was very afraid. Luckily I met an old woman who was going to Chibi.* I explained my story to her and she said she would give me one of her dresses to wear. I looked like an old woman. She told me that if we met the auxiliaries, she would say that I was her daughter-in-law and we were travelling together. In this way no one would know that I was a *chimbwido.* We walked and walked and we got to a place where we stayed with one of her relatives for the night. The next morning we got up early. We walked a long distance and I was hungry. Then, luckily, we got a lift to Mashaba which cost us two dollars. But I had to go from there to Zvishavane and I had no money. At Mashaba the old woman had to leave me. There were no buses to Zvishavane. All buses were going to Harare for a Muzorewa rally. I was crying. I wanted to

* Now Chivi.

go to my mother but I didn't even know where she was. There were soldiers. I couldn't look at them.

I had not eaten anything but a woman gave me a pint of milk which her little girl wouldn't drink but I couldn't drink it. There was a big notice at the station which said that no one should be there after six p.m. and it was about five p.m. I didn't know what to do or where to go. I had no money. But then luckily at about five-thirty p.m. a combi driven by two young boys stopped. They were going to Zvishavane. I explained that I had no money and asked them to give me a lift. I said I don't even know where I'm going but I have this address. These two boys gave everybody a lift, and only those who had money paid. When we got to Zvishavane they helped me look for my aunt's son. They were very nice to me.

When I told my story to my cousin, he felt quite sorry for me and the next day he bought me a nice dress and a jersey. I stayed there for a month and then I felt that I wanted to be with my mother. It was the time of the cease-fire. My cousin said I should wait until after independence when things had settled down. So, I stayed and sometimes I felt better in the evenings when we went to sing liberation songs. Then my father heard that I was staying in Zvishavane and he wrote a nasty letter to my aunt's son, saying that he mustn't keep me as I had wanted him killed by the freedom fighters. He said that he never wanted to see me again and, if he died, I should not attend the funeral.

After that I felt bad, I couldn't eat. When I saw food I felt I wanted to vomit. So I told my cousin that I really thought I should go to my mother as I felt it was the only place where I would begin to feel better. So my cousin gave me money to travel and I went to my mother but she was not there. I stayed with a brother for two weeks and then I decided to find my mother's sister in Harare.

By then my only thought was to find a man and get married and get everything over. I was not sure whether the war would really end and I thought that if it didn't, then the freedom fighters would get us to cook for them again. I thought that if I got married, I would be a woman and I wouldn't have to go and cook because I would be a mother. I never thought that if you fell in love with a man, and he made you pregnant, that he would then say he didn't like you. I thought that if I got married I would be happy. I met

Brian's father in August 1980 and I quickly became pregnant but then he said he didn't like me any more. I didn't know what to do. He told me that I should have an abortion and, if I didn't want one, then that was my problem.

And then my difficulties started all over again. I couldn't go to my mother because my father would tell her that I caused nothing but trouble and he would also blame my mother. So I went to 88 Manica Road. They tried to help me. They told Brian's father that he should take me to my parents and pay damages and that if I had a child, he should pay maintenance. They told him that he couldn't just throw me away and that he had to give me food.

Then Brian's father decided to take me to my father and pay damages. But I couldn't tell him the whole story because I thought he would think I was mad. He would believe that I wanted my father killed by the Zanla forces which was not true. So I thought we should see my father's sister. We went to Chilimanzi with Brian's father and his brother and sister and we visited my aunt. My father said he didn't want to have anything to do with me. My aunt didn't tell them this. She told them that my father had said that we must go to my mother. My aunt thought that my mother should try to speak to my father. And, if he refused to listen to her, then she could go the village court. So we returned to Harare where Brian's father showed that he didn't like me at all. So I went to fetch my mother.

I had forgotten her a little bit. When I arrived she was doing something in the yard. Then a woman came over to me and greeted me and I asked if the woman I could see next door was my mother. I was not quite sure. At first I couldn't talk to her, I could only cry. Then, after a bit, I told her the whole story. I was very upset because I felt that if I had been with my mother none of these things would have happened.

Then my mother went with me to see my father. He wouldn't listen and so my mother took the problem to the village court and spoke to the people. Then they decided to speak to my father. But he said he didn't want to have anything to do with them.

So then I said that I was prepared to tell my father about everything that had happened. But, I said, "The truth is I don't even know how the Zanla forces heard the news that my father had returned to his home. If my father doesn't want to believe me, there's nothing I can do. The truth is that I am innocent." Then the village court said that my father had not been nice to me. They said that if I had not stayed at home during the war, his home and all his possessions would have been burnt down. But as I had remained there, I had saved most of his things. They said he should thank me instead of chasing me away and treating me badly.

Then I think my father tried to understand and he said, "All right, she can come and talk about it." So I went and my father was a little bit understanding but my stepmother refused to believe me. She thought that I had made everything up. I tried to ignore what she said because it was painful. Then Brian's father paid damages but he said that he didn't want me as his wife and he left me with my father. My father said I could stay with him or I could go to my mother and I went to her. After the baby was born, I went to see Brian's father. I thought he would change his mind when he saw the baby, but he didn't. So I started to work as a housemaid and I have been working as a maid for different people ever since.

During the war a lot of women had a lot of problems. I am not saying that men didn't but for women it was very difficult. If you had a son in the liberation struggle – even if he was with the Rhodesian forces – you never knew whether he was alive or dead. Most mothers were always worried about their children and their husbands.

Even if your daughters were *chimbwidos* you never knew what might happen to them and if they would return home. When you heard that somebody had been killed, a mother always wondered if it was her own son or daughter. I think the women really suffered.

Now that we have got independence, I personally feel that all the things I thought would happen are not what I am seeing today. Since I was a *chimbwido*, I did do a lot of important things during the war and I thought I would receive more than what I am seeing today.

6   **Maudy Muzenda**

Mvuma

I WAS BORN in 1928 in Masvingo district. I grew up on a farm owned by my father but I was brought up by my grandmother because my father and mother had separated. My sister died when I was three years old, so I never knew her. When I was ten years old my father remarried and after that he and his new wife looked after me. They had four children of their own, but we were one family. My stepmother was very good to me. She brought me up and educated me. She was a Xhosa, a South African. My father and I were Karangas.

I went to school at Gokomere Mission in Masvingo and, after I had completed standard six, I went to train as a nurse at Makumbe training hospital in Chinamora. This took three years and, when I had finished, I was over twenty years old. After my training I went back to Masvingo and stayed with my stepmother for a year and then I went to work at Murewa Hospital.

By that time I had become engaged to this husband* of

* Simon Muzenda: now Vice-President of Zimbabwe.

mine. He had completed his secondary education in South Africa and then he done a three-year course in carpentry at Maryville College in Durban. It was there that he became interested in politics.

When he returned in 1950, we got married and lived in Bulawayo. I worked in one of the municipal hospitals and my husband started his own carpentry business in Barbourfields. We had twins later that year. They were premature and had to be kept in hospital for three months so I stopped work in order to look after them. I only began to nurse again three years later.

My husband had already become involved in politics and he worked with Benjamin Burombo in a party I think they called the Voice Association*. I did not play a participating role but I supported him, because he was working for the good of the people†. I encouraged him to continue because I understood that what he was after was for the good of Africa. While we were in Bulawayo, there was no police harassment because their organization had just started. People were not very active as they were only just beginning to organize themselves.

We lived in Bulawayo for five years and then we moved to Mvuma. We wanted to go back home, and business in Bulawayo wasn't too good at the time. We thought it would be better to start a business in a place where not so many people had already begun to do this. Mvuma was just a small place. I began to nurse again at the local hospital and my husband began his carpentry business. But most of the time he was out educating people about politics. You see the National Democratic Party‡ had then been formed and my husband became an active member. People in Mvuma did not know anything about politics and so my husband informed them about such affairs. He often travelled from Mvuma to Masvingo, Zvishavane and Shurugwi. Sometimes he even went back to Bulawayo. He travelled with people like Munodawafa, Takawira, James Bassoppo Moyo and others whom I cannot remember.

When we left Bulawayo I had three children but we had another five while we were living in Mvuma and so I had eight children altogether.

---

* The British African National Voice Association (BANVA) formed by Benjamin Burombo in 1947.
† In 1953 Simon Muzenda became Secretary-General of the BANVA.
‡ The NDP was formed in 1960.

It was difficult to look after all of them while my husband was travelling. In those days the nursing salary was very small. We were underpaid but we worked hard.

Then they started ZAPU which involved all Zimbabweans. My husband was arrested in 1962. He was arrested in Zvishavane and I only heard about it from other people. First he was put in prison in Zvishavane and then they moved him to Harare Central. He stayed there for two years. It was very hard for me. You know it is difficult for a mother with so many children to look after them alone. There was really no one to help me because my husband only had one sister, so I had to look after the children on my own. I managed to put the children through their primary education but I could not afford to pay secondary school fees, because they were much higher and I could not get any assistance from the Smith government. But while my husband was in prison, he found friends in Sweden who helped me educate the children when they began their secondary education. They gave us money and clothes. My colleagues at the hospital were kind but they could not help.

You know that if your husband is under arrest, people look at you in a funny way. They think that whatever you do is a bit odd. But the white doctors, especially the lady doctors and the sisters, were good to me.

I visited my husband once a month. I was permitted to see him for only five minutes, even after travelling all the way from Mvuma to Harare. I usually travelled on a train which took all night or a whole day and half because you had to go via Gweru. After all that time travelling I saw my husband for five minutes, and then I waited for the next train home which took another day and half. If there was a patient being transferred to Harare sometimes I travelled by ambulance. But mostly I took the train so that I could take one or two of the children with me.

My husband was full of courage. So when we visited him, if I was unhappy, I tried not to show it, because if I were to go and complain he would worry. He was doing good things for his country so I did not want to discourage him. I used to take him food to cheer him up.

He made friends with Comrade Takawira but the authorities only allowed one visitor at a time and so I never saw them together. I made friends with Mrs Takawira. Sometimes we even used to stay with her in Harare.

The police in Mvuma used to come and ask me what my position was and I always told them that I supported my husband. Then they would caution me and tell me not to become active in politics. One day the police came to arrest me. They said that they had information that I was supporting the guerillas. Of course I used to do so, but people did not know that because I did it in such a way that they should not know. They put me in a cell for one day and asked me what my husband was doing, although they already knew he was a politician.

Although he had been sentenced to twelve years imprisonment, he was released two years later. He was healthy and strong. He took up his carpentry business, but he was also very active in politics*. Then he was arrested again. But, after ten years in prison, he went to Zambia to join the rest of the politicians there.

During those years when the children were going to school, I became used to being a single mother. I used to talk with a relative of my husband's, Philip Maramba. He gave me a lot of advice. I also used to get assistance from the Roman Catholic priests from Driefontein Mission.

People were active during the time that my husband was in prison. I also became involved in politics. I discussed our position with other women and gave them ideas about what we should do. We were a sort of underground movement. Even now I support the politicians but I am not a very active party member.

Sometimes, about twice a year, the comrades came to the clinic to ask for medicines and I would supply them with what they wanted. Once I remember a guerilla with a broken arm came to the hospital and the male nurse and I plastered him up and sent him off. The white sisters and doctors did not know what I was doing. Had they done so they would have reported me to the authorities. They supported me with kindness because my husband was in prison, but they did not support the struggle. It was very difficult for me and that is why I could not give help openly. Everything I did, I did secretly. I had to be careful.

It was hard to work with people who supported me personally but did not support the struggle. I remember one

---

* Following the ZANU Congress in 1964, Simon Muzenda became Deputy Organizing Secretary to the party.

of the doctors did not even want to see me but he could not do anything about it. I kept to myself. I was a quiet person and never talked much about things to anyone. I only talked to Mr Gurajena, the male nurse at the hospital, and to Mr Maramba, my husband's relative. I could not confide in anyone else. Sometimes I had the feeling that other people just pretended to support me.

Once a certain doctor called me into his office and asked how it was that my husband was a politician but that I was not active in politics. He said that usually a husband and a wife did the same thing. He warned me that if the authorities ever found out that I was doing something to help the guerillas, I would be in trouble.

Freedom fighters, the Zanlas not the Zipras, who were in our area for a long time, came for medicines and, sometimes, money. I always gave them what I could.

It was hard for me alone to clothe, feed and educate the children. That was my biggest worry. But it was a problem that did not only apply to me. I remember one women whose husband was arrested and sentenced to twelve years in prison for allegedly damaging the railway line. That poor woman did not have a job, and so she lived by begging, working in people's fields, and growing and selling vegetables. I share sad memories with that woman.

When my husband was released ten years later he was brought home by a friend. He stayed with us for eighteen months. During that time the police often came to check on us and kept watch on my house at night. If they saw anyone coming to the house they always wanted to know what they wanted. I was constantly afraid something would happen. We had to tell our friends or visitors not to stay long at the house, for fear they could be harmed.

Then my husband left the country to join the rest of the fighters in Zambia. He went on the same day as Comrade John Nkomo. They flew from Harare. No one tried to stop them. I did not see him again until after the war.

Some time later he called for three of my children to go to Zambia to join the struggle. My eldest two daughters and my son left to join him. I felt very sad that they should go although I knew that the cause was a good one. After a little while in Zambia my husband took them to Mozambique where my daughter, Teresa, was killed at Chimoio*. It was very, very painful and I grieved for her. She was only eighteen years old.

One day I was wanted by the Special Branch who came to fetch me from my house as it was my day off. I was put in a small cell and questioned. They said they had heard I was collecting money from people to feed the guerillas. I asked them to give me the name of one person who had given them such information. I asked them to say where they had seen me collecting money and to whom I had given it. The CIDs said that I was not supposed to ask them such questions. So I asked them how they thought I could keep quiet when I was faced with such accusations.

They then said that I was a courageous woman, like my husband. But they also threatened that they would put in me in prison because we were under martial law. They said they would put me in prison without food. I told them that it was up to them to do what they wanted and that if they wanted to put me in prison, they could do so.

So they left me alone for about an hour and then they came back and questioned me again. They kept on doing this, questioning me and then leaving me alone. They said that they wanted answers from me. I kept telling them that I had nothing more to say: I had said everything I had to say.

Then they asked about my family and I told them. They wanted to know how I managed to look after so many children and I told them that I was employed at Mvuma Hospital. They then said, "Are you working under the government?" I told them that I was. So they said that the wife of a politician could not be a government employee and they telephoned the hospital to find out if I was telling the truth.

The matron confirmed my statement and asked them what they were doing with me. The CIDs told her that they had a few questions to ask me. Then the matron asked them how they could arrest a government employee, a nurse, and not inform the hospital. So the CIDs told me that they would release me because the matron had told them that she wanted me on duty in the theatre the following day. At that time I was a theatre nurse. The CIDs said they would call me in again for questioning. But they never did so.

* In 1977 the Rhodesian forces attacked Chimoio, a complex of military and civilian camps in Mozambique. Over three thousand people were killed.

The war was quite hot in Mvuma area especially in the Chirumanzu district. Sometimes the guerillas came right into Mvuma which was just a small place. One day they came into the beer-hall and blew up a part of it.

Casualties also used to be brought into the hospital from the area. Most of the people killed were men, civilians. The soldiers who were injured during a contact were sent to Chivu or to Gweru hospital. Civilians came to Mvuma Hospital although serious cases were sent to Gweru for amputations. Sometimes, but not very often, people were given amputations without an anaesthetic. A lot of people were injured in contacts.

People in the rural areas suffered. It wasn't too bad in Mvuma itself because it was a small town. It was much worse in areas such as Chirumanzu. A lot of people were killed.

I remember one of the school boys from Holy Cross Mission was killed in a cell at Mvuma. They interrogated him because they said he was a guerilla. But he was a schoolboy and he died in Mvuma hospital. The police would not believe what he said, so they beat him very badly in the cell.

Sometimes people were also thrown into a pit called an *mbidzi**. It was a big pit into which people were thrown and tortured so that they would confess. It was very deep. After throwing people into the pit, the authorities left them there for some time. They only pulled them out if they were ready to confess. If they refused they would be left to die in the pit. Sometimes people's homes were burnt down and they were left with nothing. These were some of the things which happened in the Chirumanzu area.

I used to get messages from my husband but not letters. He sent messages through people who went into the field like Father Fidelis who was with the Justice and Peace Commission.

When independence came it was a very exciting. My husband came home from Maputo with my son and my eldest daughter who had survived. We met him at the airport and I was very excited. I went with my two children to meet him. We had not seen each other for five years.

Now, after independence, I am living in Harare with my family. It is a big change for me. I worked at Mvuma Hospital

Mbidzi – deep pit (Karanga).

for twenty-five years and I still miss some of the friends I made there. When I came to Harare I had to make new friends, but now I am quite happy here.

I do not think the war would have been won without the women. Women played a very important role in the struggle. It was a very big role that they played. Now women have to liberate themselves. We should not accept our husbands as our superiors. We are equal and we should be seen to be equal because we all did a great job during the struggle.

7   Rhoda Khumalo

Glassblock

I MARRIED in 1952. At that time I had nothing of my own, and my husband and I were very poor. My husband was working for a white man in Bulawayo who was teaching him carpentry. He had a very small salary. So we decided to help ourselves. My husband left his job and we worked for people, ploughing and herding their cattle. They, in turn, would loan us their cattle to plough our own fields. Our neighbours helped us a great deal in our new home, and with their experience and advice, we learned to work for ourselves. My worst years were between 1952 and 1954. During that time I had nothing and life was almost impossible. When I married, my husband had nothing and no cattle at all but by farming, sewing and selling clothes, I managed to raise some money to buy a few cattle. Sometimes I made about twenty dollars from my sales and we would put this with whatever my husband had earned from selling furniture, and then I bought cattle at the shows.

I now have ten head of cattle, including two oxen which I use for ploughing. I manage to get enough food for my children from my fields. Our lives are easier now as my husband also makes a bit of money out of carpentry. Farming has really made us better people because now we are able to educate our children and buy them enough clothes.

I was a member of ZAPU and at meetings we talked about our lives and shared our misery because we had no freedom at all. We discussed what could be done to ease the situation, since we could never have what we wanted. We never had the opportunity to express ourselves and make our needs and wants known. Today it is different. If, for example, I am ever in need of anything or if I need advice or have questions I can ask our leaders.

I have ten children of whom seven are boys. The first was born in 1949 and the last in 1970. My eldest son first left the country in 1969. He had not done well at school and could not find employment so he went to South Africa where he worked on the mines. But when, two years later, he returned home he found that he, like many other young men, were being harassed by the soldiers and made to go to call-up.

What happened was that sometimes the authorities told us of employment vacancies, but they said that before our children could apply for them, they had to register. Parents were told that their children would be sent to do courses. We would then register our children in the hope that they would be given work or sent for further training. Only afterwards we would discover that our children had been called up. My son thought he would be forced to join the security forces, so he left the country and went to join the liberation movement.

He did not discuss his decision with me at all. I was so happy to see him after he had returned from South Africa and rejoiced, as one would, for a son who had come home. I did not think that he might go away again so soon.

After he'd left, I looked for him and wondered what could have happened. A lot of children in the area had begun to disappear and we simply concluded that they had gone to join the liberation struggle. We knew that the boys who went to fight for the country left for Zambia, Mozambique and Botswana. So we just assumed that that was where our children had gone.

What happened to us was that it was rumoured that my eldest child had come back into the country and that he had come back to fight. The soldiers went to my house in

Tshabalala in Bulawayo, where it was said that my son had been seen, and they destroyed everything and killed the lodger. Fortunately my husband was out at the time. As my other children were then very afraid of being questioned and harassed, they left as well.

In all, my husband and six of my children went to join the struggle. My sons left one by one on their own, as did their father. The two girls went together. The problem was that if the authorities knew that you had a child or children who had left the country, they gave you a very hard time. The soldiers used to come regularly to enquire where your children were and they could be hard.

The soldiers, both black and white, were very rough and sometimes they even killed people. For instance, my neighbour was beaten to death by soldiers. In my case, sometimes the soldiers came to my home in a helicopter and they always asked where my children were and accused me of feeding and harbouring the guerillas. They beat the children who were at home and, once, they beat the boy who was looking after my cattle so much that his teeth fell out.

It was a time of great troubles and problems. I cannot clearly express how I felt. My whole family had left the country, so I had to be strong because I had no alternative. It seemed better for me to stand by their decision, even though it did make things very difficult for me. The children who remained with me were very small and would often cry. They wanted us to leave our home and go somewhere, to my brother's or sister's, just anywhere that was safe. But I couldn't do that because, had I gone, I could have caused problems in someone else's home. You see, the soldiers came so often.

I never heard from my children or my husband. Sometimes I thought they must be dead and sometimes I thought they – or perhaps one of them – might return. That was another reason why I felt I couldn't move: what would my children do if they returned and found that I had left?

The children who had remained with me were too small to do anything to help me. I got most of my help from my neighbours who collected donations and bought my family food and saw to its welfare. I am really grateful to them because I could not have managed on my own with no one but my small children.

The Smith government also sometimes used spies. A person might come to your home as a visitor and yet they'd be after something; or a person would stay with a neighbour, or in the neighbourhood, and they would be quite friendly but really they were trying to find out information about a particular family. Sometimes someone might say something quite unintentionally which could be used against you. Also people might agree to statements that were untrue simply because they were afraid of being killed.

The only group in our area was the Zanlas and they came towards the end of the war and were here for about a year. There was no difference in the way they treated us, whether we were ZAPU or ZANU. This was because we received them kindly as our children and we too did not discriminate between the two parties.

When they first arrived they called us together and addressed us. They told us what they were doing and what they wanted from us and expected us to do. But, thereafter, when they returned they would go to someone's home and the owner would notify the rest of the village of their presence and tell us what they wanted, food, clothes, information about the soldiers and so on.

They only asked for money to buy beer and cigarettes and this we contributed. We never actually bought them clothes; they just took what they wanted from civilians. If, for instance, we were at a meeting and they saw somebody wearing something they liked, one just had to take the garment off and give it to them.

The soldiers often came and demanded information about the Zanlas. But, somehow, the two groups always missed each other.

One day the Zanlas came to base at my home and, as I was in the fields, a neighbour came and told me that there were people in my yard. I went to see who they were and found six groups. The freedom fighters who had first come to our area had told us that we should not welcome people without knowing who they were. So I questioned each group, although I was very frightened as I went among them asking who they were: but I had to know before I could receive them. The first group told me who they were, but I did not know them. Neither did I know the second group, but when it came to the third, I recognized one of the boys who had been a member of the very first group to come to our area. I will never forget that day.

The freedom fighters left the following morning and, as they left, the soldiers came down from the top of the mountain. They followed the comrades' footprints right to my home. Fortunately I heard them coming. Hurriedly, I put the blankets under the maize stocks and threw the dishes and pots into our well which was full of water. I opened the cattle pen and let the cattle walk all over the yard in order to cover the footprints. I have never worked so quickly or been so frightened.

As soon as the soldiers arrived, they said they'd heard that the freedom fighters had spent the night at my home. I told them that was true, but that they'd left. The soldiers followed them but fortunately the comrades had changed direction and they never caught up with them. It was a terrible moment because I realized that either I or the freedom fighters might have been killed. They missed each other by just a few minutes.

I was chosen by ZAPU to be a branch chairperson. Then I was nominated to serve in the district and later on I became an official in the province. My job was to help formulate plans and advise on ways in which we could protect ourselves and to see what could be done to help us lead a better life. At cease-fire, as I was one of the leaders in the province, I heard that the freedom fighters were returning and going to the assembly points.

On the day that my husband and children returned from Dukwe* I felt terrible. I was really hurt, although I was happy. Sometimes my heart so pained me I thought it was breaking apart – now I can say it was heartbreak – but I tried hard not to show my feelings to my family. I believed in prayer so I prayed that the Lord would help me to be strong and not show my family that I was suffering. The Lord helped me and I managed to welcome my family happily although I could see they were afraid of me because they did not want to look into my face. They knew that I had had troubles because they had left, but to be as kind and loving as I could be, I heartily welcomed them home.

This war would have not been won without the women. They did a great job during the war. The comrades would have not been able to shoot a gun if they hadn't been fed. We cooked for them, washed their clothes and even protected

* Dukwe – a refugee camp near Francistown in Botswana.

them, because it was we who gave them information about the security forces. Women worked hard.

Now that it is all over I am very pleased because I can see that everyone feels happy and free. At the time, the war was necessary because we could only get what we wanted by fighting and now we are free and not afraid of anything. Normally war is very undesirable but, at that time, it proved necessary.

When my children first came back, those who had been in Zambia and those who had been in Dukwe, they were very strong. They wanted to work and build their own homes, but they have not been able to find employment and they have become discouraged and feel powerless. They are still dependent on me. However, my eldest son is now a tailor in a clothing factory in Bulawayo. Three of my girls have married and one of them has a job. Another two of my children also have jobs and so, at least, four of my children are now working.

I am now involved in various projects. We are building dams, we keep chickens for sale and we also build and equip our kitchens to make them more convenient. In other words, we are learning to modernize our homes, and this has made our lives easier.

My wish and prayer is that all women should feel free and be willing to participate in everything that pertains to development. All women should feel free to think, as they like and say what they think so that we can help one another to develop our country. Every woman should feel it a duty to be concerned about our country so that what our children inherit will be good.

8 Thema Khumalo

Esigodini

I WAS BORN in Mzinyathini, the last child in my family. My mother died when I was very young and my aunt brought me up. I went to primary school in Mzinyathini and then my married sister Elizabeth sent me to St Augustine's, Penhalonga. However, in my second year, I became pregnant and so I left school and returned home.

When I was nineteen I married Enoch Khumalo and I lived for a long time at my husband's home while he was working in a factory first in Bulawayo and then in Mahalaphe in Botswana. During those years we had a good life and I had eight children.

I worked on the land, ploughed, looked after the cattle, took care of the garden and cared for my children – all the work that had to be done at home. My husband visited me at weekends. In our time, nearly all the home work was done by women although sometimes we hired people to help us, especially when we wanted to erect thorn fences around our homes, fields and gardens. When the war started my husband was still working in the factory.

At that time, we had very little money but we also had no knowledge of how to use it. We did not organize ourselves into good productive groups. We were ruled like tamed animals. We did not have the opportunity to do things on our own. We did what the white man told us to do. As a result we had no confidence in ourselves and we had no chance to prove ourselves worthy people. We doubted our abilities and could never see ourselves doing something worthwhile. We did not think that black people had rights and could use money as they wished. We thought that money was only supposed to be used profitably and satisfactorily by whites. We did not think that any black person could be engaged in business. For instance, even though I was educated enough to read, write and work for myself and might have known how to save and invest my money, I – and not only I but all blacks – never tried to do this because it seemed so remote from us.

My son was sixteen years old when he went to join the liberation struggle. He went on his own. I do not know if he joined others later. I had sent him to Bulawayo for money to use for grinding. When he left we were worried because we did not know where he had gone. Neither I nor his father were happy about his departure. At that time no parents wanted their children to leave. The children were doing what they saw other children doing, that's all. Everyone was worried. We had nothing to say, we looked at each other and cried, because we did not know where our children slept, what they ate or what they did each day. We never had any letters from them.

In our area, many children left at that time. They were fed up with the way the boers were treating them. The soldiers would beat both the boys and the girls to try and force them to say where the freedom fighters were. All my neighbours' children left – four families were left without any children at all. One of my neighbour's children have never come back. Most children left in 1976 and came back in 1980. When they returned, they were mature and more knowledgeable than they were before.

Neither my husband nor I ever considered running away from the war, although some people left. We never thought of abandoning our home to go and stay in town because we knew that our children were also fighting. If we had gone to live in town, who would have welcomed the children when they brought independence? We helped the Zanla freedom fighters until we attained our independence.

We women also fought the war and I still feel proud of this. Even our children are proud of us because they saw that women were not the cowards they had thought we were. Instead they discovered that women are very strong. We women used to wake up very early in the morning to go and find food for the *vakomana*. If I had no food, I would ask my neighbours for mealie-meal.

As the bases were very far away, there was always a danger of being spotted by planes, so we would put the food into bowls and then tie them into head scarves and on to our backs, as if we were carrying babies. Unfortunately, sometimes the bowls had holes in them and the soup would leak out and burn us. Sometimes planes would fly overhead and then we would have to rush for cover and, while we were lying down, the hot food would burn into you but you could not cry out. We were always determined to arrive with the food so that the freedom fighters had something to eat. Sometimes if you carried your plates or bowls in your hands, the other women would complain and say we saw a 'star' – that was to say, a soldier. We did not mention soldiers by name but used this term. If someone asked you whether you saw stars anywhere and they replied, "Yes, I saw stars everywhere," then you knew there were a lot of soldiers about.

The women provided everything the freedom fighters wanted: cigarettes, soap, clothes. The women were very courageous and strong and fought to the end.

Both Zanla and Zipra were our children and they fought equally well. Zipra was the first group to come to Sigodini* before they passed on to the mountains beyond. We wanted to see them with our own eyes and satisfy ourselves that they really were our children. The Zipras remained in Mzinyathini and did not come to our home area.

When the Zanlas came, we never heard them say anything bad about the Zipras. They called them their brothers and said, wherever they were each fighting, it was the same war and, in due course, together they would take and win the whole country whether the boer wanted it or not. However, when I talk or think of the liberation struggle, I am actually

* Sigodini – officially called Esigodini. The 'e' is a locative meaning 'at'.

talking about the Zanlas and Smith's soldiers because these were the two groups in our area.

I will never forget the day the Zanlas first came into contact with the boers, who had grown a lot of hair all over their arms, like some kind of animal. The Zanlas were in a mountain called Dombo. I don't know how the soldiers knew this but, when we saw their trucks, we thought all the freedom fighters would die.

We heard the sound of a gun, a bazooka, and we all ran away and hid ourselves. We lay down quietly: there wasn't the slightest movement, no coughing, nothing, everything was silent. All we saw was smoke and fire. During that gun battle two freedom fighters were shot, one died and the other was seriously injured. We never knew how many Smith's soldiers were killed because they never made it known; but we heard from those who had gone to carry the injured boy that a lot of the boers had been shot dead. I will never forget that day as it was the first time I saw a gun shooting out fire.

We did not bury the freedom fighter who was killed because he was taken by the enemy and used as an exhibit, showing him to people and saying, "You see, this is a terrorist we have killed. Today, we killed him." He was tied on to a truck and dragged along. It was their way of telling us that they had killed a 'terrorist'. We could not do anything because we were not allowed to touch him. They never gave back the body.

The boy who was killed called his gun Sibongile, which means 'thank you'. So we used to call him Sibongile's father. He was a kind boy and we missed him. All the children in the village felt the loss.

If any civilians were killed, the men went and collected the bodies and buried the remains. In our village we were lucky: no one was killed because of sell-outs. We were really very co-operative and the Zanlas did not have to help us solve our problems because we worked together. If there were misunderstandings we solved them among ourselves. Those were hard times. People were dying and we knew that if we sold out on one another we would only cause more death. In surrounding villages many people were killed. They would be taken from their homes and then you would hear a shot. I don't know how many people died, but a lot of people did. There are families where both parents were killed and today their children are all by themselves.

The sell-out business was a way that some people used during the war to get rid of others they didn't like. For instance, someone might go and tell the Zanlas that Zipras stay at so-and-so's, and someone else might do the opposite; or someone might tell the freedom fighters that the soldiers had come because so-and-so had called them. As a result, a lot of people perished. Even though most of us were co-operative, there were some people who were like snakes – a snake will bite a person but will not eat him. They caused the death of a lot of people but they gained nothing. That is how the word 'sell-out' came into being.

The soldiers who came to our area were both black and white. It would not have been appropriate for the latter to come on their own. Although all the soldiers harassed us, it was the black soldiers who were used by the government, and by the white soldiers, to communicate with us and make us suffer. Since the country was being ruled by whites, the black soldiers had to do what they wanted and, in order to please the whites, the black soldiers were actually responsible for unspeakable beatings and torture.

Both black and white soldiers beat us. It was war. The situation was bad: each person killed the next, sometimes in self-defence. So when soldiers, even black soldiers, met with the comrades, they killed each other; colour did not matter. It was the same with civilians: we were beaten and harassed by all soldiers, even the black ones. It was always the black soldiers who came and asked where the guerillas were. Sometimes we said we hadn't seen them and sometimes we said we had, in the hope that the soldiers would leave us alone, but mostly they would beat us anyway.

As a result of the soldiers we could not do much to help ourselves. We hardly ever slept at night because we worried about who would be killed next and we wondered if we would live through the night. Then, in the morning, as we prepared to go to the fields – sometimes even before we had finished preparing the oxen for the plough – the soldiers would be everywhere. This was very hard, because if we couldn't plough, there was no food. No food for us and no food for the freedom fighters. Sometimes we could get a few vegetables from the fields; we tried to keep chickens for relish and we could milk our cows. It was in this way that we managed to feed the freedom fighters.

They did not give us money, even if they wanted soap or cigarettes. We had to find it ourselves and this was difficult because our husbands did not come home very often. As for clothes, we usually just gave them whatever we could find: even our husbands' clothes. We had no money for new ones. When my husband did come home I would tell him what I had given away – a shirt, trousers or a pair of shoes. My husband never complained – he knew the comrades sometimes needed clothes. The soldiers would, of course, have killed us if they'd known.

We became used to people dying at that time and so we were ready for anything. We accepted death and even became reconciled to the idea, because we knew that war meant the death of people not animals. We became almost immune to it because a lot of our children and neighbours died. But somehow we resolved never to go backwards but to go forwards until we won our country. And so we fought side by side with the men, falling down, getting injured and getting up again.

We were never supposed to tell the boers where the freedom fighters were. For instance, if you met the soldiers, even if you were returning from visiting the comrades, you had to say you were looking for your children who were looking after the cattle. The soldiers would always ask if you had seen the freedom fighters, sometimes you were threatened with a gun but you had to be strong. If we had not acted in this way we might have never won the country because all the freedom fighters would have been killed.

Some civilians who were killed were fortunate to be found and buried by their neighbours. But sometimes people would be killed and taken away by the soldiers in order to show others that they had killed 'terrorists'. They generally never showed a body to people who knew that person but took usually took them away to display in an area where the person was unknown. In this way, people were led to believe that the dead person had been a 'terrorist'. So it happened that when the situation was very tense, people found dead in their own areas would be buried just anyhow. Later, if the situation changed, we would exhume the bodies and rebury them properly in coffins.

In our village, not many people were killed but in the next village some girls were killed. We never buried them because they were carried away and displayed. They were alleged to have been collaborating with 'terrorists'. It was an astonishing claim, because if they had been found collaborating with 'terrorists', the comrades would have died with them, but not one was ever found there.

One of the most painful things was that we could not give our condolences, as we could not travel. People could not visit other villages because if it were to have been discovered, the soldiers would say that you were travelling for the Zanlas. So, even if you met a bereaved person, you did not mention it. We just looked at each other without comment. However, after the war, we went to different villages and gave our condolences to those who had lost members of their family. But even then we did not say much: we greeted each other and then shed tears, because we felt that if we talked about it, we would bring back the pain of loss. I think that a person who didn't undergo this experience is better off than those of us who did.

It was a really difficult time. Another problem was the *mujibas*. For example, you might be in your house, when suddenly you'd get the surprise of your life, when a child from next door acted fearfully like a lion. Your door would be banged, opened and then you would be forced to leave whatever you were doing to go a meeting or something. The *mujibas* came into our houses and demanded that we prepare food for their 'brothers'. Sometimes they weren't even sent by the comrades. Some of the *mujibas* turned into hooligans and cheats and they lied about many things. Sometimes they said that the comrades had demanded chicken, or goat's meat, when they had said no such thing. Those *mujibas* caused a lot of people to die because they told untruths to both the comrades and the parents. For example, they might say that such and such a parent had refused to provide food, or this or that shop owner had refused them cigarettes.

The *mujibas* caused a lot of problems and hardship, especially if you remember that we were their parents and they, our children, from the villages. Now we regret that we cannot do or say anything to or about them because all they did happened during the war, and although they misused their power, we cannot reverse those events. They lost direction and did not follow the instructions they had been given by the comrades. Often they were the same people who took our daughters and slept with them. I think that even some of those children, whose fathers we do not know, are theirs.

Even today there are children in the homes in my area who have to be looked after, sent to school and provided for. We do not know who their fathers are and we cannot turn to anyone for help. As you know, many things happen in a war: rape, for example. Some of our girls were raped by soldiers and some were impregnated by the *mujibas* or the comrades and now we have to look after their children.

In our custom, every child's father should be known for, if a child becomes ill, it should be treated according to the father's tribe. But we do not know who the fathers were and so we do not know their ancestral spirits and we cannot help to heal children who become ill.

Sometimes, when they knew the boers were not nearby, the freedom fighters called us to their bases which were usually on top of the mountains. It was there that the comrades gave us rules and, when they were leaving the area, they would tell us that they were moving and that we would be told by their *mujibas* what would happen next. The most important rule was that we should never divulge any information about them. They also told us that they did not like sell-outs: they wanted us to work together. They said again that when they asked for our daughters – the *chimbwidos* – we should not say they were doing this to make them their wives. They said that they just wanted their company as sisters. They gave quite a number of rules that we were supposed to follow and they told us that if we did not follow them then we would be sell-outs.

When they told us not to work with the boers but encouraged us to work together, that was an indication that someone had told a lie or that there was a sell-out amongst us. After the meeting, we would sing and sing and the songs always made us feel like dancing. We sang until our voices were hoarse. We felt as if we had already taken the country and we felt renewed. On those occasions, our morale was usually very high. One of the the songs went like this:

Mai na baba chengeterai Zimbabwe.

Zimbabwe yakatouya.

Mai nababa tarisai Zimbabwe kumaoko enyu.

These words mean: Mother and father look at Zimbabwe. Zimbabwe has come. Mother and father Zimbabwe is in your hands. This song was really very nice; even the old men enjoyed it because you could hear and see them singing with all their might in their deep voices. When we came to the part where 'hands' are mentioned, we would all display our hands.

The freedom fighters respected every elder person as a parent. They mostly talked about how they were going to take the country and the way of life after independence. They did not talk about the role of women. They said that they were fighting so that everyone could have a better life. They said that we should have land and that the children would have good and better education, and we would lead a more human life.

It was only after the war that we started to hear discussions about women.

Then when we realized that women were being recognized, but it was no big deal because women should, by right, have this recognition considering what they did during the war. Mothers, women, are the people who fought this war and I feel proud about it. We women fought together and even now we do things together. Some men ran away and went to towns. They only came back after the war was over and then only to ask what happened to this and that. Some men in the villages were helpful, but we women were the ones who knew what the boys ate, what they put on, and it was we who made sure that they had enough cigarettes. No men ever got directly involved in the problems of how to get this and do that: things like carrying food on our backs.

If our affairs were now to be decided on how each of us had fought, I can tell you that all the homes would now belong to the women. Men just went away to live in town and left their wives to suffer alone. Some sent parcels and money at weekends but still they never came home because they were afraid of being killed. The women stayed, whether it meant death or life, because we wanted our country.

So I say women are heroes: all over Zimbabwe women are heroes. Before the war women were not seen, but now we have been noticed. Some women are even members of parliament and have posts in the government.

There was also a great change in our own children when they came back from the war. They are much more loving and understanding and they are willing to teach others about the liberation struggle. We can see that they are courageous and have self-determination. We can see it in what they do.

When my own child came back from the war, we told him everything that had happened and he told us about their struggle. I had nothing to complain about when he returned. He was very knowledgeable and now he is a policeman. I notice that he wants everyone to be free since our country is a free country.

In our area all the children came back. However, what I now realize is that the children who did not come back immediately after the war, and have still not come back, must have died.

Those children who refused to return worried us because we did not know what else they wanted and how they could be helped. Some people, in some areas, say that some children went back to fight after the war, and that they became the dissidents. They say they were very frightening. Civilians were afraid of them and they wondered why they had gone back to fighting. So, although they did not want to give them food or water to drink, they ended up doing so, after asking themselves: why did he go back to fight; and what is his aim in doing so? There must have been a reason. Of course, they were also afraid for their lives. But some, a lot, of homes were burnt down. I cannot say how many and I also cannot give names because I am still frightened. There were also men who were killed for nothing, nothing.

Unity has really helped us because previously we were not settled in our homes. Unity has made us more co-operative than we were before when we grouped ourselves into Ndebeles, Shonas, Mazezuru, Karanga and Kalanga, but now we are one people and our leaders are working together towards the same end.

Previously some people were afraid to stay in their homes and went into hiding. Now no one lives in fear, no one leaves home in search of a safer place and no one wonders why we fought the war. This is because 'unity' means getting together and becoming one thing. So we are working together. There is no longer anything to frighten and intimidate an individual because we are all Zimbabwean. Anyone can go to any district regardless of where they come from and that I come from Matabeleland does not hinder me from going to Mashonaland and feeling welcome there. Unity has brought in a new Zimbabwe: it's as if we'd just become independent. A lot of bad things were happening in the villages in Matabeleland, but now many development projects have begun. Unity has changed everybody's life. Now things are going well and we can now work towards the development of our country because the children who remained in the forests have come home. At one stage we were worried that the people who were fighting were not our children, but others from outside our country, who just wanted to trouble us, although we had attained our independence. But when the call came for everyone to return home, surprisingly we saw them coming: so, indeed, they were our children.

Now I wish that the bad spirit that had entered into them will never return. They should realize that since they fought for Zimbabwe, they should work hard with everyone else to promote development and enjoy the fruits of their hard struggle. Such fruits will not come without hard work. In the end, everyone will appreciate the good that comes out of hard work. So I would like to stress that unity is a good thing, because now the war has really become toothless.

9 Loice Mushore

Wedza

MY FATHER was born in Wedza in Ruzane's kraal – Ruzane himself is of Rozwi origin but my father is of the Mbire clan, of the house of Choto. His surname is Kachenhere. My father and mother grew up in the same village where later they courted. After my father married, he went out to work and only came home occasionally. My father and mother had three children; two girls and one boy. I am the second child in the family. My older sister died and my young brother Cuthbert is now in Zambia.

Our father died when we were still very young. But he asked his mother-in-law to look after us, so we were brought up by our grandparents, who sent us to school. Our relatives on our father's side were not concerned about our well-being, and my mother paid for my education at St Anne's Mission. She earned her income from moulding clay pots and being the local midwife. She earned a dollar for each midwifery duty.

Later my mother married a man who could not afford to

send both my brother and me to school, so I left when I had finished standard two. My mother managed to continue to send my brother to school and I did not mind because I knew that later he would be able to look after us. He was extremely intelligent – once he did two grades in the same year. Later he went to Mount Selinda in Chipinge where he took a course in carpentry.

After I'd left school I stayed at home for a while but then I decided that I wanted a job so that I could pay for my own education. My father's older brother had refused to help me because he said it was a waste of time educating a girl. After I had discussed the matter with my grandfather and my mother, I started working as a child-minder in order to save money for further schooling.

But, after a while, Joshua Mushure began courting me. He had a job escorting a missionary doctor on his rounds. Later Mr Mushore approached my father and requested my hand in marriage. I objected because I wanted to continue with my education. But he was very persistent, although my stepfather explained that it was impossible for him to accept *roora** as he had no authority to do so. Joshua then spoke to my grandfather about his intentions and, subsequently, he was introduced to and spoke to my aunt. She approved of Joshua and initiated marriage proceedings by taking him to see my uncles.

I was married properly in the traditional way and afterwards, for several years, we lived on the farm where he was working. But then his boss decided that he wanted to work as a doctor in town and he sold the farm to another *murungu*† to whom he recommended my husband as a worker. So, when the new owner – whom we nicknamed Chamuka‡ – established a farm store, my husband was made the manager. He worked well and was soon promoted and sent to Borongwe and then to Wedza and later Buhera. By then I had two children, Felicitas and Teda, and so I went to my husband's family home in Murewa.

At first my husband's family liked me and I stayed there for a whole year. I was allocated a plot of land to work on and they even gave me my own hut to discourage me from going back to my husband. They wanted me to help them

* *Roora* – lobola, payment made to bride's father by her husband to be.
† *Murungu* – white man (Shona).
‡ Chamuka – the one who rises early (Shona).

in the fields and they thought that if I stayed with them, my husband would visit me and they would see him more frequently. In the year that I was with them, I harvested five bags of rapoko, three bags of rice and four bags of maize – a bounteous harvest which was due to my youth. When my husband wrote and told me that he had been transferred to Buhera, I wanted to join him but I did not know how to get there. I told my father-in-law what I wanted to do and he advised against it because he thought I would get lost. But I did not think that it would be difficult to find my husband as I had his address. So my father-in-law agreed, but he made me promise that I would return to tell them of my journey.

So I went to Buhera and stayed there for about six months and then I returned to Murewa to till the land. But my sisters-in-law had become unfriendly towards me because my husband had supported them before we were married. At the time I was pregnant and I became very sick and had to be taken to hospital. Then my husband recalled me to Chisasike and told me that we should settle there because he disliked the hostility amongst us ladies. We had found a place at Jokoto but my uncle advised us against it as he thought the people were evil as they stole from each other's fields. So we moved to Chirinda's kraal where we lived for a long time. It was close to my parents' home and they often used to visit me.

Then my uncle, who had received my *roora*, decided to return it as he said that he couldn't spend the money; he suggested that it be kept for my brother. My husband was unhappy because he thought that his *roora* had been refused, but I told him that I would always remain with him, as I didn't want to become a loose woman. So another of my uncles accepted the *roora** on my brother's behalf and, after my brother had finished his carpentry training, it was given to him. We were then able to have a civil marriage in the Wedza DA's office.

My husband then started a tailoring shop at Mukamba while I remained at Chirinda. So we were able to fend for our children – we had nine in all – as my husband had a steady source of income.

I was the only person who farmed the land as Chirinda,

---

* Seven head of cattle and $10.

the kraal head, was working. Later we farmed together and grew maize, millet, rapoko, groundnuts and sweet potatoes. Mr Chirinda was our group leader. He showed us how to use the irrigation scheme which, unfortunately, is now obsolete. Workers from Agritex came to our area and gave us advice. Then, several men, including my husband, were chosen to attend a course on farming at Silveira House. They were each from a different village and they were told to share their knowledge. So we soon realized that individual effort would always result in low yields as the overheads were high. So we formed co-operatives and we ordered fertilizers and seed in bulk. My husband became one of the leaders of these groups, so we lived very happily, we sent our children to school and my brother Cuthbert assisted us with the school fees.

During the early sixties we began to hear about Nkomo, Sithole and Chikerema. I saw Nkomo at Mukamba. I believe he was on a familiarization tour. We were rather scared as we had heard that he was the leader of ZAPU. He was accompanied by two ladies. We also understood that there was going to be warfare and one day, in 1964, a young boy was shot at Matsika. He had been told not to take cattle to the dip but he did. There are now a great many versions of this story: one of them is that he was shot by one of Nkomo's men.

Many years after that in 1975, Macmillan, my son, who had been attending a secondary school at Waddilove, went to join the struggle in Mozambique. It happened this way. A friend of his told the headmaster that his father was very ill in Marondera and asked for permission to visit him. This was granted, as was permission for Macmillan to accompany him and they left together one Friday afternoon. But, by Monday, the boys had not returned and the headmaster grew anxious, so he phoned St Mary's and left a message for us. I cried. I felt very distressed. I thought that perhaps my son had been murdered. Although I heard that many children were leaving their schools to go and join the struggle, I didn't really believe it of Macmillan. He had gone to school to learn. I was so worried that I couldn't eat. We heard nothing more but some time later we were asked to go to Waddilove to collect my child's clothes.

It was, I think, the following year that the comrades came to Chief Ruzane's area and only the year after that, in 1977, that they came into our area. All the adults in the village were summoned to the headman's house and we were told that the comrades had come. We could not see them clearly at all. Their faces were shadowed by their hats. After that we did not see them again for some time. But they used to pass through our district about once every two months.

However, the night after they finally came to stay in this area, they arrived at my house at around ten p.m. We heard sharp knocks at the door. My husband and I opened it and they told us to get up and follow them. We carried a lamp into the kitchen hut. The comrades ordered us to go and wake the children and then they were ordered to stand outside the kitchen. My husband and I sat in the kitchen with the comrades. I offered to cook for them but they refused. I asked if I could light the lamp, and I did. The comrades then ordered me to go outside. They started to interrogate my husband. Unfortunately he had always had a stammer and the comrades interpreted this as an attempt to lie. They accused my husband of being a sell-out. They alleged that he had spent the day at Chisasike with the soldiers. I heard everything outside and so I stood in the doorway and demanded to know what they wanted. They refused me entry into the kitchen. I told the comrades that they were being unreasonable and I reminded them of what they had promised when they first arrived – that they would thoroughly investigate each accusation before punishing anyone.

At that, one of them opened fire on my husband who was seated cross-legged by the fireplace. The comrade was standing at the doorway. The comrade fired four shots but they all missed my husband who asked, "Why do you want to kill me? What have I done?" The comrade did not answer but aimed his fifth shot. This time the bullet pierced my husband's neck. My husband collapsed and I saw blood begin to flow. I could not believe what was happening.

The children were then told to move out of the yard and the comrades set all our rooms alight, including the two granaries and the storeroom, although they took our wireless and my husband's special pair of shoes out of our house first. I just stood there, in the courtyard, with my baby on my back. I had nothing with which to cover it. The comrades had removed the baby from the house before they set fire to it, but they did not bring anything like a blanket with them.

The comrades then said they wanted to kill our cattle. So I explained that the cattle were my mother's. In fact they were *mombe dzemai**. So, in the darkness, we went to the kraal. When we got there, one of the comrades said that, no, he didn't think it was right to shoot the cattle, but others disagreed with him and they argued amongst themselves. Then they told me to go and tell the soldiers what had happened. I told them simply that I would not go, I did not know any boers and I did not understand their reason for killing my husband. So they went off in one direction and I went in the other.

I did not go back to my home, although the fire was dying down. I collected my children and I went to a friend's house. I only had on my dress without a petticoat, headcloth or shoes. I felt terribly confused. The next day I was treated at the hospital and I stayed there for two weeks. I felt I was losing my mind. Our neighbours were very kind: they looked after the children during that time. At the hospital I was given some clothing. After I was discharged I went back home and I was told by the comrades to go elsewhere. So I went to my mother's at Mutambirwa. After a few days the *mujibas* came and informed me that the comrades said I should return to my house. My husband had done no wrong and that I ought to understand, for such is the nature of war. So I returned home. I did not mind because it was uncomfortable living with other people as I have many children. One of the mission fathers gave me a door and a door-frame. One of the rooms had not been completely destroyed, but there was no one to help me repair and thatch the roof. Everyone was afraid and so I did everything myself.

Later, as the comrades demanded, I went to their base. They did not quite apologize for the death of my husband, they just put the issue aside. The leader of the comrades gave me ten dollars and his deputy gave me five. They said I should look after my children by growing crops on the land.

So I went to a place across the Ruzawi river to buy groundnuts for seed. On my way back home I met the soldiers who took me to their camp in Wedza where I spent two weeks being questioned about the whereabouts of my son who'd gone to Mozambique. They laughed at me with scorn, saying how ironic it was that the very people we had

---

* Special cow given to a mother as *roora*.

supported had killed my husband. The CIOs offered to resettle me, but I swore that I would not go away. I was also accused of cooking for the comrades. But I was released when my daughter came to see me. She spoke to the soldiers and told them that I was innocent. We spent one and a half hours in the questioning room. Then, after a long silence, one soldier said, "What are you sitting there for? I don't want to see you. Go home." But before we left, the soldiers brought out several guns and I was asked to show them which type of gun had killed my husband. I said that as the incident had occurred at night, I had not seen the gun. There were two other young women at the camp so I told the soldiers that they were my children and we were all released. Unfortunately, the soldiers had roasted and eaten all three buckets of groundnuts which I had bought to plant.

So I went back home and life carried on as usual. I used to help in collecting food for the comrades. Sometimes I would help the *chimbwidos* with the cooking. We were required to donate a bucket of mealie-meal every week plus two dollars. Then, unbeknownst to me, some people went to the comrades and told them that I was a sell-out, that I was paid by the soldiers and that that was how I was managing to send my children to school. So the comrades said I was to be watched carefully. I heard that some of them wanted to kill me but two others said it would be better to establish a base at my home.

So this is what happened. It was winter, the comrades' cooking was done in my home, and I had to cook outside, in the bitter cold. Whenever anything had to be done, I was sent for. I even had to fetch the meat, after cattle had been killed for them. Once I had to carry the whole hind of a cow. It was so heavy that I fell over, I could not manage it. But, after several months, the comrades were satisfied that I was not a sell-out and, finally, they left.

At every *pungwe* the comrades either killed or beat somebody. But to provoke the whites, the comrades also engaged in stock theft from nearby farms. They would share the meat with us villagers and we would make it into biltong. We used to have *pungwes* which finished at four a.m. when the comrades would return to their base. Normally they stayed in the mountains during the day. Then, at dusk, the *chimbwidos* would come out to see if it was safe and the comrades would follow behind. One day, as the *chimbwidos* were coming from the base, the soldiers opened fire. Two comrades retaliated and, it is said, that they shot seven soldiers. Later that evening, as the soldiers were collecting the corpses into their vehicles, the comrades ambushed the vehicles. As my house is very close to the road, some of the bullets flew into my yard. In fact, the following day when I was collecting firewood, I found a gun which I later took to the freedom fighters. There were many grenades in my yard and these I threw into the pit latrine.

On another occasion, early one Sunday morning I had gone to wash my clothes and my children had remained at home. But they heard shots and ran away in fear towards Gumbozvinda village. They did not know that the soldiers were in the village drinking beer. When the soldiers saw the four children running towards them, they threw a grenade. My son was hit on the leg and fell down. Those who saw it happening say that he tried to crawl towards an anthill, but the soldiers threw more grenades and he was killed. I was still down by the river but I knew something bad was going on because a few bullets reached as far as the river and I had to take cover. When I saw certain women coming to look for me, I immediately suspected that something dreadful had happened. When I heard of the event, I wanted to commit suicide and tried to throw myself into the water, but one of the women caught me and they helped me home. That was how my son Patrick was killed. He was brought back to my home on a scotch cart.

During the war I received no news of Macmillan, although a comrade named Danga did once mention him, although he was very vague. But I received news of his well-being during the cease-fire and I was told that he would be at St Anne's, Goto. So I went there and spent several days waiting, but I did not see him. He came home later. He was eighteen when he left but he had grown into a big muscular man. When I saw him, I fainted I was so overjoyed.

Of course, he was most upset to hear the news of his father's death and he was very vengeful. He wanted to know who the people were who had told the comrades that his father was a traitor. He went and asked the headman, but the man was incoherent and I urged my son not to pursue the matter, because I was sure that if he found out who had done it, he would have killed him. I told my son that, even if he took revenge, it would not bring his father back to life.

During the war, Macmillan had become a very humble man and he showed me great respect. He wanted to become a soldier, but I advised him against it. I said that once was enough. I felt he had done his duty. So, instead, he took a course in nursing. I told him that, although it was good that he was looking after me, he had his own life and I felt he was neglecting it. He is now married but unfortunately I don't get on well with his wife.

The war was very tough. I had many nasty experiences. My husband's death was because people were jealous of my life. We had a big house, good yields and the tailoring shop. Even today my neighbours think that I'm well off. They refuse me opportunities to train and participate in village activities, even though it is the policy that widows or single women should be given opportunities to learn about farming. I'm struggling to make ends meet and I am not very happy. Some of my children are working and they are doing well and they do help me out, but I have such a large family that there are always difficulties. I'm looking after my widowed mother and she is now old and sick. I can't ask my daughters for money because they are married and have their own families to fend for. My husband's family is not at all interested in my affairs. In fact, they say that I'm responsible for his death. My daughter was ill in hospital for a month and I sent word to them but they did not come. When I think of the war, and especially of my husband's death, I sometimes feel it was all futile because in our area the comrades harassed and killed more civilians than the soldiers did. I'm living for my children. If it weren't for them I'd long since be dead.

But I do think that is very important for women to go to clubs and to try and improve their standard of living and that of their children. I am a member of a women's club and I am the treasurer. We are banking money, although many women still don't really appreciate the value of doing so. I think that women have to work hard to realize the benefits of all their suffering. I feel that honesty and diligence are amongst the most admirable virtues in any person. So I say, "*Pamberi ne* hard work."

Today I would really like to see the family unit preserved and cherished. All women must work together with their husbands to bring up their families.

I want my granddaughters to be dignified women. Today there is so much prostitution and promiscuous behaviour and so I want my grandsons to respect women as human beings and not to regard them simply as objects of pleasure. I wouldn't like to see them engaged in vandalism and hooliganism. I would like to see my grandchildren being educated but continuing to cherish our African culture. That's all I have to say.

10 Lisa Teya

Wedza

MY FATHER is Mr Phiri and he came to Wedza from Malawi in 1918 after fighting in the First World War. He came as an expatriate seeking employment and he settled here in Svosve and was later registered as a resident of Wedza.

It was here that he met a Zvomuya maiden, Eriza, and courted her although her parents tried to dissuade her from marrying a Malawian. However she replied, "Once love has struck, that's that. Love is not like a coat that you can keep on or take off." So she married my father and in time, we – three girls and two boys – were born.

My parents were ordinary rural folk. They raised their family by growing crops such as maize, rice, ground and round nuts. My father was a builder on a farm called Zvitondi. He would tell us that they were made to work extremely hard. They were supervised by a foreman on a horse with a troop of nasty dogs. If you made a mistake, the dogs were set on you and that was that. But they had no choice, so that's what they did for thirty pounds a year.

We children were born at Makoma but we moved to join my father on the farm in 1947 after some resettlement programme had taken place in our area. Everyone, including the young children, was required to work in the tobacco field. We picked tobacco leaves until we had callouses on our hands. But that was life. At the end of the month we got paid four dollars and each worker also got a cupful of maize-meal.

Eventually we decided enough was enough and so families trooped off the farm and found themselves homes in the local villages. Our family settled in Murariramwa village and we have been working for ourselves ever since without being exploited by anyone. And so life is good. We are living in a land of milk and honey since, at the end of the day, everything we do benefits us.

We were still quite young when we left the farm to settle in the village. On our arrival, our parents gave us a lesson in self-reliance. My father said that it didn't pay to sit on one's hands. They gave each of us a hoe and told us that it was the key to our future. We were to sweat it out on the land if we were to survive. Each of us was also given a portion of land to work on and we were monitored by our parents. Our yields were quite good. So life was quite different from the one we had led at Zvitondi farm. My father used to fatten cows for sale. We had all the food we required: milk, meat, vegetables and that's how I developed into a nice round woman. My father taught us that we had to work hard for ourselves. And so when I married I put his teachings into practice – in fact, all his children who took his advice have done well for themselves.

I attended school but only up to grade five. You see we hadn't the opportunity in those days to advance in education as one can today.

I was twenty-five years old when I married a man of fifty-seven from Buhera. After my marriage I was blessed with three sons, Abraham, Misheck and Thomas. Then my husband suddenly had 'a dozen eyes' and left for Botswana. He was an Apostolic, the type that shave their heads bald. So when he arrived in Botswana, he was given three more wives and life was very good to him, so it was no wonder that he never came back. I returned to my father's home and I raised the three children single-handed. I relied on a poultry project which gave me sufficient money to see the boys through primary school. For their secondary education, my father had to sell some cows to pay for the boys' school fees. He was very annoyed with my husband.

But eventually I got fed up with my loneliness and went to the chief to discuss my problem, saying that I wanted to take it to the *dare**. I told the court that for twenty-four years I had been living as a legally married woman but I had not once seen my husband during that time. They laughed but I went on and on and asked them to grant me a divorce as was the custom under such circumstances. The court granted me it and I could not believe my luck to be free and single again.

A little while later I married Mr Nhekairo who already had a wife and I bore him a son, Tendayi, but his father took him back to his home. And from that time I have lived alone.

When I was staying with my father I became a member of the party. Previously I had been an Apostolic, like my husband, and had gone to church and made baskets as the Apostolics do. But I joined the party because it mobilized people to form co-operatives and other joint ventures. We did crochet work to sell but we mainly relied on growing maize. To this day we continue to implement the teachings of the party because we still conduct our business ventures as co-operatives.

We did not really discuss politics in earnest until 1976. That's when we first really knew about the party. Of course, we had heard of ZAPU but I personally never even saw a ZAPU card. The people who were said to have led ZAPU are Chitepo, Chikerema, Sithole and Nduna but we did not get any real details until we heard that Chitepo had died in a foreign country. As for Nkomo . . . well, we have an obscure picture, but from what I heard, Chitepo's leadership was way ahead.

The war started in Chigondo in 1976. This is when we first met the combatants. We were working in our gardens when we saw the young men. At the time I did not think much about them. But, later, when I was returning home it dawned on me that there was something odd about them. Why, I thought – they were dressed like everyone else – clothes, boots, caps and all. Even the way they walked was the same. So I paused, pondered and concluded that the

---

* *Dare* – village court.

boys were not local. I went to my garden and sat down for a while.

A little while later I heard gunfire. I ran but didn't get far. I fell down, got up and picked up my basket to run again, but I was too frightened to do anything. I was weak at the knees. When I heard ululating from a distance, I also ululated and immediately joined the celebration for the arrival of our young warriors. I got up and jumped up and down with joy. Then I bolted.

A few days later we heard more gunfire. Later a certain 'bird' came to our village and asked for food. So we prepared it and took it to the comrades. On our way back we met the soldiers who asked us where we had been. We told them that we were returning from a funeral but they broke sticks from a nearby tree and gave us each a thorough beating. Afterwards a black soldier suggested that a helicopter be sent for, but a white soldier asked why, and when he was told that the plane would be used to take us to Rusape for further interrogation, he ordered the other soldiers to allow us to return to our homes.

Some time later the *vakomama* came round to our village asking for blankets which they called *gudza**. We agreed and we each gave blankets according to our means – you only gave one if that was all you could afford – and the *chimbwidos* collected them.

Generally the girls cooked the food that we provided. A man would be there to supervise the cooking and monitor everything. Those who were on the roster to provide food would get it to the base at about three o'clock and by four the cooking would have been done and we would be safely back in our homes. That's how things went. The boys were not cruel to us. We didn't see them often as they stayed in their *poshito*.

Being beaten up by the soldiers was our main problem. That, let me tell you, was something that happened regularly. We went about our daily business on the trot because we were afraid. Even the simple task of going to fetch vegetables from the garden was conducted fast. I wish we could still do our business as briskly as we did it then! We took very little time to get food from here to Chigondo.

As soon as we had taken the food to the base we would

---

* *Gudza* – mat made of woven bark.

hurry back home so as to get on with cooking for our own families. But a bit later you might hear knocking on the door. "Who is it?" you'd ask.

"It's us. The soldiers. Have you seen the *gandangas*?"

"No, my son, I haven't seen them," you'd say.

"Are you lying to us?"

"No, my son, I didn't see them."

But, no matter what you said, at that point they would beat you with the butts of their guns and we would fall down in embarrassing positions. The soldiers gave us hell. We suffered for this country, I can tell you that.

Sometimes we attended *pungwes* late at night where we received political as well as social education. They taught us the virtues of co-operative enterprises and extolled the virtues of hard work. They were against lazy people. On the political side, they taught us to unite and join hands against the enemy so that we could achieve national independence in Zimbabwe. I can very well remember our first *pungwe*, because what we were taught then is still relevant to our lives and we are still applying those lessons. So, today, we have sufficient food, clothes, blankets and we even drink tea which was once a treat for the elite of our society. After the *pungwe* we would say, *'Pamberi nayo'** and then disperse – but if it was your duty to provide breakfast, you would rush home to get it ready and bring it back to the base before daybreak.

We were all rather frightened at the first *pungwe*. We nearly retreated but word came from the *vakomana* that we had to go. The *chimbwidos* and the *mujibas* rounded us up and we each fetched a blanket to keep us warm. The astonishing thing was that no ill befell any of us on our way to the *pungwes*. The few who slipped and bruised themselves can only blame their *vadzimu* because the majority of us had no problems. Some would get lost – the unlucky ones I have already mentioned. But we had a nice time at the *pungwes* although we were initially afraid to go.

One day we returned home from a *pungwe* and quickly prepared food – rice and other nice things – and took it to the base. Suddenly we were surrounded by Dakotas and there were helicopters and jets everywhere. The *vakomana* ran in all directions, dodging the planes and disappearing. They were like people possessed by their *vadzimu*.

* *Pamberi nayo* – forward with information.

We, the onlookers, started singing traditional songs such as *Tatoranyika taramukai** and *Mikono inorwa*†. And so it was: a battle of the fittest. There was heavy gunfire all around us. We sang the praises of our ancestors and urged them to give courage to our young fighters. So we sent our pleas to *Mbuya* Nehanda and *Sekuru* Chaminuka‡ and then went back home.

One day we went to the base and cooked sadza but we had no relish. The comrades asked us why this was, but before we could reply they called the *chimbwidos* and told them to dish out the sadza to us, so that we would know what it was like to eat sadza without relish. So we sat and ate and ate and ate the tasteless sadza, but one old man could not do so and so he slipped it into his shirt. But when we stood up to go, the sadza fell out of his shirt and the comrades saw it. They said, "Old man, what do you think you are doing?"

"I-I-I was trying to eat the sadza, my children," he stammered.

"Is this what you call eating?"

"No . . . nnnno . . ." he stuttered.

Then the comrades asked us whether we agreed that he be beaten, but we didn't. So instead we were lectured about our role as parents in the struggle. The comrades said they disliked eating sadza without relish just as much as we did. They told us that we were supposed to ensure that they got decent meals. Afterwards we sang:

> *Mudzimu woye mudzimu woye*
> *Makaita basa.*
> *O here mudzimu woye*
> *Makaita basa.*§

When word reached us women that the comrades wanted clothes or cigarettes we secretly called the community together. We would then decide on how much was required from each of us to contribute towards purchasing the items. Cigarettes were not difficult to get as they were relatively cheap. We always discussed what contribution each family

---

* *Tatoranyika taramukai* – We are taking the country/Move away!

† *Mikono inorwa* – Bulls are fighting.

‡ *Mbuya* Nehanda 1862–98 spirit medium who encouraged the rising against the white settlers. She was executed with Kaguvi. *Sekuru* Chaminuka possibly the greatest *mhondoro* (guardian spirit of a tribe) in Shona oral history. He is believed to have been a miracle worker, magician, prophet and psychic force.

§ Oh Spirits, Oh Spirits,
You did great work,
Oh Spirits,
You did great work.

should make, but if someone indicated that they genuinely could not provide their share, we understood. The community always asked those families who had sons in the struggle to contribute more, as they felt the sons were the comrades that they were having to feed. But our *vadzimu* usually made sure that we had something to contribute.

It was a difficult time, but we managed to overcome our problems. Sometimes we would kill chickens and goats to provide relish because that's what they wanted. We were consoled in the knowledge that we were doing everything for the common good because we felt that these young men were sons to mothers like us – mothers who would give the best to their own sons. So, we felt we should treat the comrades as their own mothers would have done.

Occasionally the odd soldier would arrive and ask for sadza. Once, I remember, there was a bit of *rhopi** left after our meal, and a soldier entered our home, immediately dipped into the sadza and took the *rhopi* for his relish. It surprised us. On other occasions the soldiers would ask for food and when we told them we did not have any, they beat us. Oh yes, we got quite a good bit of beating from those people.

The soldiers were a mixed group of blacks and whites. But sometimes the whites painted themselves green. One day we met a group of soldiers and the girls amongst us immediately ran away and we did likewise. But the soldiers stopped us and asked us why we were running away. They asked us what was wrong with soldiers being in the village, and we replied that we were afraid because the soldiers had a reputation for beating people up. During the panic one of the girls who had run away had dropped her child on the ground in her haste to get away from trouble. So I picked the baby up and was slapped in the face for doing so. I put the child down and explained that I was only doing the mother a good turn. Then one of the soldiers suggested that I should be taken for interrogation because he said that earlier that day he had seen an overalled man approach my home and was convinced I was collaborating with the comrades. I denied having seen such a man, and this invited a second slap. I immediately fell down. But then a white soldier arrived and demanded to know what was happening.

* *Rhopi* – pumpkin puree.

He was informed that I had been beaten because I was a collaborator. But the white man ordered my immediate release saying there was no real proof. So I picked up the Zambuko baby, put him on my back and left for home.

On another occasion, two days after a contact at Zindi, my son disappeared. When I enquired about his whereabouts, his younger brother said he had no idea where Misheck was.

But the following morning Thomas found a note amongst his bedclothes and brought it to me. It simply said, "I have gone, goodbye." So I enquired further and found he had left most of his clothes behind. He hadn't even taken a jersey with him. I was worried and set about looking for him – first to Ganga; then to Rukucha; then to Mukamba where the DAs were stationed. They asked me where I was going and what I was doing and I told them I was looking for my son who had run away from home. The DA told me to be brave and face reality – my son had decided on his own to leave home. They told me there were many mothers in my situation. So I retraced my steps and went back home, consoling myself with the thought that there were many women with broken hearts like mine, many mothers whose sons had gone to fight. In war some people die and others survive. I knew my plight was not unique – many young men, like Misheck, were risking their lives. I must say, however, that at first I was cross with all my *vadzimu* for allowing this to happen. I was cross with the whole lot of them from my mother and my grandmother to my *sekuru*. So my son was away for years and when he came back it was all of a sudden. This is how it happened: knock, knock, knock, went the door. "Who's there?" I said.

"It's me."

"Me who?"

"It's me, Gilbert Murasirarwa."

"What's the matter?"

"Your son Misheck is back from the war." Then all I could do was ululate: ooh, ooh, oooooh, and I walked on my knees and sang the praises of *Mbuya* Nehanda and *Sekuru* Chaminuka. I said to myself, "Well done, Zimbabwe." Others ran to meet him but I was too overcome with joy to be able to stand up. So I remained there on my knees until he entered the house.

I was really very grateful for the role my own son had played in liberating our country. I ululated and ululated and my joy was boundless.

When I saw the comrades returning triumphantly, both men and women in their combat gear, I wished I'd been young enough to have gone to war. So I sang,

> *Urombo hwe iye iye we*
> *Tafirenyika ije ije woye ye*
> *Aiwa Aiwa Aiwa*
> *Ngindi Ngindi Ngindi.* *

Misheck is now a policeman and the bodyguard to a Minister. He is a giant whose strides are huge and he is always smiling. He has married and my daughter-in-law . . . well, she is not my wife so I can love her. Misheck tells me he earns so little that he can't spare much to provide for us, and there are a few of us: myself, my crippled brother, his wife and child.

He is now a much more caring and understanding son, very different from the Misheck of long ago. He is respectful not only to me but to all elders and I attribute this positive change to the education he received in Mozambique.

Indeed independence has meant a lot to us. It means we must celebrate our nationhood but it also calls us to bow our heads in memory of those who died for it. So we have mixed feelings – feelings of joy and sorrow. Our lives have positively changed for the better. We were oppressed and we had no real development but everything has changed and we are all a lot happier than we were before.

I am attending adult education classes to improve myself. I do not know whether I will succeed but I am trying my best. I sing and pray and study at the school for adults. But I have my problems: I am a single parent with a crippled brother to look after and I have not been well. So I have been asking God, "Is it not enough that you gave me a crippled brother to care for? Do I have to bear the added misfortune of illness?"

I sometimes wish that people would offer me help but nowadays everyone has their own problems, so I resort to crying and going to church. If I keep in touch with the church, maybe they will give my crippled brother and me a decent burial when the time comes.

* Oh sadness,
 We've died for our country
 Oh no, oh no, oh no
 Boom Boom Boom

My father died earlier this year and I am definitely going to have problems when the ploughing time comes, as I will not have anyone to help me. My father used to head the span of oxen and I would hold the plough, but now I am all alone. Otherwise, when all is said and done, I am quite all right and I shall pray to God and my *vadzimu* to help me.

11　Margaret Nkomo

Nyaje

I FINISHED school in 1961 and then did a two-year teaching course. Afterwards I taught at Manzimabi school in the Nkayi district. Later I transferred to Bulawayo where I taught at Hellem government school.

My husband was a carpentry instructor from Gwatemba. We first met at Hope Fountain School when we were students. For a while after we were married, we both taught at Hellem. But, because life was so very expensive in Bulawayo, particularly as I was responsible for four of my husband's younger brothers and sisters – I had to send them all to school in addition to looking after my own child – I thought it would be better to live and teach in a rural area. So I found a teaching post at Nyaje school in the Gokwe area. My husband was still living in Bulawayo. He would visit me when he could, and as he liked the district, we decided to settle there. We started building our home in 1974.

It was easy really. There was a bus from Bulawayo which goes to Gokwe and it passes though Nyaje, so transport was not a problem. The people of that area were very friendly because I had already been teaching there for five months when we decided to build a home. So when we started building, people already knew me although they did not know my husband very well, because he came only for short periods, and they welcomed us. We looked for people to help us build our home and it was easy.

By that time my husband was no longer teaching. He had left to join a company but he felt that he was paid badly and, after that, he worked for a contractor in Bulawayo. Then he stopped work altogether. I'm not sure what happened but sometimes I would receive a message to say that he had been arrested for political reasons.

I never really knew why he'd been arrested. I didn't know what was happening in Bulawayo. I think they were holding meetings and that is probably why he got himself into trouble. On one occasion I was called into town and went to the Central Police Station to find out why they'd arrested him, but he had just been released. When I asked him to explain to me why he'd been arrested, he always said that it was none of my business. Women, he said, were not supposed to be involved in men's business. He never told me anything although I tried to find out more from him on several occasions.

I think he was seriously considering joining the liberation struggle but, although I could see he was dissatisfied, he never showed his feelings. I tried not to worry about it. In fact, it did not really affect me at all. I would complain a little and then just let things be.

Before the war we did not talk about 'liberation' although people would say that our country was not a free one. They complained about taxes – dog taxes, cattle taxes and so on – and digging contour ridges. But it was just talk no one had solutions. It was simply said that all our troubles were caused by the white man who had colonized us. I first heard of the suggestion of war when I was in Bulawayo and I was very frightened as I imagined a conventional war when a whole town might be destroyed, just like that. I often felt it would be better if our children lived apart from us, so that if anything did happen, we would not all die at once. When I went to live in the Gokwe area, I never thought it would be affected by war. I had never heard any rumours of war in the district and I thought we would be safe.

Indeed, it was not until 1978 that I first encountered the

war. The white soldiers were the first group to arrive in the area. They often came either to the school or the shopping centre. They asked many questions. One day a large group of soldiers came to the school and called out first the headmaster and then the teachers, one by one, and asked us questions.

I can't remember what they asked the others, but I do remember what they asked me. They asked me what grade I taught. I said, grade one. Then they asked me whether we sang songs in class. I said that we did and then they wanted to know what kind of songs I taught the children. I said that I taught the children many songs in both Ndebele and English. They asked me to sing them one of the songs, so I sang, "Buy, buy my buns,"and some of the soldiers sang along with me.

Then they asked me what kind of Ndebele songs I taught the children and they wanted to know if I taught them *Nkosi Sikeleli Africa**. I said that I didn't because it was too difficult for them. Then they asked if we ever sang it at the school. I told them we didn't, which was true, as we always sang hymns during our assembly.

They then wanted to know about a place called Sekusile, how far away it was and so on. I said I didn't know. This was true because I had never heard of it. But they asked me if I was really telling the truth and I told them it was as I did not travel, being busy during the week and returning to my home at weekends. Then they wanted to know where my home was and I pointed out the direction and they let me go. They were not rough with us and asked their questions nicely.

Sometimes they did not call out all the teachers when they came to the school but would only talk to the headmaster. Sometimes they would come as often as twice a day, early in the morning and again in the evening.

I was afraid of them. I was particularly afraid of their guns. Then a bit later, the guerillas came into the area. I had heard many stories about them but I had never seen them. It was said that they could turn into anything: trees, cabbages, all sorts of unbelievable things. So when they came to our school for the first time, I was looking forward to seeing

---

* *Nkosi Sikeleli Africa* (Ndebele)/*Ishe Komborera Africa* (Shona) – God Bless Africa: a widely accepted anthem of national liberation throughout Africa which originated in South Africa. The song was banned in Rhodesia.

something of this, but they did not turn into anything at all. They were just people. Three of them arrived at the school at about ten o'clock. They told all the school children to return to their homes because they said they were closing down the school. All the teachers were told to remain behind.

Once all the children had gone, they told us to give them wrist-watches, radios and so on, but we did not have such things. They also ordered the headmaster to surrender his gun to them, but he didn't have one. We had nothing they wanted. They said that, since this was the case, we should burn down our school. So the school was burnt down with everything still in the classrooms: but we were able to remove all our property from the teachers' houses before they were burnt down as well.

I will never forget the date, the 31st of January 1978. I was the only lady teacher at the school and I was expecting my third child. Having destroyed the school, they then said they would also beat us because we hadn't given them what they wanted, and we were to lie down. But one of them told me to go and burn down the one remaining house instead. I did this but I removed all the property first. In the meantime, the three boys gave all the other teachers a thorough beating. They beat them so hard that our headmaster almost died. Then they told us to pack up our things and leave the school. That was the first time I met the guerillas.

We were all very unhappy about the incident. At first we did not think they could have been the freedom fighters, but they were. We could not understand why they should beat the teachers when they were supposed to be freeing them. Most of the teachers didn't come from that area so they left for their homes soon afterwards. Only I and the headmaster had homes in the neighbourhood although he soon returned to his original home. Everyone else in the area felt very sad because their school had been burnt down, but they were afraid and would never have dared ask the guerillas why they did this. I think they believed that one day the school would open again.

Personally, I think the guerillas acted out of anger. They wanted us to respond to their demands and when we couldn't, they retaliated. Initially they had simply told the children to return to their homes, saying they were closing down the school and that it would re-open after independence. It was only when we couldn't give them what they wanted that they became so angry and told us to burn down our school.

I did not try to look for another teaching position because I realized that we were at war and I could not leave my home. I had children, property and cattle and I had to stay and look after everything as best as I could. The villagers did not do anything to try and rebuild or re-open the school. Children remained at home because the guerillas had said that no one was to go to school. They said that they would let people know when they could re-open the school.

My husband was still living in Bulawayo but he used to come home to see me from time to time and, fortunately or unfortunately, he never met the guerillas.

There were many groups of Zipra freedom fighters in the area. We fed them. What happened was that if they came to your home to ask for food, you then went to tell the other villagers. Then, after we had provided the food, the 'youth', as we called them, meaning both boys and girls, did the cooking. They ate whatever we had available; they weren't fussy.

The youth were responsible for cooking and for watching out for enemies. Some of them were always on guard and would inform the guerillas if they saw the enemy. The children did not spend nights with the guerillas singing or addressing people. They were needed to cook and to watch out for the enemy.

I cannot say how often the freedom fighters came to our village because there were so many groups. It might happen that one group would come today, another tomorrow and so on. Some groups did not ask for food at all, they just passed by after asking for information. But whenever food was requested, all the villagers co-operated. We never left one person or one home to take care of everything.

When they came into an area sometimes they would call a whole set of homes or the whole village – depending on its size – together for a meeting to explain their plight. While the meeting was being held, the youth would patrol the area to watch for the enemy. They would address us and explain how much they needed the support of the villagers and what sort of things they wanted: clothes, soap and food. They said that we, the parents, should provide these things. They also explained that they were fighting to free the country. They never said much about how they'd joined the liberation struggle, but rather that we parents had sent them to fight for our country's freedom and that they had returned to do so. They said that the gun would free us and that when we were free, we would be able to have all the land we needed, since we had so little because it had been divided into farms. After independence, they said, everyone would own land.

In my area we also contributed money which was put aside for things like cigarettes. But when they came to my home they also wanted soap and those of my husband's clothes which he'd left at home. They would just open the wardrobe and look for whatever they thought would be useful to them and take whatever they found. They especially wanted khaki clothes so, in the end, only my husband's suits were left.

One night two of the freedom fighters arrived and asked for soap. I told them that I didn't have any as I had a baby which meant that I used a lot of soap and had run out. They wanted to beat me and said they would do so, because I had not been beaten alongside the other teachers. I told them they could do whatever they wanted, if they considered it reasonable. But fortunately they didn't beat me.

A long time after Zipra had come into the area another group called the *madzakutsaku* arrived. I'm not exactly sure when or how they came because I only met them after they had been around for some time, although I had heard of them previously. They came to our village from the Gokwe office. They were after the Zipras and sometimes they were very rough when they made their enquiries. They usually beat the youth, no matter what they said. For example, if they asked where the Zipras were, and the youth either said they didn't know or that they had passed by on the previous day, they were beaten. They constantly alleged that either the youth were lying or that they had cooked for the Zipras and were harbouring guerillas. But they did not kill anyone.

During this time my husband was in Bulawayo but one day I received a letter from my son who had been staying with him to say that their father had disappeared. As he had told the children that I would collect them, my son wanted to know when I was coming. My first thought was that my husband would probably return and I waited for two weeks to see if I would receive a letter from him, but then I realized that he would not return.

So I went to collect the children. The journey from here was very difficult. Buses had stopped servicing our area, so I had to walk from Nyaje to Nkayi and then I took a bus to Bulawayo. Finally, when I arrived, I found that the children had been looked after by our lodger. I returned home with the children, taking a scotch cart to get from Nkayi.

It was very painful because I realized that my husband had gone and I doubted that he would ever return. All his clothes, blankets and belongings were in the house; he had taken nothing with him except a skin blanket. The children said that he had left with two men in a small car. They had come to collect him and after talking with them for a bit, he had bid the children farewell, collected his blanket, and left. I have never heard from him again.

I managed because my husband had left some goats and other domestic animals and I also had some savings which I would withdraw, if ever there was a need, from my bank in Kwekwe. But travelling there and back was a big task. We would go by cart to Gokwe and then take buses from there. When I had used all my savings, I began to sell goats but I had to keep some with which to feed the freedom fighters. They frequently asked for this and that from me because they'd been told that I had once been employed.

I always gave them what I could, when I could, but sometimes I told them I could do nothing for them. On these occasions a few of them would sometimes threaten to beat or kill me but fortunately no one ever did. All I can say is that the Lord protected me.

When I returned with my children, some people began to question me and hinted that my husband had joined the guerillas. I could neither confirm nor deny what they said; I told them that I did not know. Some people disbelieved me. They thought I knew where my husband was and suggested that sometimes he came, with the other guerillas, to see me in disguise. I denied this but I could not help noticing that some of my neighbours shunned me. I was classified as one of those troublesome people. From that time, I was always asked for something whether it was my turn or not. For example, even if the cooking was being done at another home, I was always asked for sugar or salt or something, yet they did not do this to anyone else. I was always expected to give something extra although I made the same contributions as everyone else. The implication seemed to be that, as my husband was one of the freedom fighters, I had to make an extra contribution.

As far as civilians were concerned, especially at the beginning, the freedom fighters were quite troublesome because they were always demanding this or that. But as time went on, and the comrades explained their purpose, people cooked and fed them happily because they knew what the freedom fighters were fighting for. I used to hear people say,"No hungry soldier will fight a successful war. They must have energy to fight and win."

The freedom fighters would sometimes ask me where my husband was and I would say that I didn't know as he was no longer in Bulawayo. I did not say that I suspected he had joined the struggle because one could never be very free when talking to those people. Also, as he had never told me anything, I could not say definitely that he had joined the struggle. The only thing I know was that the year he disappeared, was the year when the war was at its peak. It was a time when many people left Zimbabwe for the liberation struggle.

At first, I hoped that he would return, but many years have passed and he still hasn't come. It has not been easy. My first child was a temporary teacher, but they have been asked to stop teaching and she is not doing anything. My other two children are still at school. I still also look after one of my husband's sisters. It is difficult to be a mother and play the role of father as well.

Life since independence has not changed very much for me. I am still educating my children and taking care of my home on my own. The freedom fighters used to tell us that we would have plenty of land but I am still tilling my field and I haven't been given any more land. The same applies to everyone else.

The people who died during the war had to die because there is no war without death. One side must win and the other side lose and, in the process, people die. All I can say is that the Lord was with me and has kept me all the days of my life. But I have also tried to use my hands. I have had to work hard to provide for my family. I used to tell my children that unless we worked we would not survive because we were at war. I managed because I worked hard, I used these hands of mine.

12 Anna Madzorera

Nyaje

I WAS BORN in Mhondoro but after my marriage I went to settle at Roseday* with my husband. Then the government forced us to leave Roseday. They sent the police with big trucks to move all our property, which they loaded on to the lorries and they forced us into other lorries and brought us to Nyaje. They had to force us as we had not agreed to move to a place we did not know. We lost a lot of property in the process because the police just threw our things into the trucks. They were very rough. At the time I had three children who were still small. I don't remember what year it was because I didn't go to school.

My husband, who had been interested in politics for a long time, had been taken to Kwekwe prison. I don't remember the reason but I think it was because he refused to dig contour ridges. He told me that one day, when he was in prison, he went into the laundry room and painted 'ZAPU' on the back of all the prisoner's shirts which were in one of the storerooms. He was punished by being put in a cold room for the whole day. He was only taken out for an hour

* Possibly Roadsdale.

113

at a time before being put back again and he was not given any food. This happened for some weeks. After his release, he did not stay very long at home. He ran away because the police were after him for political reasons.

So, when we were moved from Roseday, my husband was not there. The white people who forced us to settle here, in Nyaje, kept checking on us to see if he had returned home. They were sure that he would come back to his family and then they planned to arrest him.

I lived here with my mother-in-law and my children for a long time before he did finally return and it was only a short time afterwards that he was arrested and taken to Gonakudzingwa. He spent a whole year at the restriction camp and, after he was released, he came home and married a second wife. But it was not long before he was arrested again and taken to Wha Wha, where he spent another year. Then I remained with his mother and his second wife. My children had, by this time, grown up and left home.

I did not complain or feel unfairly treated because my husband had told me that he was being arrested for political reasons. So I knew that he was working for his country and I accepted the consequences. Of course, it was painful to live alone at home, it would have been nice if he had been with us.

I used to visit him when he was in Wha Wha. I would take the bus and when I arrived at the prison gate, I would tell them who I had come to visit. Then I would be given a note to take to the office. There they would write down what I wanted and then they would allow me to see my husband. We were allowed to bring food in for the prisoners. But I did not always go to see him, sometimes his other wife would go and sometimes relatives would visit him. He was only in Wha Wha for a year.

When I went, I met many other wives who were visiting their husbands. We would talk about our problems. We wanted our husbands to be released and return home to live with us. But there wasn't a solution and I never really felt strengthened by being able to discuss my problems with other women. To my husband it did not matter how you felt, or whether you suffered: he was determined to fight for the country and he was determined not to retract, and so I just had to accept the consequences.

But when I had problems I did discuss them with him.

When I ran short of money, he advised me to sell some oxen so that I could send the children to school. He gave me plans. I also ploughed a lot and grew crops to sell.

Not many of our neighbours could be free with us. Obviously they thought my husband caused them trouble, although there were a few people who sympathized and helped us, especially with ploughing. During the war, we used to visit each other in our own village to talk and help each other. We even went to church.

In fact, our neighbours here were nicer than those at Roseday. There, when we were moved – it was only my family on that occasion – everyone in the neighbourhood ran away. You see, it was only those families who had something to do with politics, who were moved, although there were some others who wanted to come this way, as they'd heard they could have big pieces of land to plough.

There were schools in this area and I sent my children to be educated. My eldest daughter completed standard six and my younger daughter form four. My son did not do very well. He left for the struggle after the war had started and the freedom fighters were already in the area. I did not know where he'd gone because he didn't tell me. I was distressed, but after a while I comforted myself with the thought that a lot of children had gone to join the freedom fighters. His family was my only worry because he left a wife and two children and they had to be supported and it was a problem to do this.

Of course, had my son asked me if he should go, I think I would have refused because he is my only son. But I remembered the biblical story of Abraham who was asked to sacrifice his son. That helped me a lot because he was my only son. He was just like Isaac and he was given as a sacrifice. I told myself that I would, God willing, see my son again. My daughters never spoke about it, but they did help to support his family.

I think both Zipra and Zanla were in this area but I did not know the difference between them. All freedom fighters were the same as far as I was concerned. They did not distinguish themselves when they came. They told us they were fighting to free the country but they did not say which group they belonged to. Because I was alone, I was not really involved in providing for the freedom fighters. Everyone knew I was alone so they did not bother me.

Of course, we gave the freedom fighters food, mostly chicken because it was easy to come by. When they were in the area, the men would inform us that 'our children' had come and ask for meal-mealie or chicken which they would then collect. It was always only cooked in one home by the men and then carried to the base. I contributed whatever I could, even though I was alone. I had to because everyone else was doing so and the war was being fought to free the country which belongs to everybody.

Sometimes the soldiers came and asked where the freedom fighters were. We always said that we didn't know and never saw them. Nothing happened to us but, in a nearby village, the soldiers had contact with guerillas. We heard the gun shots but, because it was dark, we did not see what happened. My one real fear was of the gun. We were all afraid of the gun. It is a fearful thing to see one even if it is not going to shoot you.

Once the schools were closed for a while, but I am not sure who closed them. It could have been the soldiers or freedom fighters. I just heard that children had been told not to go to school. My children had left home by then. On another occasion, a dip tank was destroyed, but again I never heard who did it. It was not good to know too much about these things.

My husband was released during the time of Muzorewa's government. I was pleased that he was out of prison where he had been for a long time. His mother had died while he was at Wha Wha and he mourned her loss. We, I and the second wife, did not see so much of him then, as he moved around with the comrades. I did not know much about it. Even after the cease-fire, he did not come home to live for a long time. But now he is back and he can help me to do those things which I had to do on my own.

It was almost sunset, on the day my son came home, some time after the cease-fire. I was in the fields and I saw him coming. He was with another boy from this area. I just greeted them normally but I was very pleased that he had returned. Everyone was glad to know that our children had brought us the country we wanted.

My son went to his home and and straight away began to plough his fields with his family. Now he is working at Gokwe with the contractors who are building the hospital. So he is looking after his family and that's fine. He respects me as a child should do and that is all I expect from him. My husband is now doing what I would have done, and what I used to do alone, so my burden is much lighter.

Now everybody is free and we are working together as one. There are no more problems of division. We are all free and enjoying ourselves. I was pleased that, after independence, there was unity. Life before unity was difficult and my husband was sometimes afraid to stay at home.

Now we are also being taught by the agriculture workers the proper way of doing things and we know what to do. For example, today we dig contour ridges. The agricultural advisors have told us that they are good because they prevent the fields from being washed away. Long ago we were just ordered to dig them, but we did not understand why. We thought the authorities only wanted to trouble us and so we didn't dig the contour ridges. My husband was arrested and taken to prison because he refused to dig contours. The war was fought because of this.

The agricultural workers have explained a lot of things to us. You see, during the war we planted and sold a lot of shelled nuts to shopkeepers with stores in the area. Now we are not producing enough nuts to sell and so we have been advised to plant maize and sunflowers. We are no longer selling our grains to the shops but we take them to the GMB* where we get a much better price for them. The shopkeepers used to give us very little money. Sometimes we only got six or seven dollars for a whole bag of shelled nuts.

Life was tough before independence; but now it is much easier.

* Grain Marketing Board.

13 Meggi Zingani

Zinhanga Village, Buhera

I WAS BORN in Rusape district in Chief Chiduku's area in 1927. My father's name is Tsoka so I was known as Meggi Tsoka. I have three sisters and four brothers. It was a long time ago and mothers did not worry about anything except bringing up their children and we did not worry about anything at all: we passed our time roasting dry maize. That was before people knew about the white man's food. Later when people got to know about it, we found that sugar cost sixpence* and dresses a shilling: if you had as much as three shillings, you could buy the most expensive dress in the shop.

We swam in pools in the rivers. Boys and girls swam in the same pool but boys swam on one side and girls swam on the other. Afterwards we lay on the river sand to get dry. We swam without wearing anything, there were no such things as swimming clothes. When a boy was old enough to propose love to a girl and she was old enough to have

---

* The denominations of currency used until 1970 in Rhodesia were those of Britain: pounds, shillings and pence.

119

a boyfriend, he would visit her home. He would pretend he had come to see or to play with other boys in her family, but really he would have come to see her. After a while he would indicate that he was interested in the girl and, after a time, she and her sisters would accompany the boy home, so they had time to talk to each other. Parents somehow always knew that the boy had come for one of their daughters, so they did not fuss. On their return home, the girls would collect firewood. Once the girl had fallen in love she would tell her sister and then the two of them would inform the girl's aunt. Then the boy and the girl would give each other love tokens in the presence of the aunt. Today this does not happen, but this is what we did in those days.

In 1940 my family moved from Chiduku to the Buhera district and we all stayed at home for a year because there was no school nearby. Then my parents initiated the idea of schooling for children and our first lessons were held under a tree, later they built a grass shelter as a classroom. But we only went to school in the mornings. We were back by noon and then we went swimming. School was not very important to us, we did not care very much whether we went or not. I did not progress very far as I was not interested in going to school. I took advantage of the fact that I was the seventh child and it was not very easy for my father to send us all to school. So I decided to leave.

My parents tried to force me to go but I played truant and eventually they let me be. Only two of my brothers are educated: the rest of us did not bother with school, although we all can read and write. We did not understand the importance of education and thought it a waste of time. Although our parents wanted us to learn, they were not very worried when we refused to be educated. We were also much older when we went to school. I got married when I left and I was over twenty.

My married life was very difficult. Problem succeeded problem from the time that I married until the war. Buhera was then a poor, backward district. People did not wear dresses, they covered themselves with skins, and they did not know how to till the land. But I had committed myself to living with such people.

My husband did not have parents: he had grown up in his grandfather's house and we lived with them, which was very hard. My husband's grandmother was very cruel to us.

Sometimes she would go away for days and leave us with nothing to eat at all. Her children had all married and my husband had done all the work for her. So she did not like the idea of him marrying and leaving her and so she mistreated us. My own parents sometimes had to help us with food.

Three years after I married I had a child, and a year after that I had a second. It was a year of drought and there was no food to be had, so my husband decided to go to South Africa soon after the birth of the second child. He spent three years there and during that time it was very difficult for me to look after the two children, who were almost the same age, on my own.

I had a hard time. Every night I prepared the children's food and, early in the morning, I carried the older child on my shoulders, the younger one on my back; in one hand I carried a basket of food and, in the other, a stick to hit the oxen with. I went to plough on my own. People planted millet because in Buhera they knew nothing of maize. And, if anyone tried to suggest doing anything different, they were very resistant. They thought that people from Rusape district were troublesome because they tried to introduce many new ideas. In the end I just planted millet like everyone else.

When my husband came back from Johannesburg he had only eight pounds in his pocket. But at that time it was a lot of money. We used it to buy what we needed for our home and he had also bought me some new clothes because I was still wearing the ones that I had brought with me from my home before we were married.

Then my husband helped me to till the land and we began by ploughing a small piece of the earth. As time went on our ploughing improved and we had better harvests. We even began to sell our grain at a store in the Buhera centre. Once we harvested two truck-loads of groundnuts and sold them in Dorowa. We then bought goats to sell and this gave us enough money to buy four cattle. The following season we ploughed and harvested three truck-loads of nuts and then we bought some more cattle. They were not very expensive then: one could buy an ox or a cow for seven or eight pounds, so we bought ten cows and two oxen. Our cows had calves and then we had a lot of cattle. But that was the very year that the government, or the council, made a rule that each family should only have a certain number of cattle so that the land would not be overgrazed. So we sold some and reduced our herd to eight, which was the maximum we were allowed. If people refused to sell their cattle, the council said that they would shoot them.

We have nine boys and a girl, two other children died. We managed to send them all to school because we sat down and planned how we would do it. We put the money we got from the sale of our cattle into the saving's bank at Nyazura. Later we used some of that money to open a little hotdog shop at Watekama township in Chiweshe, which is where we live now. When our children started going to school, our shop was well established and had become a grocery and that is how we managed to send our children to school.

In all that time I knew nothing of politics or the liberation struggle. After the rule about cattle, the council began to divide our fields and each family was allowed to have only a certain number. The demonstrators or agriculture extension workers forced people to dig contour ridges. Some of these officers were understanding and helpful but some were very cruel: they also treated people differently. Sometimes they were kind to some people but harsh on others. Sometimes they would not allow people to plough if the ridges had not been dug. But we dug all the contour ridges that were required for our twelve acres. They were supposed to stop erosion. Then we harvested more grain – both maize and millet – than we needed, so we sold it and this all helped to educate the children – by then we had five at school.

My first child went to school at Nyazura Mission. At that time it was a rule that, in order to progress beyond grade six, you had to have a good pass in certain exams. If the child did not do well, that was the end of his or her education. I think my son was worried about this but he did not say anything to me. When he left school he stayed at home for a while and tried to join the police force but he was not admitted. Then he left home and said he was going to Gwelo* where his younger brother was working. We never saw him again. He had gone but no one knew where or what had happened to him. He had been about to get married before he left. But the woman's parents had not agreed to it and so his 'wife' returned to her parents. There she gave birth to a son whom I raised as my own. He was just a bit younger than my last born.

* Gwelo is now called Gweru.

Then policemen from Masenga police camp came and asked us where my son was and we could only tell them that we did not know. They came frequently, so we began to wonder if perhaps our son had stolen something from somewhere and was in hiding. One day, after several visits from the police, they said that they had heard that he'd been seen on a hill close by called *Munwe waMwari**. They said that he lived there and was often seen wearing a white garment. I told them that I did not know anything about this but the allegation was constantly repeated. We were really in trouble with the authorities over that child.

Mozambique was known to us as Portuguese East Africa and apparently my son was heard on a radio broadcast from there. I do not know exactly why, but I suppose he knew that we were very worried because we didn't know where he was, and made an announcement. The police heard it and then they knew he was in Mozambique. The officer-in-charge came to our home at night and he called from a distance using my son's name, "*Mai mai mai*, answer me, I am your son, Fanuel." But I did not answer. My husband was not at home, and I kept quiet because I did not know who it was. Then the policeman went away and returned the next day. He admitted what he had done and said that since they now knew my son was in Mozambique, they would no longer bother me.

After that, nothing happened for another year and I had still not heard about the war. Later I began to hear rumours that there was a war in Portuguese East Africa. Then quite a long time afterwards we heard from a home boy with a radio that my son had again broadcast from there. Only then did I begin to believe that he was still alive. Later still, the police again drove up to our home and told us that our son was a terrorist. We wondered what this meant, because the police officer used the word 'tororo'. "What is that?" I enquired. Then they simply repeated what they had said and told us that my son had crossed into Mozambique. I said that as he had not told me, I could not know if this were true.

From that time I was considered as a 'terrorist mother' and I was in trouble. Often, when the police officers passed by, they would say, "Hello, *mai vatororo*," meaning, 'Hello,

---

* *Munwe waMwari* – finger of God.

terrorist mother.' We heard that the war was very intense in Mozambique and then we heard that the country had been liberated. Next we heard that the war was here, in Rhodesia. We were told that there were many terrorists, and then I recalled that the police officers had said that my son was a terrorist.

I think there were rumours about terrorists for about a year. Then we heard that they were called guerillas and we heard that the *magandanga* were in the Chipinge district. I wondered who they were and was told that they were the same people who had once been called terrorists. We all waited anxiously to meet them. We heard that they could foretell things, that they could detect witches and they knew everything. So we said let them come and catch witches and liars. Finally they arrived and we met them, but my son was not amongst them.

I first saw them in 1975. At the time we still had our shop and were residing at the shopping centre. The first time they came it was dark. I was preparing the evening meal when one of them arrived. He just came to our house and told my husband and me to follow him. We left the house and followed him to his friends. They asked if we knew them and we told them we did not. Then they asked if we had ever heard of the guerillas and we said we had, but that we had never seen them. So they explained that they were the guerillas and that they wanted things from our shop. They told us to open it up. My husband did so and we all went inside except for the two older ones who remained outside. Then they took what they wanted: sweets, biscuits, soap and a lot of other things – they filled up a cardboard box. Then they told us that we should keep their visit a secret and asked us to accompany them to Muringani store where there were lots of other guerillas.

They came back to our shop the following afternoon. We had a big radio: it was an attraction to a lot of youngsters at the centre who loved to come and play records there. So the guerillas came to dance as well, though at the time we did not know who they were. It was only after they'd gone that we asked one another about them, as my family were suspicious that they were the same people we had seen the night before.

At that time I think they were based in another village. The first group to arrive was always the one which alerted people about their presence in the district. After the first group another group always followed and those groups addressed us at *pungwes.*

When they first came into this area, they followed the river, Mwerahari, and based themselves at a hill called Chikunga which is near the river. They saw a little boy in Rukweza homestead and sent him to go and tell the headman that the *vanamukoma* had come. We were informed at sunset and everyone from Zinhanga village was told to gather at Chief Chiweshe's. Everybody went. Some people were afraid but we had to go because we had been threatened that business people were always sell-outs, so we had to be seen at the meeting otherwise we would have been in trouble. At the meeting all those who were running businesses were asked to stand up, so my husband and I stood up: we were the only ones with a business.

They told us that they were the same people who had come before, and that whatever happened at the meeting should only ever be known to the ones who were there. Anyone who broke the secret would be killed. They said they were 'our children' even if this was not literally the case as our own children were fighting elsewhere. They said Mozambique had been won through war and now they had come to fight and free our country. They said that they dedicated themselves to liberating us and that they were receiving assistance from friends whom they had also assisted. They said that after independence everyone would be free from colonialism. No one would be forced to dig contour ridges; we would have as many cattle as we wanted; a married woman without a marriage certificate would have the right to be treated as legally married; and that we would be treated like human beings. They said that we must be united and co-operative in fighting for our land. They said we could only succeed if we worked hand in hand with one another, because 'parents' were the people who were aware of all the dehumanizing things done by the government of the time. They cited the sort of things they felt bitter about, that, for example, most of them had been prevented from continuing with their education because they were said to be too old to do so. Thus they were forced by circumstances to go and work on the farms for next to nothing. They said that we parents had undergone many such unhappy experiences and so we should help them to defeat the system.

We agreed that they were right because we were being forced to dig contour ridges, if we wanted to plough. We were pleased the guerillas had come and decided to co-operate and work closely with them.

In the process of co-operation we cooked for them, we gave them bread, we killed and cooked chickens to feed them. During those first days the *vakomana* never came into the villages. They just stayed in the bush. We carried sadza to them in buckets, as if we were going to fetch water. Each mother brought her food in water containers and it was then shared amongst everyone present. They were very generous in sharing their food with everyone else. After eating the mothers carried their containers back home and the girls and boys remained with the comrades.

After a long time, when the war was at its peak, they changed their strategy. They said women should not bring food to their base and they formed a 'base committee'. I was a member of that committee. Its responsibility was to see that the comrades had enough food, that it was well prepared and that their clothes were cleaned and mended. From that time I never cooked for the comrades, my duty was to supervise the women who prepared the food. Every time the comrades came into the area, I knew which women were on duty to prepare food. The organizer, who was also a base committee member, was the first one to know of their presence, having been informed by the chairman. The organizer would then inform other committee members and each member knew their duty. So everyone was organized, the women cooked good food and the girls cleaned and mended the clothes well. Sometimes the comrades left clothes with the committee and the next group would take them, after they had been washed and mended.

Sometimes the *vanamukoma* looked very smart. Had you met them you would never have been able to tell that they were 'terrorists'. Sometimes even the soldiers could not tell. At times the comrades even used the *mujibas*' registration certificates to go to town. The situation was very tense: all the roads were out of operation and soldiers didn't drive here, instead they came by helicopter. If we wanted to go to town, we walked all the way to Dorowa where one could get transport because it had a police station. This became a war zone. There was war and nothing but war. We talked of war, we sang war songs; we concentrated on the war and nothing else.

Occasionally soldiers came on foot but only if they could call in air reinforcements if there was fighting. I can recall one incident when the soldiers came and took people quite unawares and many died. Girls were brutally killed, having had their breasts cut off. One of those girls is still alive but she is crippled: both her legs are paralysed. Nonetheless, the soldiers were defeated and we did not see them in this area for days afterwards.

Another time the soldiers came on horse-back and were all killed in Madzire village. We only saw one soldier on a horse who managed to get as far as our well, the other horses were riderless. I don't know what became of that soldier. So the people in this area – Chiweshe – filled in the well in order to stop horses from drinking there. After that we never saw the soldiers again – our area became the comrades' territory in which they did just what they wanted.

People who were jealous also caused problems. Some people did not like others who were better off than themselves. Many people died – they were killed because the sell-outs were jealous. They did not like those who were successful and said they collaborated with security forces who gave them money. As I said before, Buhera was a backwater. People who had moved there from Maungwe district were the elite because they generally had more education and worked harder and so they were made to suffer during the war.

People had different reasons for hating others. Some people supported the oppression which existed in Rhodesia: people being forced to do what they didn't want to do, to plough in a certain way, to eat food they didn't want to eat, and so on. The comrades told people to do what they wanted and plough where they chose. But some headmen and kraal-heads were very unco-operative, (many still are). They wanted people to abide by Smith's rules. Now, when you look back, you find that those were the people who were sell-outs during the struggle. They told the security forces a lot of untruths about others.

Unfortunately, the comrades were not aware of this. We, the ordinary people of the area, were not willing to report the sell-outs because they would have been killed. We felt that if this happened it would bring great misfortune to our families. When the comrades killed a person for being a sell-out they washed their hands of it and said it was not their fault but only their duty. It was the person who had reported someone to them that was held responsible for his or her death and many people were afraid of the *ngozi**, and that is why they said nothing. As a matter of fact, some of the people who sold out on others were mad.

My husband was one of the people who was sold out to the comrades. He was beaten and left for dead but fortunately he did not die: others beaten that day died. The night after he was beaten, I kept him at home but the following day I moved him from the house and hid him in our sunflower field. We had built a little hut there and two of my small boys spent nights with him. I treated him until he recovered. It would have been dangerous to keep him at home, as the soldiers might have come.

When the war became very intense, we closed our grocery shop and built a home about half a kilometre from the shopping centre. We moved everything from the shop into the house. My son, our fourth child, had a small pocket radio and some people thought it was a radio system for communicating with the security forces. They told the comrades that my son was a sell-out and that he was in touch with the security forces. So two comrades came to my home to fetch him and find out about the system. My husband was at the shop, so my son and the comrades went to see him and then together they went to see the radio which he had left at a friend's grinding mill.

After the comrades were satisfied that it was not a radio system, they let my son free but they passed a rule that they did not want to see any soldiers in the area. They said that, if they did, they would know that they had been called or informed by my son. Unfortunately, a couple of days later, soldiers came into the village and took some of the children away with them. But, because our home was a new one and we had not cleared the area around it, they did not notice it and did not take my children away. So we quickly moved our son to Harare where he stayed with his brother until the war was over. After this, the soldiers came again in a Dakota and were dropped in Bonde village which is just next to Zinhanga and people were beaten by them. So a man in the village went and told the comrades that my son had gone to join the security forces at Dorowa and that

---

* *Ngozi* – unhappy spirit of dead person who can return to visit the living.

he was now a soldier and the one who had led the soldiers to Bonde. This is why the comrades beat my husband. They said that my son had joined the security forces. My husband was beaten hard but he stuck to the truth that his son was not a soldier. They hit him very hard and at last one of the comrades said that he must be telling the truth and so they stopped beating him.

I did not blame the comrades. I knew that it was because of the other people, neighbours, certain village people who did not like my family. I knew the comrades were not able to divine the truth although, before they arrived, we had been told that they could do this. I knew that whatever they did, resulted from what they had been told by people in the neighbourhood. I was very hurt and worried, not by the comrades but by the behaviour of my fellow people. From the time the comrades came to enquire about my son's 'radio system', I knew the comrades had been informed and so I knew that someone had been spreading misinformation about our family. It was a terrible period and I was very hurt and very troubled.

By that time comrades had been in the area for two years and considered it their own zone. Soldiers only came into the area by air. We had moved everything from the shop into a little room in the house. When people wanted food, salt or sugar for the comrades, the organizer of the base committee came to collect those goods from the house. We stopped operating as shop owners. Many businesses closed down because things were just being taken from the shops and some shop owners were killed after being sold out. Schools also closed down. No one said very much, pupils and teachers just went home quietly. This last very intense period of the war was called *Gukurahundi**. Then the country was won and the war ended.

After my husband had recovered, he was again chosen to be on the committee. It was a committee formed by the comrades after they had realized that they were killing people for nothing. It was supposed to look into people's problems in the whole area. So, instead of people just being killed because a report about them had been received, a court was called and it determined what should be done.

---

* *Gukurahundi* – the rains that came after threshing, often accompanied by a strong wind. The last intense period of the war.

In this way a lot of lives were saved. My husband was a sort of judge on that committee. The comrades said that anyone who was found guilty was to be beaten by the committee. They were allowed to give people from 25 to a 100 cuts but committee members did not do this because they were afraid that people might die. They told comrades that they had beaten the guilty, but they really only gave them warnings.

The comrades often said, "*Pamberi nana mai.*"* Mothers were co-operative they prepared good, clean food for the comrades. The men were not as careful as the women. Sometimes a whole committee of men was beaten for neglecting their duties. At times, comrades got angry because the men did not handle them well: they treated them as if they were dirty, people with lice and yet they were fighting to free everyone. Women always took great care over what they did for the comrades. The comrades wanted their 'parents' to be considerate: they felt that they were our children. At first we also used to contribute money for cigarettes and beer for them, but we had to stop doing that because a lot of boys were killed by soldiers when they had gone to buy cigarettes at Dorowa.

I don't think the comrades knew that our son had gone to join the struggle. Personally, I never told them. I could never have done so because they were frightening: you could not talk to them about just anything. I think that, even if one's son had been amongst them, one could never have talked with him freely. They were very fearful people. They had been in the bush for such a long time and some of them were almost like animals: I mean, they were not as warm as ordinary people who stayed at home. It was hard to get used to them.

In some areas people took their children into town to live with relatives, but it did not happen here. The comrades had made a rule that anyone who moved their children away could not bring them back after independence: they were no longer considered to be from the area.

During that time, my seventh child was still only a small boy. He was the smallest *mujiba* and used to be sent many times to fetch a lot of things for the comrades. Sometimes he was sent as far as Rusape because the soldiers did not

* *Pamberi nana mai* – Forward with women/mothers.

suspect him of anything, as he was so small. For instance, one group came and said they wanted tape-recorders. Shop owners in the area contributed money and sent my son to Rusape. He bought the recorders, returned and the comrades came to collect them. He had no problems on the way, not even at road-blocks. The soldiers did not tell him to get off the bus even when they searched everyone else. He was very clever: you know, children who grew up in the war learnt all the tricks and knew what to do.

I was very worried about him. I was always afraid for him and thought that one day he would be killed. He was too small to be so involved. He was somehow affected, because when he tried to go back to school, he did not get very far. He completed form two but some of the habits he had picked up from the comrades hindered him. I cannot blame him because my son was so small when he got so involved in the liberation struggle.

I was troubled but the comrades had always said that the war was being fought for everyone. Some parents had children who went to fight and never returned, so I just accepted the consequences, there was nothing else to be done. A lot of children died at Nyadzonya and their parents never saw them again. They never even saw their graves and they were children like mine. I know that in some ways I was lucky because I still have my son.

As I said before, I was chosen to be a member of the base committee. I can now see that this was because they thought I might be killed as it was a dangerous position. If anything had gone wrong, I would have died and people knew that and some were banking on me being killed by comrades for having failed to perform my duties properly. When they chose me, it was a way of pushing me to danger-point.

In the same way, I now realize that when they selected my husband back on to the committee after he had been beaten, it was because they hoped that he would be killed. They thought that, since he had no training in either solving cases or any training similar to that which the comrades had received, he would never be able to do what was required of him. There were many people who did not have good motives right from the start. It took me some time to understand this. But right at the beginning, when the police came to enquire about my oldest son, people had wanted us to get into trouble.

After the war, the comrades went into the assembly points but I never saw my son. Two years later it was rumoured that he had been seen in the barracks in the Charter district. Then, a year later, I heard that he had been seen on a farm at Wedza. I went to look for him without my husband's knowledge. I told him I was going to visit my home and once there, I asked my sister to accompany me to Wedza to look for my son. I did not find him. I thought that he was probably dead. I lost all hope of ever seeing him again. Then, in the fourth year after independence, he came home.

I had gone to the river to wash my clothes when my son arrived with a wife and son at our old home. He introduced himself and asked a neighbour for our whereabouts and the woman accompanied him to our new home. As they approached, the lady started dancing and calling out to me. I came home and found him there. It was like I was watching a film. I felt as if I were dreaming.

I invited my son and his wife into the house and we just sat there. I did not even greet him properly. I was silent for a long time, I somehow could not comprehend his presence. Then my son asked me why I was so silent. I asked the lady who was with him to tell me again who I was speaking to, and she told me he was indeed my son.

He did not look at all well. He looked worn out and finished. It was terrible. I sent another son to Harare to fetch my husband who was visiting people there. Before his return, I killed a chicken because I had heard that, if a child has been fighting, he was not supposed to spend the night at home without having seen blood.

When my husband arrived, we went to consult n'angas about having my son cleansed: he looked so worn out and ill that we were both distressed. We were told by the n'anga that my son had been purified and that was why he had taken such a long time to return home: he had been cleansing himself.

My son had changed so much, he had been so many years in the bush, that it took me some time to adjust and accept the person he now was and put behind me the boy he had been. He was always moving about. He could never sit down for long, it was as if he were afraid of something – a gun maybe. He would sit for a few minutes, then stand up, walk about, sit down again, move again and so on. Sometimes, when he danced, I could not believe he was my son and at times I was even afraid of him. He had left in 1973 and returned in 1984. He had fought in the Mozambique war and then he had joined our liberation struggle and that must have worn him out. I was even afraid to look at him, but you always know your own child, there is that bond of motherhood.

He never talked about the war. All he said was, "We fought, that's it." He never explained exactly what took place. He would just say, "I'm alive and that is the important thing. I have brought a family home, so why do you want to know about my problems?" What distressed me sometimes was the way he danced, moving for a distance on his tummy, like a snake. I knew that that was the kind of training they had received, but it still really upset me.

When I now think of the war, I feel frightened. I suffered a lot. I suffered from the beginning, even before the war started and I suffered until the war was over. Now I am happy. People treat me like a human being. I feel I am safe; I do not think people will do anything harmful to me.

After independence, village committees were formed and my husband and I still serve on them. First I was on the village committee, then I was elected on to the branch committee and after that on to the district committee. Then I became the vice-chairwoman, and after the chairwoman was transferred, I took her place. Unfortunately, there are still people who are jealous and frustrated because their plans to have us killed or removed have failed and my husband is now a presiding officer and I have become the leader of the women in the district. Some people still feel that we are outsiders and have taken jobs from them in their area. However, the majority are the ones who elect us and they seem happy with our leadership because we never caused anyone to die, rather my husband saved a lot of lives when he was a judge on the base committee. He was very fair: he did not wish to take revenge for what had happened to him and people appreciate that kind of leadership.

The district chairwomen are supposed to teach women proper ways of behaving, good manners: to know their place and position in the home. Some women do not understand what independence means they think they should rule others and their husbands. We encourage them to look after their children properly and teach them good behaviour. We also encourage women to work hard to help maintain their families. If a woman has nothing productive to do such as keeping a garden, or sewing and selling her wares, then she will start to make mischief and want men with lots of money and divorces will follow.

During the war people were spoilt – everyone was behaving in the same way – married women, single girls, men and boys. When they danced, even the married women, it was in the same undignified manner. Everyone said they were fighting, everyone was a guerilla, that was what they said. You see, the comrades had told us this because we were all fighting for the country.

But now people are still behaving in the same way. So the village and district committees were formed to teach people, especially mothers, to behave like mothers. The young women were the most affected by the liberation struggle. The war caused people to behave wildly. The comrades said that, when people danced as they did, it was good. They said it was a way of appeasing the dead. But then people went too far. We try to keep women busy and bring them back to the old normal way of life so that they do not spend time following things like music groups.

But since independence some things have got much better. We used to sell our crops to shop owners but now we can take our grains to the Grain Marketing Board which, before independence, was only for whites. Now we can see the advantage of being free, we can sell our crops, get cheques in our own names and we get better prices. Long ago we gave our crops away for nothing: imagine, six dollars for a whole bag of shelled nuts!

Since the war, we have not been told to dig contour ridges but we have been prohibited from ploughing some of our fields. Sometimes the headmen do not even give us alternative land to plough. This is not what the comrades told us they would do. They said we would have land. Once you have been told to stop ploughing, that's it. I do not know what the government has to say about this because the same headmen give their smallest children land to plough.

The village and district committees do not discuss such matters. I think the problem is that the party has no say in the leadership of the villages pertaining to such matters. The same headmen and councils who were there under Smith just continue to act as they did before: they don't seem to understand why we fought.

The war liberated us. If there had been no war, our status would have deteriorated. I do not know what the future holds for us, but now we feel that the war set us free.

But I want to say that the government should unite the rulers: the old chiefs who were there before the war and the present presiding officers. If the government does not do this, a war will begin again. Some people are saying, "Forward with war" because they are not satisfied that people like my husband, who is not from a family of chiefs, is a presiding officer. Maybe the government does not know this but it is really a problem here in the communal lands. Since the day the government announced that the chiefs should be re-installed, there has been misunderstanding because in practice the presiding officers are still solving cases and the chiefs do not like this. So we are still waiting for the government to take an action in this regard. The problem must be solved quickly because now there is war – a war of words among the people here.

The comrades fought the war and got their rewards. Some are in the army, some got demobilization money, but some of us got nothing. First I served on the base committee and I am still serving people, but I have not received anything, no matter how small, as a token of appreciation. All we hear is, *"Pamberi ne basa"*: but we work and work and work, and everything ends up with the council. We are being overlooked. It is said that we are working as volunteers and yet we do a lot of work for the people. Do you think it's fair? Those who mocked us during the war, saying that all we ever said was, *"Pamberi neZanu; Pamberi neZanu,"* are now the ones who are getting paid. We who suffered, killed our chickens and goats, had children who died; we, mothers, who carried food on our heads to the guerillas, while others hid in safety, now we see that they are the ones who are getting paid and we are getting nothing. It is most unfair.

14 Mary Gomendo

Chipinge

I WAS BORN and brought up at Chikore Mission in Chipinge. My father was a chief by the name of Mhanda. He had two wives and eighteen children. I was the sixth child in the family. I was very fortunate because my father allowed me to go to school. In those days people did not often send girls to school because parents, fathers mostly, wanted them to get married, so that they could get lobola. But our father wasn't like that: he was good to us.

Since our family was large, my father was not able to give us enough money for the fees. We had to work to get our school fees. I went to school while I was very young. Miss Torrence, our missionary, who was at Chikore school, was very helpful to me. I worked for her and she helped me with the fees. Many girls in those days made baskets to earn money for school. I was not able to make baskets as I was very young. Instead I collected leaves for manure. If I filled a sack with leaves I got half a penny. It was very diffficult for me but I was very thankful because they thought of something for me to do in order that I could have education.

After I had finished standard one I was able to make bad baskets but Miss Torrence, who was a really wonderful lady, always bought those bad baskets from me. When I had completed standard four I thought it was the end of my education as I knew I would not have enough money to go to a boarding school* which meant paying for my food, accommodation, blankets and other things. But Miss Torrence said that I could bring my own food, relish, pots and one blanket. So I did this and I was happy to do so, because I wanted education.

I slept on the floor on the mat while the other girls slept in beds because they had enough money for the fees. When the bell rang for us to go to our rooms, I had to start cooking my own food. The others had it prepared for them. I often had nothing to eat because there was not enough time for me to cook and eat before I returned to class. It was a problem but I managed because I wanted education.

When I had completed my primary education, Miss Torrence and Mrs Dysart said they would pay for me to go to secondary school at Mount Selinda. They paid my fees and bought my uniform and books but I did not go home for the holidays, instead I worked for my education. My mother came all the way to Mount Selinda carrying a basket full of mealie-meal, mufushwa† and, sometimes, a few eggs for me to eat during the holidays.

I worked very hard because I felt I was very poor but I wanted education. I worked very hard in order to pass. I am glad to say that I never failed because I was working hard. When I was in standard six I even came first in class and then I did a two-year teaching course. After that, the authorities said, "Oh, this girl is really concentrating on her lessons. Let her come and teach at Chikore Mission." So I went to teach at the mission and when I got my first pay, I tried to give Mrs Dysart and Miss Torrence some money but they refused to take it. They said all they wanted was for me to be a Christian. They must have prayed for me, because I am now married to a church minister!

---

* At the time, many schools required children to become boarders after they had completed standard three. Schooling took the following form: kindergarten for two years; primary school through standards one to five; secondary school through forms one to four. Only a small minority of black children ever managed to complete nine years of education as there were very few secondary schools, rigorous, disqualifying examinations and the fees were too great for most families to bear.
† Mufushwa – dried vegetables.

I enjoyed teaching at Chikore very much. It was the first time that I had earned my own money and could buy what I wanted. Since I am the oldest daughter of the second wife, I was very responsible. I wanted the younger ones to go to school and I paid their fees. They did not go very far, but I tried to do something for them.

I met my husband Fred, who was a builder, at Mount Selinda before I started teaching. We were in love for six years before we got married.

After our marriage I continued to teach, first at Chakohwa, a school near Mvumvu river, and then at Emerald primary school near Mount Selinda. This is where we bought a piece of land after our marriage and where our home is now.

It wasn't easy to be a teacher, a housewife and a mother at the same time. Once we had a visitor who said, "Mrs Gomendo, if you want to be married and have children, stop teaching and, if you want to teach, stop having children." That was because the baby was very dirty when I arrived home from school and this visitor had already arrived. It was not easy. By then we had a bakery and my husband was away working as a contractor. I had to take care of everything: home, school and business. You know, women always work very hard, they work very hard.

My husband decided to join the ministry in 1966 after we had been married for fifteen years and had five children. When he told me, I couldn't believe it. I said, "Am I dreaming, can it be true?" Nothing ever made me so happy as his decision to join the church. He trained at Epworth Theological College for three years. I was not very happy during that time as I was often sick. You know, where there is light, the moths always try to put it out.

Then in 1969 we moved to Bulawayo, which is where my husband first served. We lived in Bulawayo for four years. We enjoyed the ministry and the church members and women's meetings. We women met together through the clubs, and taught each other how to cook and make biscuits and baskets.

During the years when I was at Chikore and Mount Selinda people talked about politics but we were not involved. We just thought it was the business of the older people. I heard of politics, of people going out of the country. Right up to the end of war, people were still leaving the country to fight.

I was not happy about the war. When I heard that so-and-so had left, it pained me as a woman. Women cried when their children disappeared because they did not tell their parents that they were going. You would simply look around and see that your child had gone, and you began crying for your child who might never come back. It was a terrible time. I felt for the children who had gone.

Apart from children and people leaving the country, I heard about many other things. People were killed. Boys who tried to cross the border were shot by the soldiers who were always watching out for them. Even parents were killed by the soldiers who said that they should not have let their children go, and yet parents were also worried that their children were leaving.

After we had been in Bulawayo for four years, we were sent to Chisumbanje. It is very hot there and we had to use water from the Sabi river which was not good for us and the children often got malaria. We stayed in Chisumbanje for two years and then we were moved to Chibuwe which is also in the Chipinge district. In Chibuwe there was good transport and good drinking water from taps, but it was still very hot and there were a lot of mosquitoes.

At Chisumbanje, as in Bulawayo, we heard about people leaving the country. But while we were at Chibuwe our sons left. My older son, who was a temporary teacher, left in 1975 and our last born, who was then about eleven years old, left in 1976. The departure of children had nothing to do with parents. It had to do with general feelings, the atmosphere, things they had seen and heard from friends and acquaintances, things which they saw happening. My older son saw many people crossing the border while he was teaching at Rimayi and I am sure this is why he made the decision to go.

But when my youngest son left, it was terrible for us. He decided to leave with others: just a group of about six small children crossed the border into Mozambique. We were so worried. We did not know where they were. We looked here, there and everywhere, but we could not find them. Then someone told us that they had seen them crossing the border into Mozambique.

I did not feel free. I did not really know why they left. I worried because I knew that they were going to fight and I didn't know whether they would ever come back, young as they were.

I am sure that these children had discussed how difficult things were, how they were treated by whites, and whether it was fair or not. They decided that it was better for them to fight for freedom in the country. We never discussed politics in our family and the departure of my sons tasked us terribly. Some children even died on the way. They were killed by soldiers, or they were bitten by snakes, or drowned in rivers. There were so many things that could happen to them.

It was a difficult time. The freedom fighters ordered some churches to be closed. We were very fortunate because we were not ordered to close down our church. The freedom fighters said that they did not mind the Lord, they did not mind who was God. So we continued to worship but we did so in fear. Once, when we were at Chisumbanje, I was preaching at a women's meeting and a freedom fighter entered the church and cried, "Freedom!" I stopped. I couldn't go on. Everybody was quiet. He shouted, "*Pamberi!*" and *"Pasi naJesu!"** People did not respond to that slogan. They wouldn't say, "*Pasi naJesu!*" They did not respond. Then the freedom fighter spoke about this and that concerning politics, and then he went away.

In 1977 my husband was elected president of our denomination and we moved to Houghton Park in Harare. While we were there we heard that my elder son had been ambushed. It was a sort of rumour. We did not know exactly what had happened, but we were told he had been killed. My husband tried to find out through the official channels. But he got nowhere. At that time people were talking secretly to each other.

Later, when the freedom fighters were told to go to the assembly points, some people said my son had not been killed. My husband went from one camp to another trying to find our son. He did not find him. No one, not even the officials, knew anything about him.

Later, after independence, when my husband and I were in America, we heard that a list of comrades, killed in the struggle, was being shown to people. My daughters tried to find my son's name on the list, but it was not there. It is a great worry because we really do not know what happened to our son. We do not know whether he was killed,

---

* *Pasi naJesu* – Down with Jesus.

or bitten by snakes, or washed away in a river. We are stranded. When we think about him, we become very downhearted.

We know our son went away to try and fight for freedom but we do not know where he is. In the camps, when the young people arrived, they kept a record of who they were, so that if anything happened to any of those children, they could inform their parents. But we are in darkness. This is our problem.

The eleven-year-old returned. When he reached the camp in Mozambique, they said he was too young to join the struggle. So they sent him to school in Sierra Leone. He studied there until he had finished form five. But we did not know where he was through all those years. It was only in 1983, when we were in America, that he returned. My daughters wrote and told us that he had suddenly arrived home. It was amazing news and we were very happy. We thank the Lord that one of our sons returned home to us. He still has the feeling of politics in him, but he is training to be a teacher.

Because the freedom fighters were fighting against soldiers at Chibuwe, the authorities thought of putting us in what they called 'protected villages' and many people were driven behind those big fences. Those who were not willing to go into the villages were shot dead by the soldiers. People were forced into these villages: they ran to them, because they were afraid of being shot.

The villages were very overcrowded and, as a result, diseases spread easily from one person to another. Many people died. There was no sanitation. Conditions were very bad. It was not easy to live in those villages and, although they were called 'protected villages', they were not.

People's homes were burnt down so that they would not return to them. Everything was burnt – their corn, their fields, everything. Many people were tortured. Children could not go to school. They could not because people were flung together from faraway places and it was a long way for their children to walk back to their schools. Many teachers had also left their schools and everyone was frightened of meeting either the freedom fighters, or the soldiers, on their way to school. It was a really terrible time. Shootings! Ah, people were shot and the targets were chiefs, teachers, businessmen and bus drivers. They were shot by both the soldiers and the freedom fighters. They were targets for both groups because they were in between. The soldiers said they kept and looked after the freedom fighters, because when they looked for them, they could not find them, although they knew they were active in our area.

If they suspected you, they shot you or took you to jail without trial. People were even tortured at a place called Chibonore. Many of my relations suffered because they were taken to Chibonore. They were beaten and sent back home. The authorities suspected businessmen and bus drivers because they had money and the soldiers thought they gave it to the freedom fighters. "If you don't do this," they said, "why is it that the guerillas are not starving to death?" The soldiers killed people that they suspected.

On the other hand, the freedom fighters always wanted to know why there were soldiers in the area. They said that people were informers. We heard the freedom fighters sometimes did terrible things to people they thought were informers: cutting off ears, or lips, or breasts. Sometimes they even asked you to dig your own grave and then they killed you and threw you into it. Sometimes, if they suspected that you were an informer, they tied your legs together and your arms together and they called everyone to collect firewood and make a big fire. Then they threw the person, alive, on to the fire. They said they wanted everyone to see what would happen to an informer.

Everyone had to sit and watch the person die. You were not even allowed to cry. It was terrible. I personally never attended such an event, but many people witnessed such things.

The time was not easy for people. It wasn't easy.

After independence things are better, although sometimes people still kill each other here and there. But it has got nothing to do with war. Life is easy now. We wish it to continue like this. No one likes war.

Women did a good job of taking care of their families while their husbands were away. They went away to war or to work in town and women had to remain at home with the children and try to look after their homes and their property. Their children went away to the struggle and they just had to try to maintain what was left.

Today, in Chipinge, there are many widows, young and old. Some young women have only one child. After they had only been married a year, their husbands would be killed in one way or another.

Some older women are living alone with no one to help them, both their husbands and their sons were killed. When we have Women's Fellowship meetings, we usually call for such widows so that we can give the little we would have prepared for them. We see many widows. Now we are planning to build a home for those who need assistance, those older women who have been left alone. Money is a problem but the Women's Fellowship are trying. It is our project.

The young widows are better off than the older women because they will marry again. But the old ones need shelter and food. They have been left stranded by the death of their husbands. Yes, women did a lot, but no one recognizes what they did.

15 **Margaret Viki**

Mtshogwa

I WAS MARRIED at an early age. I was eighteen when I married and in our custom that is considered quite young. I married an old, mature man who already had a family and I was the second wife. I had eleven children with my husband, seven girls and four boys. My husband died when my last child was two years old. My husband was sick for a long time and died of cancer.

At that time we were staying on a farm. But, after my husband's death, I realized that since I wasn't the elder wife, my children had no chance of a good life, because my husband's first wife had her own children and they inherited the farm. So I decided to look for somewhere to build a home for myself and my children and requested permission from my husband's sister to do this. She wanted to know whether I would stay with my children, as I was young enough to marry again. I told her that I would because I had a large family which I could not leave or expect someone else to take care of. So I looked for somewhere to build my own home, and this I found at Moyana's village. It was just before the war came to that area.

When the freedom fighters first came, we could not tell what kind of people they were because they wore belts with bullets in them, and we had not seen bullets before. We had heard about the *vakomana* being in other areas but still it was frightening. The Zipras were the first to come. As time went on, they told us who they were and why they were there. We did not anticipate any problems since we were excited and thought things would run smoothly. But when they came it was hard.

The problem was that the freedom fighters wanted food and soap from us. Movement became very difficult as there were many different groups in the area and life got even harder as Smith's soldiers – some white, some black – also arrived in the district. The soldiers did not want us to feed the freedom fighters, while the comrades expected us to continue preparing food for them, in spite of the presence of the soldiers. Life continued under these hardships for a long time and it seemed unbearable.

Then, after a long while, the Zanla forces came as well. So we had two groups in the area, the Zipras and the Zanlas, and the situation became even worse because they did not like each other. So, in all, we had three groups of fighters, the Zipras, the Zanlas and Smith's soldiers. Of course, we did not prepare food for the soldiers, but we had to feed both Zipra and Zanla. Later, Sithole's soldiers also came for a while. Because life was so unbearable, we almost ended up hating the freedom fighters.

For instance, on the farm where we stayed, there was a borehole and the Zanlas camped on our farm, although the Zipras did not. The Zanlas stayed because they wanted to have water nearby.

One day the Zanlas had come to my village to ask for food. We prepared it and took it to their base. Then, at about ten o'clock in the morning, the soldiers came to the village and said that they had heard that the Zanla guerillas were at my home. I denied that I had seen them. We could never admit that we had seen them because the Zanlas said that if anyone ever admitted their presence they would kill us. The soldiers then questioned the small children who were around and they beat my young son. They pressed him to tell them where the freedom fighters were. My son refused to say anything.

While the soldiers were still harassing us, they spotted

a boy who had been sent by the Zanlas to come and check on the noise of trucks which they had heard. When the soldiers spotted the boy they shot at him three times. The Zanlas, on hearing the shooting, returned fire and were firing towards my home where the soldiers were. Fortunately no one was hurt.

That was a tough day, I tell you. The bullets flew everywhere and I had small children. It was a really dangerous moment. I cannot really express the fear and difficulties we experienced during the war.

Our children were used as sentries. They were always on the watch, looking out for soldiers and then informing the Zanlas if ever the soldiers were around. If they heard the sound of trucks, the *mujibas* and *chimbwidos* ran around to see what was happening and where the trucks were going. *Chimbwidos* also washed clothes for the freedom fighters. Our children, by that I mean any child over the age of twelve, would also stay at the base with the freedom fighters so that parents would not sell them out to the soldiers. They took our children, so that if ever the soldiers came to shoot them, not only would they die, but so also would our children. They said it would be our fault for selling out on them. That was very painful.

The children were not happy about this. They only went to the bases because they were afraid. Each group that came took the children to their camp. There was no way out. It was a great risk because, if the soldiers had come, the children would certainly have been killed.

The children would stay at the base for as long as the group of Zanlas or Zipras was around. They returned to their homes when the group moved away. Then, when other groups arrived, the children went back to the bases again. But if there were no *vakomana* in the area, the children had a rest.

The children had enough to eat when they were at the base. They ate together with the *mujibas*, *chimbwidos* and the freedom fighters. If there was not enough, the mothers would be asked to go and prepare more. The women always had to taste the food first, before dishing it out.

Some of the girls had children by these freedom fighters. At first they seemed to be good young men, but later on a lot of girls became pregnant. There was nothing the parents could do because they were afraid. They couldn't even ask the *vakomana* for fear of being killed.

The comrades were fighting for the country, in a way they were fighting for us, but they were also capable of killing. If ever, for example, a parent refused permission for a child to go to the base for a day, one could be killed or thoroughly beaten. That was frightening: so parents never said a word if their child became pregnant by the *vakomana*. That was that. The father never, to my knowledge, came back to help or see the child or the woman. Both Zipras and Zanlas were the same in that regard.

In most cases Zipra and Zanla did the same things in the same way. Sometimes the Zipras came and asked for many items of clothes. We had to find the money to buy them. Afterwards the Zanlas would come, because they had heard that we had done something for the Zipras and would ask for whatever they wanted. There could be no excuse, because we had already given provisions to the Zipras. The great difference between these two groups was that Zipras did not mind what kind of relish you gave them. They ate anything. The Zanlas only wanted meat.

The Zipras did not want any children to go to town, even if a child was going to school. They wanted all the children to be at home participating in the war. If parents sent their children to school in town, we were forced to bring them back. The Zanlas were better in that regard because, if the child was in town at school, they did not require us to bring the child back home. All my children were at school then. They went to school in Gweru. My sister's son took my girls because the situation was bad at home. I stayed there with only the small children.

I had a very hard time in those days. I had to go to the fields and look after the cattle as well. I did sometimes have men to help me but, because of the curfew, they often came late. Then I would have to get up very early to go and look for my cattle if they were lost. Occasionally the cattle spent the night in a camp which was quite a long way off. One morning I met the soldiers while I was looking for my herd. They asked why I was out so early, before the stipulated time. I explained that I had to find my cattle as they could be eating in the fields. They did not do anything to me, and they let me continue. Then they went to my home. As they arrived, so did the men who worked for me. The soldiers asked why they had come so late to work, but they did not do me any harm and, that day, they did not harass the men either.

Those were tough years. The Zipras were still in the area but they rarely came into the villages, because there were a lot of Zanlas. Zipras went to other homes in a different area but in the same district.

One afternoon the soldiers and the Zanlas met again at my home. The soldiers had been told that I had cooked for the Zanlas and that some chickens remained. That was true because those chickens were still in the house. The soldiers came to my home to ask where the Zanlas were. As usual, I denied knowing anything, although I had just come back from giving them food. That was the day I should have died, but I was very fortunate they did not kill me.

The soldiers entered my house and searched and, sure enough, they found the chickens tied up. When they asked me why I had tied up the chickens, I replied that someone wanted to buy them. One of the soldiers said that he knew all my chickens and so he would check to see if they were really mine, as I said. This he did. Then he told his friends that I might be telling the truth since all the chickens were mine.

Then they used their machines which they use for watching [binoculars] and, after they had spotted the freedom fighters, they followed them. But the *chimbwidos* had also seen the soldiers and they hurried to warn the comrades. So, by the time the soldiers reached the base, all the freedom fighters had run away and only my cups, plates and pots were scattered about. They smashed everything except the pots which they brought to my home. They asked me who they belonged to but I said that I did not know. They would have killed me if I had said that they were mine. The soldiers took all the pots to their camp. I was fortunate they did not beat me.

But one day I was beaten. Again the soldiers had come to my home and asked whether I had seen the freedom fighters. As usual, I told them that I had not seen them. If one ever admitted this, the soldiers would ask you to show them the way to the *vakomana*. It was very frightening. The soldiers walked around my home, examining it closely, and they noticed footprints. They made it clear that the freedom fighters had been to my home. Finally, I admitted that the comrades had passed by, but I said I did not know where they had gone.

The soldiers asked why I had not said so in the first place.

I told them that it was because I was afraid. Then they beat me. A white soldier called me into my house, picked up a small axe and swung it as if he were going to chop me down. Then, suddenly, he threw down the axe and beat me thoroughly with the back of his rifle instead. He hit me again and again until I grabbed the rifle in protest. I held my grip and we struggled until we were both outside the house. But I had not seen another soldier who was just outside the house. As I came out he hit me and I fell down.

The soldiers wanted to take me to their camp but, because I had a sick child at home, they let me be. They told me that I should be thankful for the sick child and the crippled old man who was also there, otherwise they would have taken me away to their camp.

The following day I could not move an inch. My whole body ached and the rifle blows had bruised me badly, especially around my tummy. It was terrible. I did not want anything near my body. I could not go the hospital because I couldn't leave the small children alone at home. But after some days I healed.

Two days afterwards the freedom fighters came to find out how I was because the *chimbwidos* told them that I had been beaten. They were relieved to see that I was recovering as they thought that I had been killed. Those were tough times.

The women always prepared food for the freedom fighters at one home and then carried the food to the base. We were always afraid that the soldiers might come while we were cooking, which would mean that everyone would be killed. Cooking was always done at my home because there was water in the borehole nearby. That is why people preferred cooking there: afterwards it was easy to wash the pots and dishes quickly. Everything was done fast so that we could disperse quickly in case the soldiers came along.

Since I was the owner of the home, the soldiers always came to me and I would be alone after everyone else had gone. We had to do it this way because we were afraid of both sides, afraid of the soldiers who would kill us if they found out, and afraid of the freedom fighters because if we refused to feed them that would also mean we would die. We often discussed what would happen to us. We said we had seen and experienced so many problems and we wondered if we would ever lead a normal life again. Sometimes we comforted ourselves by saying that, once the freedom fighters won the liberation war, we would sit pretty. After such a thought we would laugh, imagining ourselves being remembered by the freedom fighters after the war when they would be sitting in their high places.

We said, surely the *vakomana* will not forget us, after we have done so much for them. Such a thought would comfort us for a while and yet we were still quickly gripped by fear. Such ideas were just day-dreams shared amongst ourselves. Now some of those freedom fighters are in high places and they have forgotten that we helped them. Today when we talk among ourselves we remember how we suffered and lived under such hardships and yet those freedom fighters have forgotten us.

The soldiers killed people. If ever they came and found the freedom fighters in your home, you were a dead person. The soldiers shot everyone. Sometimes it happened that the freedom fighters ran away unhurt since they were used to fighting and they knew what to do, but the civilians died. Sometimes the freedom fighters also died and sometimes the soldiers did. People died. It was a war.

We did not help each other to bury the dead. Each family did whatever it had to do on its own. We could not even go and give our condolences. If, for instance, a person was killed by the freedom fighters, only the people who witnessed that death were supposed to bury that man and do it there and then. Only those who saw the incident conducted the burial and they kept quiet. If ever a civilian was killed, each family buried their dead. If anyone was killed at your home, the relatives would come to collect the body for burial.

The soldiers let us bury our dead but, if a person was killed at someone's home, the owner would be thoroughly beaten. Sometimes you would be taken to the camp and beaten for as long as they felt like it.

Freedom fighters killed people because they said that people sold them out. If the soldiers came along they said it was because someone had told them. Then they would make enquiries until they came up with a name. Even if that person had not sold them out, but was not in the area or village when the soldiers came, that person could be said to be a sell-out. That person would be killed. Yes, sell-outs existed but many people were deemed sell-outs when they were not. A lot of people were killed who were not sell-outs.

Many people were suspicious of one another and people told a lot of untruths. If someone had gone away for one reason or another, it could be said that they had gone to report to the soldiers, when it was not true at all.

Sometimes a person might ask someone else for something – sugar, for example – and, if you did not give it to them, they might tell the freedom fighters that you were a sell-out, to get you into trouble, although what they said was not true. You could be killed for nothing, just because someone wanted you dead, and told lies about you, all because you did not give them something they wanted.

It was common, especially among women, for them to sell out on each other. For instance, if one worked very hard and acquired some possessions, one could be branded a 'witch' by those who were jealous. The freedom fighters were against witchcraft, so that was a sure way of having someone killed. Witches were killed mercilessly. Sometimes a bonfire was made and a person who was said to be a witch was thrown in and burnt to death, dying for a bag of sugar, or just because someone was disliked by someone else. In most cases it was due to nothing but jealousy of somebody who was successful.

Clinics and dip-tanks were closed down during the war. What happened was that when the freedom fighters came to an area they told people that they should destroy them. They said that schools should be closed because they did not want schools. They said that traditionally our grand-parents did not dip their cattle and the cattle survived. They said they wanted life to be as it was at that time. But it was the villagers who did the destruction.

We just did as they said because we thought they were right and that they knew what they were doing. Later we regretted it because our cattle died of anthrax. A lot of cattle died and people even died after eating contaminated meat. It was bad because we really were not aware that we were damaging ourselves. We were destroying our own possessions.

Schools were closed down and window panes smashed because the freedom fighters said that we paid school fees to a government that was fighting against us. They said that children should not go to school because if they did, we had to pay school fees and the money would be used to buy the bullets that killed the freedom fighters.

Clinics closed down because, when the freedom fighters came to a clinic, they took all the medicine and then, because there was no medicine, there was no point in opening the clinic. They never told us what would happen after independence in connection with these things that we destroyed.

We agreed with what they told us and we did not worry whether it was true or not. We thought they knew what they were doing and so we did as they said. We went ahead and destroyed things. We did not stop to think that we would need educated rulers after we attained independence. During that time all we were concerned about was the war and doing as the freedom fighters told us. Now, after independence, we realize that we acted foolishly. Now we know that we need educated people to run the country and we regret that we destroyed our own facilities because now we have to rebuild them.

One afternoon, not long after the war had come to our area, I sent my oldest son to the shops to buy some sugar. I did not realize that, in this way, I had sent him away. He never came back.

The following day I went to the shops to find out if anyone had seen him. I was told that they had, but they did not know where he had gone. The shopkeeper gave me the sugar my son had left for me at the shop the day before. I went back home and for a long time I did not know where he had gone. I felt sick for days afterwards, but this did not help me.

Our leaders had explained to us that the liberation war would give us the country. We understood that, when it was over, we would be free and we would rule ourselves. So, much later, when my nephew came and told me that my son had left the country with his cousin, I was happy, as most of us were. We thought that our children were helping us by going to fight for our country. We knew it could not be free if we did not fight for it. Someone had to do it.

My son, who was in form two, often listened to the radio and was fascinated by what he heard. I think that, when he failed his exams, he decided to become one of the freedom fighters as he had often heard of them on the radio. I think children were excited by the idea of holding guns and fighting, even if the Rhodesian radio reported adversely on the guerillas.

For parents it was painful, but we hoped that our children would return and we thought we would be happier still, as they would bring the country with them. I thought we would have a hero in my family. I did not know how things would turn out. Now I am very grieved.

During the cease-fire, when the freedom fighters had been gathered in the different assembly points, my son wrote me a letter asking me to come and see him together with my last born. I asked my brother to accompany me because I did not know where his assembly point was. We left Gweru and spent the night in Harare. My son had instructed me to take a bus from Harare to a place called Papa which is somewhere near Karoi. But instead of boarding a bus we got a lift.

We did not see him on the day we arrived: but we registered at the office and they told us that we would see my son the following day. The next morning I was called to the office and they sent someone to call him. He came. He was very thin. I was saddened by the sight of him and I asked him why it was. He told me that the burden of war had been heavy. Fighting was not an easy job. Every time I looked at him I could not reconcile myself to his appearance, as if he were not my son. I felt tired and powerless, I think he felt the same too. I almost cried but, because I was afraid that would make him emotional too, especially as there were so many other young men about and crying before them would put my son off, so I controlled myself. Later, when he came home, he was much better. But he resigned from being a soldier because of ill-health and was at home for a year before he went to work again.

When he was well, he went to work as a medical orderly. He worked at several clinics including Zhombe hospital as an orderly. He was then transferred from Zhombe to Ndutshane, where he disappeared. I heard that he had been taken and put in Roma camp. So I went to look for him there but I did not find him. The authorities admitted that he had been there but they refused to allow me to see him. I asked them why they had taken my son, but they refused to tell me.

After that I sought a lawyer's advice but that was of no help. The lawyer was not able to trace his whereabouts either. My daughter also got another lawyer, who is still trying to find him but so far no news has been heard. I have not seen my son again and I do not know whether he is alive or not.

There is nothing I can do now that I cannot find my son. I thought that, when he came back, I would have someone to help me look after the other younger children but, as he has gone, I have to work hard to be able to look after the rest of my children, since I have a large family.

To accomplish my goal I decided to join an agriculture group composed of men and women. Here we are taught better techniques of ploughing and planting by extension workers. They have taught us that we should make sure that the soil is turned upside down properly when we first plough. Then, when the rains come, and we want to plant, we plough again. But this time, we just scratch the surface of the land and then sprinkle the maize seed so that it does not sink deep into the soil.

You see, a long time ago, we used to go behind the oxen as they pulled the plough and put our seed maize into the furrows. As a result, we buried the seed too deeply and usually the germination was poor. But with this new method, as soon as the rain falls all the maize germinates and the roots grow well because of the first deep ploughing.

In the past two years we have each selected a portion of the field on which we plant a competition crop. In the first year, I won third prize, which was three types of cattle medicine. Last year I came second among all the groups in the area and I received a number of spare parts for a plough, including a wheel and a ploughshare. I was fortunate because my plough was old and almost useless. So the parts helped me a great deal which is why my fields look good this year.

Raising eleven children is no joke. The elder girls are now married. Two of my children did well in their education and are now working and one of my married daughters is helping me a great deal. Although I still have several children who are still going to school, things have eased a bit. My son and daughter are educating the younger ones. I am therefore no longer concerned about finding school fees for the children. My job is now mainly to clothe and provide food for the children. I consider myself very lucky that my daughter who is married is able to look after her own brothers and sisters because it is rare for a married woman to be able to help her own people. I am very thankful to my son-in-law for his good kind heart.

It is very difficult to raise children without a father to help you. I do not feel strong at all. It is a great task to teach a child to do something and become someone in life. You must teach the children to learn to respect you as a parent while at the same time you manage the home and property. I could not move an inch from home in case anything went wrong. Sometimes you feel stranded and run out of ideas and there is no one to help and advise you.

When I married, things were easy because I married a man who already had an established home. Things went very well for me even though I had a child each year. I did not mind because nothing seemed difficult. But, after all the hardship, I sometimes wish I was educated. I think it would make things much easier for me because I could then be employed and I would be able to raise my children in a better way. But, because I am not educated, things are very difficult. I cannot do anything better for myself and my family.

My own parents were very strong. They taught me to work hard before I married and that was a great asset because having married a man who was already married, life was supposed to be tough. But I worked hard and had no regrets at all. It was the influence of my own parents which gave me strength to go through hardships.

I think if the women had not been there the freedom fighters would not have won the war. Women did a great job. Cooking and providing food for the freedom fighters was a way of fighting on its own. Women cooked, and were beaten by soldiers for doing this. Sometimes, while we were busy cooking, the soldiers could come and we had to run away and hide, leaving the pot burning. But now we, the women, the 'povo' as we are called, have been forgotten. The freedom fighters have forgotten us and how much we helped them. The fact is we fought a war. Carrying hot pots of food up the mountains is no joke. I do not think that the men would have managed if the women had not been there to do all this. I think they would have ended up being killed by the freedom fighters after they had refused to cook and carry food for them. The men were around but they only used to tell the women to "Hurry, before the soldiers come and beat you up!"

There is a lot of development in Zimbabwe today because

we are now doing things for ourselves. We even built the school for ourselves. Although the government helped us, this is true development. Now we can say that Zimbabwe is free. Before independence, things were done for us. Today, women can meet, have discussions and do things on our own. For example, with the school, we decided that we would make the bricks and build it and we did just that.

16 Tetty Magugu

Zhombe

WE are only two in my own family, my sister and I. My parents lived in the Zhombe district but I went to school in Bulawayo where my father had worked as a policeman. I was lucky because both my parents were active in politics from the sixties. After I had finished school, I returned to Zhombe and, shortly afterwards, I got married.

For myself, I found out that starting a home was very difficult. I had problems in acquiring almost everything – blankets, plates, all sorts of household items. At my parents' home life had not been so hard, and the contrast made life seem almost unbearable. Once I had visitors, but I did not have enough utensils. I brewed tea for them, but I did not have enough cups and teaspoons. I had to give them tablespoons. After serving them, I went behind my house and cried. I said to myself, "Lord, things were not like this at my parents." It was these circumstances that made me use my hands. There were no other means of changing my life except by me working hard.

Then I started growing vegetables in my garden and I was

159

able to earn a little money to buy myself paraffin, sugar, soap and, if any money remained, I bought a few plates at a time.

Then I remembered that my grandfather had told me that he used to breed chickens for sale. So, I went and asked an old man with experience, how I should begin. He told me that if I could put down some money, he would make a contribution.

He really helped me, because he ordered the chickens. We ordered fifty between us, I kept twenty-five and so did he. We agreed that I would provide the chicken feed since I had the grain. When the chickens were ready for sale, I told my husband that I was going to sell them, and he said, "You cannot sell grandfather's chickens."

My husband did not know that half the chickens belonged to me, he thought that I was keeping them all for the old man. When I told him that half the brood were mine, he was surprised and wondered where I had got the money to buy them. You see, I 'stole' maize from my husband! I took some maize without his permission. You see, in our custom, maize belongs to the man and women have charge of the groundnuts. But I had sold some maize to add to my own savings, to buy chickens.

After the chickens had been sold, I managed to buy blankets, a couple of pots and plates. But I also bought some more chickens and this time I sold eggs. Sometimes I would not take money in payment. I took whatever I most needed in exchange for eggs.

Then came the good news that I was selected to go for training as a women's advisor. While at the training centre we got some money for allowances which I sent to my husband to help both him and the children at home. I started this work in 1971.

My husband and I have seven children. My only son, who went to join the liberation struggle, is my first born: my other children are girls. So when my son left I was very anxious. I could not do anything. He had gone. I worried a great deal but there was nothing to be done.

After he had left, I had difficulties with my neighbours because they suspected that my son had joined the Rhodesian army and they passed on their rumours to the freedom fighters. They, in turn, made enquiries and investigated my family to discover the truth.

I was very fortunate because someone who had just returned from Zambia, confirmed that my son was there, and that was how my family was freed from suspicion. From that time the freedom fighters took us as their parents and looked after us, in the sense that they often came to see how we were and find out if the enemy had been to our home. In this way they offered protection.

This continued for a long time. The freedom fighters felt free to visit my home and, if they needed anything, they did not hesitate to come and ask. They were confident that they could ask us because they now took my home as their own and considered us as their brother's parents.

They asked for different things. Sometimes, for example, they asked me to mend their clothes and sometimes they asked me to prepare food for them, if they knew they were going to a place where they did not expect to get anything to eat. Sometimes I baked them scones and prepared five chickens for them at once. I had a lot of chickens so I did not need to ask for contributions from anyone. I also did a lot of mending for them. Occasionally they asked me to go and buy them clothes, but sometimes I was too busy and couldn't go and I would tell them so.

I was lucky. Things were not very tough for me because I had a savings book. We used those savings until there was nothing left. But sometimes they gave me the money to buy what they wanted. I remember once that they asked me to provide them with tablets. I had a friend who worked at a hospital in Kwekwe who helped me secure them. Then I had to carry them from town to the village. There were often road-blocks where we would be searched and so this was not easy. The way we managed was first to cut a hole in the tube of a scotch cart tyre and then we put the tablets into it. After that, we mended the tube and inflated it again. That was a clever idea.

Generally, whenever I had to go to Kwekwe for medicines, I would go by bus. Sometimes we arranged with others from home to meet us in Kwekwe and they would travel by scotch cart and, on these occasions, we would put the tube in the cart. Otherwise I would carry it back on the bus and pretend that I had taken it to the garage for repair.

The boys travelled in groups. I cannot tell how many groups there were but sometimes they came as often as three times a week. Usually they came during the day or just before dark so that we could identify them. I don't remember a time when they came at night.

This went on for about six years. It was a long period. At cease-fire when the *vakomana* were leaving the area, all the groups came together to show their appreciation and bid me farewell. I was not at home because I had gone to a meeting which had been called to tell parents to encourage the freedom fighters to go into the assembly points.

So, I didn't know anything about the freedom fighters visiting me until I met a woman who told me that I should hurry home because I had visitors. She said, "Hurry all your children are at your house." I replied that I would have to kill a chicken for them, but she said, "One will certainly not be enough . . . you will have to kill an animal!" I was very surprised and wondered how many 'children' could possibly be there if they needed to be fed by an animal and I hurried home.

When I arrived I found that the whole place was full of the *vakomana*, about one hundred of them altogether, but because I was used to them and they were also used to my home, it did not bother me. I killed two goats for them to eat.

The behaviour of these freedom fighters pleased me. When they arrived they were told that I was away. So, they asked my small daughter where I kept my sugar and tea-leaves and whatever else they wanted. She pointed to the things they needed. Then they prepared some food for themselves and after that washed all the dishes. They cleaned my house and even washed my dish towels. I was pleased because these boys felt free to take whatever food they could find and prepare it for themselves. This showed me that they considered themselves as my own children and that they felt at home.

My own son was twenty years old and in form two when he left. His sisters felt lonely and missed him a lot and they wondered where he had gone. I told them that I did not know where he'd gone, but they suspected that since he had left all his clothes behind and not said anything to them, that he had gone to join the freedom fighters.

I think he just envied the fighters and, as he attended many political meetings, he was no doubt influenced into joining the struggle. You see, the freedom fighters were already in this area when he left the country. My husband was very courageous: he just said that my son was becoming a man. He was very calm and did not seem to be very worried, although he actually was.

I was the secretary for the party in our area and I was chosen by the people. My main job was to organize events and to take minutes of all the meetings that we held. A very important thing was to see that the freedom fighters had provisions and plan how to get food for them. The freedom fighters wanted us to look after them. By looking after them, I mean we had to provide for all their needs, and keep the secret. The most important item of all was not to give away any information about them, and treat them as our own children. I mean, we said that we should not see them as a burden. So the party held meetings to discuss how we could feed the comrades, find money, keep the secret and also how we should communicate with each other if the soldiers were around.

We found a way. Sometimes we went to a neighbour and said, "Ah. Hm," which was like a way of greeting. We then said something like this – it's like a proverb, *"Amahlamvu amahlamvu,"* which literally means the green leaves are everywhere, and the person you were speaking to would know that you meant the soldiers were in the area. That person would then tell their neighbours in the same way, until everyone was aware of the situation. The last person to know would take the message to the freedom fighters. Quite often we also used *mujibas.*

My own children were girls and so they did not act as *mujibas*. But whenever the freedom fighters were in the area they did their washing and mended their clothes. They also had to see what they could wash and they often did the cooking.

My husband always helped me by giving me ideas. He advised me on many occasions. He did not seem as worried as I was. He was always very strong and calm, and each time I expressed worry and fear, especially about my son, he always calmed me. His advice and strength was a great help to me.

Sometimes . . . rarely . . . parents would decide to send their children to town because they were afraid for them. But, if that happened in our area, the villagers would contact the child's parents and say, "Who do we have to fight the war if you take your children to town? Who do you expect to remain at home and fight?" Mostly people in our area knew what they wanted and we kept our children with us. We did not experience any problems with our children at all. No children were misused in this area. We also never had any problems with sell-outs here. And there were no deaths caused because we had sold out on one another. We heard about it happening, but it did not happen in this district.

White soldiers visited our area, but they weren't either the ordinary soldiers or the Selous Scouts. Mm! They were those who wore earrings. There was a group that came to our area twice. Those people, those soldiers, they were white soldiers. I do not know what kind of people they were, but what I noticed about them was that they wore earrings. They came right at the peak of the war when it was very hot in our area. Those were very brave soldiers because what we heard was that they did not retreat at all, even if they were in contact with the freedom fighters. We heard that they wanted to catch the freedom fighters – actually catch them alive. In our area they came twice asking questions, how we were living and so on, but they did not harass us. In the second group, they were mixed with black soldiers. I really do not think they were Smith's soldiers at all. I suspect that they came from other countries because of the way they behaved and looked, with their earrings. I think they came from other countries to help Smith's soldiers.

What happened once was that, one day after the freedom fighters had had contact with soldiers somewhere, they came to my home in the evening. One of them had an injured arm. I dressed the arm and gave them food, then they spent the night at my home. Very early the following morning, they went to another village for security reasons.

But the soldiers had also come into our area. The soldiers asked one young boy – a village boy – to show them the home to which the freedom fighters usually went. The boy did not know that the comrades had even been in the village. But since he knew that the freedom fighters always came to my house, he indicated another home. He thought he was protecting both our home and the freedom fighters by misleading the soldiers. But, unfortunately, the direction in which he pointed was the one in which the *vakomana* had gone that morning. The soldiers found the comrades. Four of them were killed. After that the soldiers instructed us to bury the freedom fighters in one grave.

It was very painful. They were so disfigured that we could not even identify them. One had had his head blown off. It was a great pain to the villagers because they respected the freedom fighters and wished to bury them decently, but they could not.

The good thing was that the villagers were not at all harassed by the soldiers, even though the *vakomana* had been killed in a village home. That is my reason for thinking that those soldiers came from other countries: if they had been Smith's soldiers they would surely have tortured and even killed some villagers.

Unfortunately Muzorewa's fighters came here towards the end of the war. Ah! they really tortured us. Someone had told them that we harboured freedom fighters in our home. It is by God's grace that we are still alive, otherwise we would have died. At that time, during the war, no family was allowed to have more than one bucket of mealie-meal, but we had about four buckets at home. We also had bags of sugar which we had hidden under the bed. I can say we had plenty of other provisions which were meant for the freedom fighters that we had kept under our beds.

But the one who had told on us had said that we had shoes for the freedom fighters. And, yes, the shoes were there. But fortunately, when Muzorewa's boys searched my home, they did not find them. Then they said that because they wanted to please those who had told on us, they would beat us. So they made us lie down, both me and my husband, and they beat us on our backs. They took a big stick and beat us: me first, then my husband. After that they locked us in our house and left us. My children were not at home when this happened. That was a good thing because if they had found my children at home, those boys might have done worse things. Yes, we had the shoes in the house but they did not find them. If they had found them, they could have killed us.

Women had a hard time. Mothers were faced with most of the problems because they had to provide food and we had to provide good, body-building foods not just anything because the boys had to have lots of energy to fight. Men were mostly concerned with providing the comrades with soap and clothes – we had to mend them. The freedom fighters were very smart. I feel very proud because those *vakomana* were always smart, they kept themselves neat and presentable.

But we women helped one another. In our meetings, we discussed the way that we had come. It was a long way, but we would say, we are almost home. This encouraged us because, for instance, if we noticed that a woman was getting tired and was not as helpful as she had been in contributing food, we sat down and talked about it. We encouraged her to continue, because we knew she wouldn't expect others to do all the work. We said the *vakomana* were everybody's children.

At cease-fire, we heard that my son had come back into the country and was at Makuti. I could not believe it. I was so happy, it was like a dream. Then he sent a message asking me to bring along my last child, the one I had after he had left, whom he had not seen, so that he could meet him. We did not know where Makuti was but we asked from others. They told us that when we reached Harare we could take a taxi. We thought that Makuti was right in Harare! But we discovered that it was a long way away and that the bus took several hours to get there. So we realized that we could not use a taxi, as it would have cost us a fortune to travel such a long distance.

I thought Makuti was a big place, but it was in the middle of nowhere. As soon as we got to the assembly point we reported our arrival. I still could not believe that I was going to see my son. I sat still, waiting. Some of the *vakomana* came to greet us and then, suddenly, my son was before me. He had never looked so strong and well. I was so excited I did not know what to do. My eyes were full of tears.

I cannot express how I felt on the day that my son returned from the war. When he wrote that he was coming home we organized a big party to welcome him home. We killed an ox for him. All the people around were very co-operative and kind. Many people gave him presents, especially money, to welcome him. He got enough money from people to buy himself a calf. Afterwards he became a soldier and, since then, he has married and has two children.

But, sadly, even after independence, I would honestly say that we had a lot of problems. We suffered so much that people were worried and wondered what they had fought for. Before unity, the situation was very bad. The truth is people were tortured.

I was even put in a cell. They put me in prison for eight

weeks. I left my baby who was eight months old at home while they imprisoned me. We were beaten up because we are ZAPU supporters.

In that way things were difficult. Many homes were burnt down and a lot of people disappeared. This was a blow to us women because we had worked so hard during the war, supporting the freedom fighters and then, after independence, we found we still had hardships. We have several villagers who just disappeared and cannot be traced. Several homes were burnt down including mine: the whole property that we had developed was burnt to ashes. My home was not as it is now.

Yes, it was hard for me. At first, when I was still at home, before they took me to prison, they might come at any time – and it was very often – and beat me. But, after they imprisoned me, they did not beat me but they gave me unbearable food. The most painful thing that happened is that a child in my family was shot by the soldiers. He was a married man with six children, but they shot him in cold blood because they found him at home. They claimed that he was a Zipra and therefore a dissident and shot him. Just like that. He died and left his family with no one to care for them. They shot him before I was imprisoned.

I was put in prison in Kwekwe but I was never charged. Even men had a hard time. My husband was hiding somewhere and was not at home. After he learned that I had been taken to prison, he came and asked the authorities to free me and take him instead. He insisted that I was the one who took care of the children and should therefore be freed. They released me and took my husband.

After that, I told my son, the one who had been a freedom fighter. He came and talked to them, the authorities in Kwekwe. He told them that if it was the case, that they were harassing his parents, then it would be better if he resigned from the army. He said, "What is the point of being a soldier protecting this country, if my own parents are being tortured?" So they released my husband. But if my son had not come to talk to them, he would have surely died.

Some of the women who were imprisoned at the same time as me are still not back. We do not know where they are or what happened to them. The chairwoman of our branch during the liberation war, disappeared after independence. She was taken and has never been seen again. Her home is now falling apart because there is no one there to take care of her property.

People were afraid. They could not approach the authorities. But although they were afraid, somehow they had this hope that things would be all right in the end.

As it is now, we can think and laugh about some things which at the time we could not do. We were always worried, especially during the days when we were being harassed. Sometimes we lost hope. Yes, we could almost lose sight of what we were fighting for when things were very bad. I would say the worst hardship was caused by fear. We were always afraid of the war. Food for the freedom fighters was not our problem at all. Fear was what worried us most. We lived in fear in case the soldiers came and did something to us: taking care of the *vakomana* did not worry us at all.

Today things are promising to be very good. Women are almost the same as men in many things, like doing the same job. Of course, there are husbands who still refuse to allow their wives to work and they still don't want them to go anywhere. But such men are few. Today most husbands let their wives participate in whatever they choose to do. Also I think there is a difference because now women can travel freely.

I think people are stronger because during the war they worked together and women are stronger because of their participation in it. These are some of the things I can see and appreciate now. It is obvious that whenever you see your people free you also feel free. The fact that after unity everyone became free and can move freely is a wonderful thing.

17 Agnes Ziyatsha

Zvishavane

MY MOTHER died when I was a little girl. My little brother, who is now a builder, and I grew up in the care of my father. Life was very difficult and that is why I married at an early age. But my life did not improve at all with marriage. For example, one day after my first child was born, my husband picked up a baby's knitted hat on his way back from church. It was the first hat my baby had ever had because we could not afford anything of our own.

On another occasion he found a baby's dress made of very poor quality cloth. Dresses made of that material were called 'widows' because the fabric was so stiff, that if you put the dress down, it stood up without anything to support it. But still this was the only dress my baby had and she only wore it on special occasions like going to church. There was a famine in the year in which my second child was born. When we bought mealie-meal, I would use the sack to make my child something to wear. They were hard times but I never stopped going to church.

But when my second child was of school-going age, my husband went out to work. After that our lives were not

169

so miserable as he was able to buy soap and clothes for the children. Before then both my husband and I were totally ignorant. We had no plans of improving ourselves. My husband would go out to parties at night and when he returned we used his jacket as a blanket.

He began work by starting a bicycle repair shop, but you know how difficult it is to start a business. Days can sometimes be very sour and he would return home with nothing. But other days were more profitable as people brought their bicycles to him to repair. So we made progress and, when I had my fifth child, we were quite presentable people and our home was a warm place and, by the time I had my seventh child, I was quite a reasonable person and I was ploughing and planting a lot of crops for sale. So, despite our early hardships, I became a mature mother! I was able to look after my children fairly well and I managed to send all my fourteen children to school. It was not so expensive to do so then as it is today, otherwise I would never have managed it. So all my children are educated people.

But, just at the time when my life had improved and I was considered a successful person, the liberation war began. Then my husband was forced to leave his employment and we were not allowed to go and buy mealie-meal in Zvishavane. We were told to prepare it by pounding maize. If ever you were seen going to Zvishavane you could be killed. It was the freedom fighters who stopped my husband from working. They said that everyone should concentrate on fighting the war and that those who worked were only benefitting their employers and not themselves. My husband worked for himself, but he did not say anything because he was not the only one whom they stopped. He was allowed to go and sell firewood in Zvishavane using his donkeys and scotch cart. That is how we managed to get some cash. Otherwise he was at home throughout the war.

The war frightened me. When the freedom fighters first came they used to call us to their base in the mountain. I would wonder why they called us there at night. But later I overcame my fear by telling myself that the freedom fighters were just like my two children who had gone to fight. The comrades were only doing what my children were doing, wherever they were. This thought encouraged me.

When the freedom fighters first arrived in our area, they

called the elders and asked them to stand watch for the enemy. Then we were called to meet them at their mountain base. After that we went to meetings almost every day when they were in the area. When they left we had a rest. We used to sing and dance at the meetings: then the Zanlas would address us and tell us that they did not want sell-outs or witches. They killed such people. It was usually the *mujibas* who caused these deaths and what they claimed was frequently not true. A lot of people were killed because of the lies. The *mujibas* saw what people had in their homes because they collected the food and carried messages for the freedom fighters who never came to our homes. As they went from house to house collecting food, sometimes they demanded something from you which you couldn't give for some reason or another. But they never wanted to listen to what you had to say.

My neighbour, for instance, was killed because she had no milk to give them.

It was not the old people, the villagers, who told on each other but the *mujibas*. They were the ones who sold out on people by telling the comrades stories. They would call people to meetings and even if it was not convenient for you to go, because of sickness, for example, you had to go. This is because we were afraid the *mujibas* would tell the comrades that you had refused to attend and then you could be killed. Even when it was raining we did what the *mujibas* wanted us to do, because we were afraid of them.

They were told by the freedom fighters that they could beat anyone who did not want to co-operate. But instead of treating each case on its merits the *mujibas* were worse than the freedom fighters. They were very cruel; they beat to kill. The *mujibas* were big boys. Some of them were old enough to have families, although in our area none of them was married as they sometimes were in other areas.

We worked with them because we were afraid of being beaten. If the *mujibas* came to take my daughter to be a *chimbwido* I could not refuse to let her go. Otherwise the *mujibas* would tell the freedom fighters and they would tell them to beat us, and as I said before, they beat to kill. But the truth is that the *mujibas* did not always obey the freedom fighters. For instance, sometimes the *mujibas* were given money by the comrades to buy beer. Instead of doing this, the *mujibas* went to a home and took the beer with force, and then used the money as they pleased.

Neither of my two sons told me that they were going to join the struggle.

The elder boy was working in Bulawayo and I simply heard that he had gone. The other boy was with me here and one day we went together to Zvishavane to do our Christmas shopping. He asked me to buy him two records which he said he wanted to play at Christmas and I bought them for him. He then told me to go home and said he would follow the next day. Instead of returning home he went to Masvingo, where he met others and they went to South Africa with the people who work on the mines. From South Africa he went to join the freedom fighters.

Both the Zanlas and the soldiers came to this area. The soldiers came into our homes and asked where the guerillas were but the comrades sent *mujibas*. The soldiers said that we harboured guerillas, kept them in our homes and gave them food. We always denied that we had seen the freedom fighters, even if we had just come from their base. We said we had heard of, but not seen them. We were afraid because if you admitted that you had seen the comrades, the soldiers would ask you to show them where they were. They would send you in front so that if there was a contact, you would be the first one killed. It was much safer to deny having seen them.

Whenever the comrades were in our area we had to provide food. We donated goats and chickens and we all contributed mealie-meal. We cooked at one place, usually at those homes nearest the mountain – and then carried the food to their base. We carried our pots to the cooking place and would leave them there whilst the guerillas were in the area. If you donated a goat you would take the head of your goat home. At first the freedom fighters did not eat the inner parts of an animal: they only ate the meat but later they ate the offal.

The *chimbwidos* carried the food to the comrades. Two of my daughters were *chimbwidos* and sometimes they stayed away for days and we didn't know where they were. If the soldiers came, they ran away and hid in a safe place. But sometimes the soldiers shot their long-distance guns and it was still very dangerous.

Those girls had great problems. A lot of them have children by the comrades. Some girls agreed to sleep with them but some refused. I was fortunate that my girls did not have children by the comrades. Nonetheless, it was very distressing: we parents provided blankets for the boys and then they slept with our children in our blankets while we spent the whole night singing. But some girls in our area have now married the comrades who fathered their children and occasionally others have helped the girl to maintain the child although many have had to manage alone.

I was treasurer to the party. We each contributed twenty-five cents a month and that was kept until the freedom fighters wanted to buy something – cigarettes, shoes, trousers and so on. The boys lived almost like animals in the forests. When it was very cold they sometimes had to put on three pairs of trousers at once. Often they had to spend many days without washing their clothes or bathing. Sometimes they even got lice. Those who were smart asked the *chimbwidos* to wash for them.

Once the soldiers came to our school. The comrades saw the soldiers and they went towards the school from the opposite direction. There was a fierce contact, a great war, even today some of the school walls have bullet holes in them. That was towards cease-fire when lots of people were taken by the soldiers for questioning. After such a contact the comrades wanted to walk with *mujibas* in the front line so that, in case of renewed firing, the *mujibas* would be killed first. This was very painful for parents. Sometimes we felt that it would be better if the whole world came to an end because our lives were meaningless.

The women were very courageous because we did not run away from our homes. We stayed and worked hard to help the freedom fighters. It was difficult, as from day to day, we did not know whether we would live or die. We just lived for each day as it came. I think we did a great job. We fought hard. Even old women like me who had difficulty in walking, went to those night-time meetings. Sometimes we finished very late and the sun would be up before I arrived home. Then the trick was to look for firewood, so that if I met the soldiers I told them that I was collecting wood for my fire. I was fortunate because my children returned from the war. I had not heard anything from them since they left. After the cease-fire they met in Bulawayo and came home together. When I saw them, I was so shocked that I fell down. I cried so much, that I felt I was going mad. They both came home on the same day, just like that. A few days later, I killed an ox to celebrate their return. I was very thankful that God had protected them. I felt I was fortunate because a lot of people who loved their children just as much as I did, never saw them again. They never came back. I was indeed lucky.

But things have not gone the way we expected them to: our children, even those who fought, have nothing to do. My son has married and he has nothing to do to help look after his family. These ex-combatants have families to look after, but the government has forgotten them. I think they should have taken all those children who fought the liberation struggle and given them jobs, because they fought for the country and its independence.

Yet some of my other children are teachers; one is a church minister and one is doing a course as an agricultural extension worker. That is why I say that generally, apart from the problem that I have mentioned, my life is now good. The government that we have now is much better than Smith's government.

18 Ida Mtongana

Silobela

I WAS BORN in 1935 in the Mbembesi district. My grand-mother, my father's mother, and my mother were strong church women, my father was a preacher. I was twenty years old when I married and I moved with my husband to Silobela. I had seven children between 1955 and 1970.

As soon as I got married I was told that I should join a women's church group which met twice a week, and after a while, I became first the secretary and then the chairperson.

Then in 1960 I joined the Federation of African Women's Clubs: it is an organization which tries to help women. At that time we discussed development, ways of improving our homes, women's responsibilities as wives and mothers, and so on. We were not allowed to discuss politics. We also taught one another sewing, cooking, knitting – all the things that have to do with a woman's life at home. As an incentive to improving our lives, we held competitions and the best-kept homes won prizes.

We wanted to be knowledgeable so that were we to attain our independence, we would know how to run our homes and our country. We had heard rumours of the liberation war and we told one another that we must be strong and learn as much as we could. Even though politics were not discussed directly, we could talk about the future, our future.

We used to hear a lot about the liberation struggle and there were rumours that the freedom fighters had entered the country. In the 1960s we started being organized into ZAPU party groups. Some of us did not really understand what it was all for, but after talking and discussing the meaning of liberation, we all knew what was happening.

But I can say that it was only in 1975 that the organization grew really strong. The freedom fighters had not come to our area at that time. We, the villagers, organized ourselves on our own. But sometimes the leaders went to Harare for a congress and sometimes we went to provincial meetings in Gweru. The meetings were always held secretly because they were not allowed by the government at that time.

We heard that the freedom fighters were in other areas of the country and that, when they came into a district, they taught people about the struggle. We also heard that they killed sell-outs.

We could not do anything, but we did not like what we heard. We blamed people who did not understand that we needed to be free, as it was those people who sold out on the freedom fighters. We did not understand the sell-outs, when everybody needed to be free.

Zipra came into our area in May 1978 when we were harvesting our fields. Then the organizers came and told us that the freedom fighters had arrived and that everyone was required to attend a meeting which they would address. They told us that they did not want sell-outs. They said that we were fighting a war and that sell-outs would be killed because there was no such thing as a prison where such individuals could be punished. That was the main thrust of the meeting.

Then, later that year, two of my children went to join the struggle. My daughter was twenty years old when she left and the boy was eighteen.

I felt that, if they had thought about it and wanted to go, well and good. We knew that we could not achieve our freedom without bloodshed. There was no other way except through the sacrifice of our children. It was very painful, but there were no alternatives. I cannot say where I got my courage from: the war was with us and there was no going back. We wanted to be free, so we simply had to press on.

Parents everywhere were very distressed but sometimes we got so engrossed in the war that from time to time we would forget about our children. On occasions the war was so intense that all we could do was concentrate on what was happening to us. Many things happened. We had to be constantly alert and we were always running away from the enemy. I did not encounter any great misfortune in my family, but I heard what happened to others. Some people were taken by soldiers and heavily beaten and questioned about where the guerillas were. We were very much afraid and, whenever I thought about my children, I just shrugged and said whatever happens will happen.

The soldiers were in our area before the Zipras arrived but we were not affected by them until afterwards. Then it happened that sometimes the soldiers came into contact with the Zipras and, whenever we heard shootings, we all ran away. People just ran in different directions. Sometimes children went in one direction and parents in another, and then we always worried about our children.

The Zipras were really living with us and each group would take turns to stay in the area. They always told us to be courageous and reliable. They did not bother us: all they wanted was food and water for bathing and washing their clothes. You see, in our area, we had already organized ourselves before the comrades came and so we knew that the boys would need our assistance. So we were not bothered by them because we knew that they stayed in the bush and we were the only people who could feed and help them and we were determined to help in any way that we could.

My husband was the branch chairman of the party in the district and he was responsible for buying food and clothes for the freedom fighters. It was difficult because there were not many things in the rural shops, so he had to go to town. Sometimes shop-owners in our area were kind and would give him a lift because there were no buses. He bought many clothes at once although this was dangerous; but fortunately he was never discovered by the soldiers.

The most influential person in the district was the district chairman. He really tried hard to control people so that there wouldn't be any sell-outs. He often called meetings and reminded people that they should not sell out on one another or on the freedom fighters. He would stress that he did not wish to see bloodshed in his district and he would urge people to behave well.

Occasionally, of course, someone was branded a sell-out if he or she was seen with soldiers. It might have been a person taken in for questioning but others would think that they were being friendly with the soldiers and report them. But, although this did happen in our area, there were no lives lost, even when people were very suspicious if they saw you with the soldiers.

I think it was because we had such a good chairman and we were well-disciplined and politicized.

We were never afraid of the freedom fighters. We were just determined to do whatever we could. Even when we saw them for the first time we were not at all afraid. The only thing that frightened us was that we knew they could kill people, but generally it was because they were not co-operative. In our area the youth were organized and they would inform the freedom fighters if soldiers were in the area. They also attended youth meetings where they were politicized and taught how to behave with regard to the war. Sometimes the meetings were during the day but at other times they were held at sunset. Sometimes the children came back home but sometimes they spent the night with the comrades and returned home in the morning.

As parents we were, of course, very worried when the children, especially the girls, did not come home. It is not our custom for girls to spend nights away from home or even to return home late, so we were always very worried in these circumstances. But, because we were fighting a war, there were no remedies, nothing we could say or do, even when the girls became pregnant.

It was a difficult time. When the Zipras first came into our area the shops had not closed down. So we managed to sell our crops that year. Then we started selling our chickens. We had to find money somehow, so we sold whatever we could. Most of us ended up without a chicken to our names. It was very difficult and quite a performance even to find a piece of soap. I do not know how we managed. Maybe what lessened the burden was that there were no schools and so we did not have to find school fees and many children had left so families were smaller. You see, the freedom fighters had closed down dip-tanks, schools and clinics. They said that, as we were fighting a war, there was no time for some to go to school while others were fighting. They said everyone had to put their effort into the war and that is why they closed the schools.

We accepted it because sometimes the soldiers went to the schools and asked the children where the freedom fighters were. Sometimes the children were frightened and told the soldiers things that they were not supposed to, which would then mean they were sell-outs. Also, the children sometimes met the soldiers on their way to school and they were very frightened of them. So we thought it better if the schools were closed.

Dip-tanks were also closed down. Sometimes they were destroyed. The villagers were instructed to destroy them. This was because people paid taxes and paid to dip their animals: the money went to the government against which the freedom fighters were fighting. Clinic fees likewise were paid to the Smith government and that is why they were closed down by the freedom fighters. They said that, after the war, they would be re-opened. In our area, after the dip-tanks had been closed, the cattle died of anthrax. People knew it was because they were not dipping their cattle but what could they do? There was no answer to the problem.

One day, towards cease-fire, a number of black soldiers went on a search from home to home and they shot whoever they found. We ran from our homes and hid in villages which were very far away. Of course this had happened many times before.

You see, the soldiers would sometimes go from home to home questioning and harassing people. When we heard that they were coming, we were afraid. Then, together with our children, we would leave our homes and spend the night with people in other villages. Sometimes, when the soldiers arrived and found our homes empty, they prepared food for themselves in our kitchens. They would stay the night, hoping that we might come back. But people were clever. They would watch for the soldiers to leave from a distance, and they would not return to their homes, until they knew the soldiers had left.

During the war all the women's clubs stopped operating because it would have been dangerous to be found at a gathering with others. Even women meeting about home affairs would be seen as a political meeting in disguise. We only began the clubs again after the war.

During the war, when there was a misunderstanding between husband and wife, the freedom fighters would usually hear about it because they got to hear many things. Sometimes they tried to talk to the couple and would explain that they should respect each other. That was all they did, talk and try to teach them to live peacefully in their homes. They never stood between them because generally the misunderstandings would occur when the freedom fighters were not there.

Some women appreciated their intervention, but some did not. They thought that the comrades should not interfere in their personal lives. They did not see it as being helpful. After my two children had left for the struggle in 1978 I heard nothing from them until after the cease-fire when they came home. I had trusted that God and my ancestral spirits would take care of them. They were strong and happy when they returned. They knew that they had brought the country with them and that we would all live in peace and progress and develop ourselves in the way in which we want. My children had grown in their knowledge and their under-standing. They would say, "We are all Zimbabweans" and they would try to explain what development really means to anyone who did not understand.

I was very lucky that my children returned home. My sister-in-law's son never returned and she is still grieving. To make matters worse he was not killed in the war. What happened was that at cease-fire her son sent his father some money and told him that he was back and in a camp in Harare.

They daily expected to see him but he never came home. Then they received a letter from their son's commander asking why he was still at home and had not returned to base. They did everything they could to try to find him, checking the prisons and so on. They even went to the Zipra office where they were told by a young man that their son had probably been killed and said, "I'm sorry, mama, but you had better go and mourn your son." He told them that many people had disappeared and had been killed secretly. After they heard this they gave up hope and stopped looking for their son.

But the war would not have been won without the participation of the women. They worked very hard during the liberation struggle. They cooked and they washed and mended clothes for the freedom fighters. If the women had not participated I do not think the freedom fighters would have succeeded.

I am pleased that we now have our independence. I have a job with the Association of African Women's Clubs. I travel all over the country doing demonstrations and teaching homecrafts to women. I am also very pleased that we now have unity as in 1985 we had a bad time after one of the ZANU leaders was killed in our area. ZANU supporters then burnt down more than twenty homes in our district and many people were very severely beaten, some died. It was their way of retaliation, but they did not stop to ask questions, or to find out what people thought first. They just picked on those homes where they knew people had been ZAPU supporters. My home was burnt down. That is why I say I am pleased that there is unity because during the struggle we helped both Zanla and Zipra and there was no trouble between us.

19 Elizabeth Ndebele

Silobela

I MARRIED at eighteen. At that time I was considered to be
too young for marriage but now I would be considered
grown up enough. I had a child before I married my husband
and that is why I married at an early age, even before my
elder sister had done so.

My husband was the head-teacher at our local Roman
Catholic school, St Joseph's. The minister at that school
would not allow us to live together unless we had a church
wedding and that is why we married, although our baby
was not very well. In those days the custom was that people
could not live as husband and wife, even if you had had
a child together, unless you were married. So I had to abide
by the rules.

People were surprised on my wedding day because I did
not sit quietly for long periods as a bride should do. I went
out every now and then into the yard where my mother-
in-law was sitting with my sick child. She had taken her
there because it was our custom that a young person was
not allowed to enter into a house where there was someone

who was very sick, as it was said to bring bad luck. But I felt it was better to be with my child than to pretend to be a satisfied bride. Of course, it was pleasing to be admired, but one can be admired until one dies. Had my child died, I would have lost her for ever.

I had my first born, Christine, in January 1958. She was sick for the whole of the following year and would not feed from my breast. So my mother-in-law took my child away to nurse her and that is why I had another baby, Connie, so soon afterwards.

I had a very difficult time looking after my children. My mother-in-law died soon after the birth of my first two girls, when I was expecting my third child. My father-in-law would not allow his grandchildren to visit my parents. So it was difficult because several of my children were born one after the other and, as with my first two, were almost like twins. Moreover, when Christine returned home, she missed her grandmother very much and this was hard. I had no one to help me because we could not even look for a girl, as it was not appropriate to do so in those days. My mother-in-law had two daughters, but one had already married and the other was still at school. So there was no one to help me with my children.

Clothing the children was not my problem because things were then fairly cheap. But tilling the fields was very important. In order for a woman to be called a proper good woman, she had to be strong at the plough. We also kept cows and they had to be milked. My problem was how to carry my children when I went to the fields, especially if I was pregnant. Most times I carried one on my back, one on my shoulders and then with my one free hand I carried a tin of food.

I also helped my husband by selling clothes and jerseys that I made by hand. Teachers' salaries were very low and, as the children grew older, we used the money I made to pay our children's school fees.

In all, I had nine children because our church, the Roman Catholic church, did not allow people to practise family planning. But later, before my last two children were born, I took family planning tablets as it seems the whole world is now for family planning.

Four of my children went to join the struggle: Christine, the eldest was twenty, Connie was eighteen, the third sixteen and the fourth twelve. He was still very small and I was very worried when he went. Indeed, when I went to tell my father-in-law about my children, he was very worried and said, "Oh, Alois is going to be food for lions as he cannot survive the situation at his age."

I was also very anxious about my first born because she was sick. I had visited many doctors and even went to consult herbalists but nothing cured her. Finally Christine managed to get to Botswana. They say she had problems on the way but her friends did not leave her behind, because Connie was with her. My third child, a boy, followed on afterwards with other boys.

In Zambia, by chance, the children met my cousin who was a healer. After some discussion they discovered that they were related. My cousin, the healer, said that she had dreamt that her grandfather had instructed her to heal my daughter. She did not know the healing herb required, but she knew she would find it, since in her dream she had been shown where it was. So she went and looked for the herb and treated my daughter. Christine was healed and has never again had the problems that she had before.

My children did not once reveal that they wanted to go and join the struggle. What happened was that when the guerillas came they took the children and gave them lessons at their bases. I do not know whether they also received lessons about how to cross the border or about anything else because the freedom fighters had separate meetings – some with adults, some with children. So I do not know exactly what the children were taught. They could not tell us that they wanted to go, because we brought our children up in a Christian environment which had nothing to do with politics and so they must have known that we would not let them go.

I was very worried when I found the letter they left me on my sewing machine. The first thing I asked myself was whether I had given them enough love and whether I had looked after them properly. But when I had read their letter, I felt better because I knew my children were truthful and they would have told me if there had been something else that they wanted from me. Had they disappeared because they did not like the way I was raising them, they would not have told me where they had gone. And they did. They said that they had gone to join the struggle.

My husband was also very concerned, but he and I are different. He is the sort of person who does not show his worries on the outside, but I could see that he was also anxious. He tried to comfort me in many different ways, although there was nothing he could do about our children. Sometimes he would ask me to get into the car and then we would go visiting; and sometimes he even took me to the fields in the car – such a thing was unheard of – but I think it was his way of trying to comfort me.

The younger children sometimes listened to the radio and thought of their sisters and brothers. I tried to reassure them, saying that if Christine had not made it, we would have heard. But these were merely words of comfort because I did not know what had happened to her nor did I know where my children were. I just hoped that one day, after the war, they would come back.

In fact, Christina later met Alois in Botswana and was very concerned as conditions there were so tough. Often they only had beans to eat and they had to go without water, as water is a big problem in Botswana.

I was a hard-working farmer in our district. Even after the children had gone I still managed to grow and harvest a lot. I remember that once I had to hire two lorries to carry my grain from the fields. This was the best harvest I had ever had: it was so large that even my father-in-law sympathized with me for having harvested so much grain after the departure of my children. He wondered what I was going to do with all the food because, in our custom, it was said that plenty of food in a year is an omen of bad luck. So, as far as my father-in-law was concerned, he thought it meant that he would never see his grandchildren again.

I used to attend clubs in our area. Ladies from these clubs helped me during the year when I harvested plenty of sunflowers and sorghum. Some women came from as far as Magwabi to help me harvest my crops. They sang and danced as they were trying to cheer me up so that I could forget my problems. I took my crops to the clubs so they could be transported to the Grain Marketing Board.

I noticed that in my family the children's favourite person was my brother-in-law, James. Whenever they wanted something from us, they would send him to ask us on their behalf. So, when they left the country, they wrote to James and they knew he would give us news of them. My elder daughter had grown up with his family when he was teaching at Regina Mundi. Many people thought that she was his daughter as she never called him 'uncle' but always called him 'father'.

Once James was really troubled by the police after he'd received a letter from them. What happened was that he had talked about it in the presence of some sell-out, who then reported him to the police. They even went so far as to take his daughter, Sithabile, and put her in prison for a night. There she was questioned ceaselessly about her sisters and cousins. The police wanted to know whether she knew where they were and what they had told her. She said she did not know anything.

The following day she was released but she did not have the money for a bus fare home, so she went to see her uncle. He gave her a dollar for a soft drink and she used the money for the bus. She did not tell him what had happened to her because she did not know about the people who worked with him: some of them might have been CIDs*.

We then received word that James wanted to see us. As the security situation made it more difficult for men to travel, I went to Bulawayo to find out what was wanted. I really did appreciate the support that James and his family gave us, because they never showed anger despite what my children had dragged them into. They told me, with great good humour, how the police had taken their daughter and how they had quickly hidden everything they possessed that had to do with the party.

What worried them was that they had heard that the boys who had left in the second group had been killed. We thought that this included Alexander, the third in my family to leave. But James then went to check for himself, as people were allowed to go and see those who had been killed. But he did not find my son amongst the dead and so we assumed that he had managed to leave the country. There were a lot of rumours and untruths among people in those days.

There were many groups in our area. First, Smith's soldiers – some black, some white. Then the *madzakutsaku*; and then Zipra and Zanla. We only provided food for them.

I will never forget the day when the Zipras first came into

* Members of the Criminal Investigation Department of the police.

our area. They gathered us together at someone's home where there was a big ditch which had grown into a pool full of water. They forced everyone of us to get into the pool. I felt especially awful because I hadn't been in deep water since I was a child. But I had to get into the pool because I was afraid of the *vakomana*. They seemed frightening. They had killed and we thought they had magic powers which could tell what a person thought. Actually, the reason they forced us into the water was that they wanted us to get used to it, so that if ever we met soldiers near a river, we would cross the river without hesitation.

However, when the Zanlas came into our area, they only wanted to eat sadza with chicken. So we had to look for chickens. If you did not have one, you had to negotiate with a neighbour so that she cooked chicken and you cooked sadza. Then we carried the food to the Zanlas in the forest. They ate and went away. The Zipras did not mind what kind of food you gave them: they ate whatever relish there was.

Both fighting groups, the Zanlas and the Zipras also needed clothes and cigarettes. If you did not have such things, you had to go and find them from someone else in order be able to give them to the fighters.

We never cooked for Smith's soldiers. All they did was come and ask where the 'terrorists' were and we would indicate the wrong direction. If they insisted on us telling them where they were, we simply told them that they had just passed by, so that they would stop troubling us. We were afraid that if we indicated the right direction they would follow the freedom fighters and kill them while they were still eating.

If the freedom fighters were found by the soldiers while they were still in our homes, then they returned fire but they were careful not to shoot at civilians and they also made sure they had good cover. But Smith's soldiers would shoot into our homes. They did not care if they caught fire and people died inside them.

We all felt it was necessary for us to help these young men. We knew that they had come from different places and they had left their homes and their parents in order to fight for our country which did not belong to any particular family. We knew they were fighting to liberate the whole of Zimbabwe as both old and young needed independence.

Then there was a long period when our cattle kept dying

– we lost thirteen – and we did not know why. At that time, my husband and I had moved from the family farm and built our own home. We were worried and thought we might end up with nothing if all our cattle died. Then a child also died and the guerillas called a n'anga to find out the cause of the death. This too frightened us very much because we did not understand why a n'anga should have been called to ascertain what or who had killed the child. There was a danger that any one of us might be suspected.

So, after the saga of the child's death, my husband and I went to consult this n'anga, as he was already in our area, about why our cattle were dying. He told us that my husband's dead grandmother required her name to be recognized. At first we took his words lightly as we had never consulted a n'anga before and we did not believe in such things. Nonetheless we told my father-in-law what the n'anga had said and how he had advised us to brew beer to appease our dead grandmother's spirits.

My father-in-law was a Christian and a preacher and he did not like us to brew beer in our home but, in this case, he agreed to it. We brewed beer and my father-in-law came. From that time our cattle did not die except, of course, when there was an epidemic and all the cattle died of some disease.

The day after the beer ceremony, my husband went to Kwekwe where he was teaching. My father-in-law wanted to go with him but people told him not to go, as there were so many guests still gathered at my home. But he insisted and he was given a lift by my husband who dropped him at his farm.

That was the last time we saw him alive. At sunset Zanlas in their dozens came looking for my father-in-law. They gathered people at Thabete's farm and killed him there. They said he was a sell-out because they had heard that a car, belonging to one of Smith's soldiers, had been seen at his home. They said he had been given a radio with which to report to the soldiers. After beating him thoroughly, the Zanlas said he should stand up and go. But he could not stand up and he told them that they should finish him off. Everyone from the surrounding farms in his district was there, but no one could do anything about it. They killed him at Thabethe. It was all a lie. They did not even find a radio with which he could talk to the soldiers. The Zanlas had been given this information by people who hated my father-in-law because they said his children supported ZAPU.

After he had been killed we gathered up his remains, bundled them into a blanket and buried him. It was a very painful experience. The old man had educated his children and his grandchildren but he was buried like a dog. If he had died a natural death he would have received a good honourable burial. We did bury him in a box later on because we wanted him to rest in peace.

Our Christian belief helped us a lot in the period following his death. As a family we decided not to take revenge on those who had sold out on him because he would not return, even had we done so. We knew it was a woman, one who lived nearby, who had called the fighters to kill my father-in-law. But we did nothing, for the Bible says you should not return bad with the bad. Had we done so, it would have meant that we too would have killed. We left it to the Lord to make a judgement.

If people do not believe in God they go to n'angas to seek solutions to their problems and to ask why such and such has happened. People then use herbs and magic to retaliate if they do not believe in God. Often herbs are put on the graves of their loved ones, as it is believed that this will punish the person who killed a relative. But in my family we did not believe in such things. We knew if we were to consult a n'anga we would spend all our money for nothing. My father-in-law would never return. If the person who caused his death was guilty, it was between her and her God. It was not our wish to punish her.

I know that our belief helped us because the whole family would have been disturbed and our conscience would have troubled us had we taken revenge.

There were so many lies told during the war – so many that it was as if lies had feet and could run, or wings and could fly. For example, once my husband was arrested during the war and people said all sort of things. Some said they had heard that he had been beaten up by the police and had told them to go to my home so that I could give them three guns, hidden under the mattress. This was another reason why we could not really rely on the word that my father-in-law had been sold out. One could never be sure that what one heard was true.

I was a hero, because even after my father-in-law was killed, I still continued to cook and provide cigarettes for the freedom fighters. I remember one day when Smith's soldiers were tracking Zanlas, Zipras were coming from the opposite direction. They unexpectedly met. Smith's soldiers thought that they had caught up with the Zanlas. There were five Zipras and many soldiers. They started to shoot at each other. There was a terrible gun battle: everyone, people and animals, ran away and hid themselves.

I had just come back from giving the Zanlas food. It was about nine o'clock in the morning. There was silence at my own home. You could not even see a dog. My young children were there alone. I was frightened. I did not know what had happened. But I decided that I should continue with my work and go and fetch the water we needed from the borehole. So I fetched my donkeys and scotch cart and, taking my children with me, set off. As we went down the road, I saw footprints which I recognized as those of the soldiers, but I continued. What else could I do? Then we heard shooting.

The donkeys, hearing the guns, ran away as fast as they could. Not a person tried to stop them. They only drew up at Ndlovu's gate which was closed. Then, before we knew it, bullets were flying everywhere. There was no one to be seen. Smith's soldiers were hiding in our granaries.

I left the donkeys and we ran away to Matshaka's home but still the bullets reached us. If we wanted to move we had to crawl. We stayed put and just hoped for the best. The shooting went on and on until a plane came and circled around three times. Then the shooting stopped. There was silence.

By that time, one Zipra freedom fighter had been killed and I do not know how many of Smith's soldiers. All we saw was a lorry coming to carry the bodies away but we didn't count how many of them there were because we were afraid. We were afraid that if we went anywhere near them they would pick us all up and take us with them. When we returned home we found no one.

The following morning the Zipras who had been fighting against Smith's soldiers came to ask the people to help them bury their friend. He was buried in that homestead. It was very painful because this boy was the first of the freedom fighters to be killed in our area. Although they had fought before, the freedom fighters had always killed Smith's soldiers and no one on their side had been killed.

Sometimes Smith's soldiers would return after a contact and beat the villagers. However, the surprising thing was that at night we would be gathered together and taught how to defend ourselves in case of a contact. We were always very frightened but the fighters would confidently say that soldiers would not return the night after a contact. Zipra and Zanla were really champions.

There were both white and black soldiers in our area. One day we saw soldiers on horse-back. They were wearing earrings but we never saw them again, although we thought the earrings might have been some kind of disguise.

The soldiers were very ruthless, especially if they found guerillas in a village or home. They never warned civilians that they were going to attack so that they could at least run away or try to take cover. I suppose this was because they knew the guerillas would also take the chance to run away and hide. Once the soldiers came to a home which was in the next village and found guerillas there. They just opened fire and a lot of innocent people died because all the people gathered there had no choice. They had to attend meetings called by the guerillas and anyone without a gun during that time was at the mercy of those with guns. People had to do whatever each group demanded of them. Whatever the soldiers told people to do they did, and whatever the Zanlas or the Zipras told people to do, they did. The ordinary person had no say at all, and that is why people suffered a lot.

But as time elapses, the mind accepts some terrible things and forgets others. Now we can talk and, sometimes, cry over what we went through as 'just one of those things'. But then we could hardly, if ever, talk about such things. It was not safe to talk to anyone about what was happening at that time.

During the war we were forced to go and destroy schools. As a committee member of the school board, I discussed the importance of schools with the leader of the freedom fighters. I said that schools were our children's inheritance and it pained us to destroy them. It was like fighting with walls. I told him that we should use our energy to fight the enemy instead.

During and before the war there was a lot of discrimination.

I noticed that the boers hated us. They took the good land and fenced it for themselves, so even their cattle were healthy and strong. Our cattle, by comparison, were only skeletons with big horns. We could easily tell ours from theirs simply by their looks.

Black people at that time were always looked down upon, whether they had money or not. Black children could not go to a school of their choice: they were restricted to a certain type of education. The system was that white children went to their own schools and black children went to theirs – and black children were often not allowed to go beyond a certain standard. We thought that perhaps even our children's exam papers were graded unfairly. Black children always seemed to fail, even when we knew the child was a good student.

I was pained by this discrimination. I had two girls and the younger one was brighter. Even her grandfather used to say she could be an air stewardess but it could not happen because of discrimination. She finished her 'O' levels and then worked as a temporary teacher. We were not very happy about this because we wanted her grandfather's wish to be fulfilled and that she should work with an airline. But now the job she has enables her to travel a lot. So, perhaps the old man's wishes have been fulfilled although she does not work for an airline. If her grandfather had been alive perhaps she would have made a journey with him – but it is useless crying over spilt milk.

When my young son returned after the war, he went back to school. Now he is a policeman. I do not know his rank but I often see his colleagues saluting him. We thought he would be a teacher but these days children make their own choice of employment.

When we attained independence there was great happiness and there were celebrations everywhere. We thought all was well. Everyone was happy and all our children had come back from war and we had met many of them in their family homes, even those who had joined the army. But, suddenly, without knowing it, came the terrible time of dissidents. It was a really difficult time for me. As you know, a person cannot be appreciated by everyone. There are always those who look at you in envy, and others who watch you as if they are watching a rabbit to catch for meat, and then there are also those who see you as a challenge to their lives, those who seem uncomfortable because of your success. At the time I felt betrayed. Although I had four children who had gone to fight for the country and I had participated so much during the war, I felt it had all been in vain. My home was burnt down after independence.

Strictly speaking, it was just due to jealousy and hatred. Rumour had it that my husband had carried dissidents in his car. This was not true, but was why our home was burnt down. We never saw one dissident in my home. People just created the stories out of jealousy, that is all. I had heard of the dissidents, but the truth is I never saw one, not one, that is until a little while ago, when I saw them on TV*, working on their projects.

But because my home was burnt down, I moved to Bulawayo and life is better here. I am enjoying myself very much, just as I did in the early days of my marriage. I enjoy working with women and using my hands to make things. I enjoy working with others and I meet with different groups such as the YWCA, the AWCA and ORAP† two or three times a week to discuss development projects and so on. We go out into the districts and now I have been to most districts in Zimbabwe on development projects.

After independence we noticed that people had many wishes and aspirations. Some have failed to have these fulfilled but others have achieved them as, for example, those blacks who now run their own hotels. Before independence hotels were only run by whites. Even if a black person had a thought or wish to have a hotel, one would never have tried to do so because it was useless. Now people are progressing a lot. They get donations from outside the country and then do something to help themselves in their districts.

Today grinding mills have been built near people's homes so that they do not have to travel long distances. At schools there are engines to pump water so that the children can grow vegetables and sell them to help themselves. By raising money in this way they can, for instance, buy their own diesel so that they can travel to other school competitions. They don't have to ask for money from their parents.

---

* An amnesty for 'dissidents' was declared on 19 April 1988 following the unity agreement between ZANU and ZAPU.
† YWCA – Young Women's Christian Association.
   AWC – Association of Women's Clubs.
   ORAP – Organization of Rural Associations for Progress.

It is very pleasing because, long back, only the whites used to have nice and prosperous things. We used to think that only the white man could have water in his house or in the yard and yet today things are different. We are ruling. The boers have even to ask us for lifts because many of us now have cars. We even have to queue in the same line for a doctor's appointment and have the same treatment. It never used to be this way. We were as good as dead and, as a result, our minds were not as open as they are now. I feared the war because it took away my father-in-law and many other people who had committed no crime. But after the war I was very pleased when my children returned home alive. They understood more about freedom and they have been helping to teach those of us that remained more about what we were fighting for.

Everything that happened has helped to transform the lives of people for the better. It was only after the war that people began to understand that they had rights and how to do constructive jobs to raise the standard of their lives. People in Zimbabwe are now free and, since unity, everyone is enjoying the peace and freedom without fear.

20 **Daisy Thabedhe**

Chipinge

I WAS BORN at Mount Selinda in the Chipinge district. Our home was near Emerald school. My father, Mutarisi Duna, was trained as a carpenter and he worked for a little while as a teacher. But by the time I was born, my father was already a businessman. He owned buses, stores and a filling station.

I am the second born in our family and I have five sisters and a brother. My father was from Rusike in the Chipinge area but my mother came from Mozambique. She had come to study at Mount Selinda Mission because there were no schools in Mozambique. She stayed on after her schooling and worked at the mission hospital.

Before I went to school my life was not too bad. We grew up happy: there was nothing to hinder us from happiness. Life was not too difficult. We could get food easily. I helped my parents to plough and fetch water. We had to fetch our water from a long way away. It was not an easy task, fetching water. We also collected firewood because there were no stoves. There were no grinding mills so we stamped the maize ourselves, not because we enjoyed doing so, but we

197

had no choice. That was the way life was then. Now, when we look back, we think that life was hard and difficult then, but when we were in that situation, we did not mind at all. I enjoyed my schooling and I did well. We were fortunate to go to school. There were very few schools in the country then and only the children who did very well had any education. Very few people received higher education. That is why so many people went to work after they had finished standard six.

After I had finished school, when I was about nineteen or twenty years old, I went to teach at Zamuchiya school. I liked teaching little ones, although it is not easy to teach a person how to read and write from nothing.

I taught for about two years and then I married the Reverend Lincoln Thabedhe in 1952. We come from the same area. At the time my husband was a trained carpenter. He trained at Mount Selinda Mission which provided courses in carpentry, building and teacher training. He worked as a carpenter in Highfields in Harare. That is where our seven children were born. Then in 1967 he joined the church and went to Bible school.

He was trained for three years and then we went back to work in Chipinge in the Rimbi Chibuwe area for five years and then we were transferred to Chikore Mission.

For the first three years we were working with the youth and then for the next five with the youth and with elderly people. Then we were transferred to Mbare where we worked for about three years. In 1981 my husband was away for two years at school in the United States of America. After his return, we were sent to Highfields.

The war began in the Chipinge area in about 1977. During the seventies, I heard much about politics because that was the period when students were leaving schools and crossing the border into Mozambique. There were all sorts of rumours. Not many people actually saw the children leave unless they stopped to ask for food on their way. It was quite a long time before we saw them return to the country.

Sithole was the first person who was known in our area. He was the one who started talking about freedom for the people in the 1950s. Those were the years when our people went to work in Mozambique but they were never paid. Sithole talked about freedom. He said that people should not work for nothing. That is why the very first people who went out to fight were Sithole's followers, but then when they came back we noticed that they were Mugabe's.

During the 1950s and 1960s people slowly became aware that we were oppressed. Then some missionaries were deported, for example the Reverend Neal Richards from the Epworth Theological College, the Reverend Henrick from Chipinge Mission and the Reverend Mwadira. They were deported because of their politics. The Reverend Mwadira was suspected of collaborating with the Mozambicans and he had to leave the mission.

From that time things seemed to get worse and worse and people became afraid. It seemed as if all our missionaries would be deported. Some of our people were also chased away from the missions because they were suspected of collaborating with the guerillas. People were not happy. No one liked to see people driven from their homes. It did not even matter if you were a citizen of the country. It was not a good time for our people.

Then there was a time when the Smith regime suspected that the schools were collaborating with guerillas. Some of the schools were closed and some students were arrested. Others tried to cross the border and, if they were captured by the soldiers, they were tortured. Such torture: you could be beaten or put into a drum that was full of water. They blindfolded you and then took you to an unknown place.

My father was taken away and tortured. That was in 1979. He said it was terrible. They sometimes used electric shocks which could sometimes even force you to say untrue things, things which never happened, just in order to be left alone.

When the war became really hot, I was involved in helping our people. My husband was a member of Christian Care and his duties often required him to travel to Harare or Mutare. He used to buy *maheu**, mealie-meal, dried fish, blankets and medicine. All the food was for the people who had been moved into a place the authorities called a 'protected village' or a 'keep'. The soldiers always suspected that all these provisions were not for the people in the keep but for the *gandangas*†as they called them. Once they took my husband away for three days to interrogate him. They said that they had seen someone running away from our

---

* *Maheu* – a nutritious drink made with sadza and water (sometimes with malt as well) and left to stand overnight.
† *Gandangas/magandangas* – literally a wild or savage person. Term used by the Rhodesian Front regime in much of their printed and broadcast material to denigrate and suggest fear.

house and that is why they took him for questioning. Fortunately they did not have enough evidence against him and so they let him go.

People were driven into the keep like animals. They had to go into the keep. It did not matter whether they wanted to or not. The mission people felt very badly about this and they sent a delegation to the district commissioner to complain about the conditions in which people were forced to live. There were no houses. People lived in sheds. There was no sanitation and no water: nothing. People were forced to live like animals. They had nothing to eat, they had no fields and no money, and that is why Christian Care tried to help such people.

We ourselves did not exactly move into the keep; rather it was built around us. So we actually stayed in our house while other people had to move into the big sheds. We were also inside a big fence and the soldiers camped nearby. Our house was very close to the soldiers' camp. The soldiers watched every move we made. Sometimes they surrounded our house early in the morning and said that our dog had barked during the night, or that the light had been on for a long time. They always wanted to know what this meant. Once I was taken with my children into the soldiers' camp for questioning about such things.

We gave clothing and food to the people. It was not easy to do so because each time my husband went to buy food from Mutare, the soldiers would say we were feeding guerillas. We were always caught in between. If we refused the guerillas food, they would say we were sell-outs, but if the soldiers found out that we had given food to them, they would say we were collaborators.

Personally I did not meet guerillas when we were staying in the keep. We sent food, money and clothes to the guerillas through the people in the keep who had contact with them. The guerillas always gave their instructions to one man who then passed the message on to everybody else. That person also knew where to put the provisions for the guerillas to collect. We had to do everything under the eyes of the soldiers.

One day my husband went with others to meet the guerillas. I did not go because it was a long way off. My husband told me that they had expressed their appreciation for the assistance they got from the mission people. The mission itself was surrounded by a fence with a gate. Each time we went out we were searched and asked where we were going. If the soldiers suspected you, they beat you. I was not beaten but one of my children who was visiting us was so harassed that he decided to leave the following day.

We used to visit the youth in the churches by car. The soldiers always searched the car because they thought we would be carrying food for the guerillas. The soldiers always said my husband was a sell-out who went round feeding guerillas.

One day a young boy who was looking after our cattle told my husband not to leave the mission because something had been planted on the road. So we did not go out. Later that day the soldiers detonated a land mine and so we knew we had been set up. But God did not want us to be killed in such a way and we escaped death through God's help.

Many schools were closed and many were burnt down. At times when the guerillas got information that someone was a sell-out, they were killed.

Once when my husband was on his way to Mutare he met the freedom fighters. They stopped his car and took him into the bush where they interrogated him because they thought that he was in the Muzorewa camp. It was during that period when Muzorewa was working with Smith.

After that the freedom fighters said that all ministers of religion were working with Muzorewa. My husband told me that it was a bitter situation as half the freedom fighters wanted to kill him. Fortunately their commander was the commander of the Mount Selinda area and he knew my husband and defended him. He told the other comrades that my husband had helped them with food and clothing. My husband was interrogated for at least two hours and then the commander sent him back to his car with an escort in case those who wanted to kill him, killed him.

Three other drivers who were taken by the freedom fighters never came back. My husband knows of a driver who had four hundred dollars in his pocket who was taken for interrogation and never came back. They took him to Mozambique and no one has heard of him since then.

People were afraid of both the guerillas and the soldiers because they all killed people. If the *mujibas* or *chimbwidos* told the guerillas that you were a sell-out, then you were gone.

At first the comrades never questioned the person who had been called a sell-out, they just went ahead and killed them. Later they realized that sometimes the information they received was based on lies and so they always made their own investigations before killing anyone. If they found that what had been said was not true, sometimes they killed that *chimbwido* or *mujiba.*

War is a terrible thing. People do terrible things. Once my mother told me that one day the freedom fighters entered a house and demanded money. The owner of the house said he had no money, but the freedom fighters did not believe him and they searched everywhere until they found some. They took the money and then threw a grenade into the house and killed the owner. They were angry that he had told a lie.

His wife was in the kitchen hut when she heard the noise. She ran across the yard but because smoke was pouring from the room they had attacked, she could not enter. After the smoke had disappeared, she went into the house and found her husband in pieces. The following day my mother helped her to pick up the pieces of his body and put them into a sack. They buried her husband, just like that, in pieces.

I wouldn't say that because I was on the mission I felt more protected than people in the village. One reason that I did not meet the comrades was because our house was so close to the soldiers' camp. We even suffered the soldiers' bullets because sometimes they fired in all directions and our house was hit. Whenever they suspected anything at all, they fired their guns. They did not care what they hit.

Sometimes the guerillas and the soldiers fired at each other. Then we would hide under our beds. One day a bullet came through the window and hit the wall. It was about eight o'clock at night and suddenly we heard a noise like thunder. We did not know where it was coming from. Then the house began to shake and there was a lot of dust. A bullet had been fired through the window into the wall above my husband's head. It was a very big bullet. When we dug it out of the wall, we found that it was about six inches long.

Sometimes a bazooka would be fired towards the soldiers' camp. My husband was quite often caught in the cross-fire, especially if it was around seven o'clock in the evening when people were still working at the mission. Many people died from the cross-fire. I remember one night my husband had gone to teach a class preparing for examinations when the firing started. The students could not return to their dormitories and my husband could not come back to our house, so they spent the night sleeping in the classroom, each person under a desk.

The soldiers were really against us. The youth we were working with were not happy: they did not like the way the soldiers treated them, that is why so many of them crossed the border into Mozambique. But once the soldiers noticed that they had gone, they questioned the youth's parents and they were beaten and harassed. Just once in a while you might come across a nice soldier. A nice soldier would say "That's enough!" when one was being beaten hard.

None of my own children went to join the struggle although my son had tried to leave the school once and had been stopped by another minister. But my husband's niece who had been staying with us crossed into Mozambique. She never came back. We don't know what happened to her. We heard that she had got married after the war and stayed in Mozambique. We have also heard that she died there; but we don't know. Two of my husband's young brothers died in Mozambique. One brother, his wife and a child died in the bombing of Chimoio.

When I did first see the guerillas, it was towards the end of the war. They had been sleeping and all their weapons were lying on the ground. I was frightened but the guerillas explained to us what they used all their guns for. I did not like the sight of so many guns and bayonets, as my brother had died during the war. Some people say the soldiers threw a bomb at his car and some say the guerillas threw a grenade at him. We still do not know who killed him and all the other seven people who were in the car.

One thing my husband noticed was that when things were tough everybody wanted to be together. Even those who were not Christians came to church services. People felt that they had to come together and talk to God about their problems. We think that people in Chipinge now feel good that the country is free and that they played their part in the war. Everyone who went to Mozambique passed through the area. People suffered. They were caught in between the army and the freedom fighters but still they felt that they made a contribution, even when the struggle was bitter. Many people died during the war. That's all I can say. People died in the place that I was born; people died in the place in which I was married.

The women's role in the war was hard because they were the ones who had to cook and wash for the guerillas. Husbands heard about was happening when it was already happening: women informed their husbands that they had to cook, but they were already doing the cooking. Husbands did not do anything. Women carried food to the guerillas, fetched water for them from long distances and washed their clothes.

Since independence, the situation for women has improved. There are now boreholes in some places and women no longer have to walk long distances to fetch water.

Now that the country is independent one can sleep well without fear. I do not think that the country would have got its independence without the war. Leaders in positions of power do not often want to release that power without a fight. The war just had to be fought for our independence. That is my opinion.

21　Josephine Ndiweni

Dry Paddock

I WAS BORN in Tsholotsho in 1951. We were fifteen in our family but we have different mothers. My mother was my father's first wife. She left us when we were still small and my father's second wife looked after the five of us. That is why my life was not of the kind that one would like to have. I am the oldest child in my family as my mother was the first wife.

My aunt* was very hard on us. She let me do all the work at home while she did nothing. I worked so hard it was as if I was the owner of the home. I know that every girl is expected to cook, wash dishes, fetch water and firewood and so on, but in my case it was much harder. I used to look after the cattle, pound the mealie-meal, fetch water, look for firewood and prepare a meal every day.

If my mother had been there, things would not have been so bad. I know I'd have done what was expected of me, but I'm sure she would have helped, especially as I had to do

---

* Aunt – *mama-omncane* (Ndebele) – literally, little mother, used by children to refer to their father's second wife.

all the housework after I'd spent the whole day looking after the cattle. As it was, I not only had to cook but I had to pound the maize after I came home. By the time I'd finished cooking it would be late and I would be very tired.

My mother left us when I was very small and as I had not even gone to school, I learned to do all these things the hard way: my aunt always beat me if I did not do as she said. If she told me to do something and I forgot, I was beaten hard. I had to learn to do things early in life and do them fast.

My father kept pigs until they were large enough for sale. It was his only means of making money. Of course, we ploughed and planted crops but we only planted enough for ourselves to eat. If we had a good yield, anything that we didn't need was used to feed the pigs and then they were sold.

When I was twenty-three I went to see my father's sister who had married and settled in Gwanda. She had asked me to visit her as none of her relatives had ever done so. It was there that I met Ndiweni. He sent many people to plead with me to marry him. At first I didn't take his proposal seriously. I thought he wanted to fool around with me since I was from another area. I wondered why he had not married a girl from his own district. But finally I realized that he was serious and I agreed to marry him.

When I married, my husband was employed as a salesman in a shop but when I was eight months pregnant he left his employment. From that time life was not very satisfactory at all. We had twins but I could not produce enough milk to feed them and I had no money to buy milk. Fortunately, however, the clinic gave me some to supplement the babies' diet. Life in town for a person who isn't employed and has a family is very difficult, almost impossible. We grew vegetables to sell and in that way we managed to buy a little food although it was never enough.

When my twins were four months old we left Gwanda and moved to Dry Paddock.

I remember clearly when I first heard of the guerillas: it was well before my marriage. I asked my father what and who they were. He said that I would be arrested or cause him to be arrested if I ever talked about them. But when I explained that my questions were sincere and that I really did want to know more, my father said that he would show them to me when they came. But he emphasized that I was *never* to tell anyone. I promised I wouldn't because I wanted to know what kind of people or animals they were, and what they looked like.

About a week later, a group of them came to our home at night. Because I was the oldest child in the family, it was permissible for my father to wake me at night, if there ever was anything to be done. So he woke me and took me to see them. They were not actually in our house but they had stopped quite near it. It was then their custom that, when they first went somewhere, they never went into a home.

My father and I went to see these people: there were four of them. My father told me to greet them. I was frightened. They had guns. They said "Hello!" and I answered them and they asked me what I wanted. I told them that I had come to greet them. They asked who had called me and I explained. They questioned me and seemed annoyed that my father had told me about them. They told me never to mention their presence to anyone. I kept my promise and have never told anyone, not a soul, about them – until today.

In 1974, after we had moved to Dry Paddock, I asked my father if my youngest sister could come and help me since I had a lot of work to do building our home. My youngest sister was my favourite sister: she looked very like my mother and, as she was an obedient girl, I knew I could rely on her. From then she helped me in all types of work. For instance, sometimes parents were required to work at the local school and I would send her to represent me. That meant that I was able to remain at home doing those things which needed to be done there while she worked on my behalf at the school. My children were still too small to go to school, but every parent had to work there regardless of your children's ages. Records were kept and, if any household did not participate, you would be required to make a cash contribution towards the upkeep of the school. You either contributed money or labour. A household could be asked to pay up to thirty or forty dollars and I could not afford this. That is why I asked my sister to work with others at the school.

I like working in my garden and, when I went to work there, my sister stayed at home, fetched the water and prepared meals. She did the normal household work which meant that I did not have to do everything.

My husband was, and is, rarely at home. He was always looking for a job in town. Sometimes he came home for short periods and then went back to town to look for work, but he never got a job. When he is at home, he sometimes helps me in the garden.

My sister was with me for two years and then she left to join the liberation struggle. After she'd gone I found it difficult as I had got used to having someone to help me. I had never talked with her about the struggle. Perhaps she talked with others or her friends, but she never told me she wanted to go.

On the day she left, she said she was going to the garden and she even took a tin to water the vegetables. I was surprised when it got late and she still hadn't returned home. So I went to see what might have happened. The tin was lying in the garden but she had gone. I was then told by others that she had left for the struggle.

I was upset and I went home to Tsholotsho to tell my father about it. He said that there was nothing we could do because, were we to report her absence to the police, we could be imprisoned and beaten. So we did nothing. We wondered why she had gone so suddenly but we knew a lot of people were leaving the country and she only did what other young people were doing.

I returned to my home and at first missed her a great deal, but I adjusted and was soon able to do everything myself. I still went to work in my garden and on certain days I worked at the school and I did all my housework. The sad thing is that my sister never came back. We have looked for her and made enquiries, but we have heard nothing and I do not know what happened to her.

Before my sister went away Zipras had come into our area. They always came at night and asked for food. We cooked and gave it to them. We never told anyone because, had the soldiers known, we would have been beaten and our homes burnt down. There were many soldiers in our area and they moved about in groups. Sometimes three or four groups would pass by my home each day.

The Zanlas came a little while after the Zipras. They were very troublesome. They always wanted food and they made us sing their songs. We dreaded sunset because we knew that once the sun had set, the Zanlas would arrive and make us sing. Of course, we never told anyone because of our fear of the soldiers.

Later, because the soldiers came so frequently and always demanded information about the guerillas, the Zanlas told us that we should tell the soldiers of their presence, but only after we had prepared food for them. So what happened was this: whilst we were cooking, we would send a child to tell the soldiers that the comrades were in the neighbourhood. But, while the messenger was on the way, we told the comrades that we had sent word to the soldiers. After we'd finished cooking, we served the food; the comrades ate very fast so that, by the time the soldiers came, they had finished and gone.

In this way we protected ourselves against those who wanted to sell out on others. For, if the soldiers heard from informers that the comrades had been to your home and that you had fed them, you would be in serious trouble, but if you yourself told the soldiers about the comrades, you could not be said to have harboured them.

Then the soldiers – they were always black, I only saw white soldiers once – would gather us together during the day and talk to us. They would say how surprised they were that we said we loved our children, the comrades, for after all, they troubled us so much: making us cook in the middle of the night, making us carry food into the bush at night, making us hold meetings at night, and so on, all of which, they stated, was both very dangerous and inconvenient for us.

They said that they, the soldiers, were good people because they came to address us during the day and they did not ask us to do things for them at night. They said they only beat us because we denied we knew where the comrades were and so on. The soldiers said that they never bothered anyone because they always carried their own food and water. All they were interested to know was where the guerillas were and we were foolish to deny them this knowledge.

On the other hand, when the Zanlas came they accused us of hating them and loving the soldiers. They said that only they, the Zanlas, could bring the country independence. We were caught between these two groups and we did not know what to do, because both groups blamed us and both groups were armed, but we were not.

In our area the comrades did not select particular homes: they went wherever they chose to go. Sometimes they kept going to the same home for perhaps a week – always for food. Once they came to me when I had no mealie-meal and I told them so. They did not believe me and so I said, "All right, search my houses*." So they did and they found a little mealie-meal which they told me to cook, although it was not nearly enough for them. So the following day my children had no food and I had to go begging for some from my neighbours. They were always good to me and, if they had mealie-meal, they would always give me some. Sometimes I sold my vegetables at the clinic and sometimes I bartered vegetables for beans and got food for my children that way.

Then the Zipras came to ask for food. They nearly always came at night. Sometimes one would be beaten for not having any mealie-meal with which to cook them sadza. The guerillas would occasionally get mad and say, "How can you say you have no food when we are your children?" They always told us that we should prepare whatever food was available, no matter how little it was. Then they would eat and go on their way. Sometimes, at the next village, they asked for food again.

It was a very bad and painful time. We hardly slept when they were around. Often, after preparing food, we were asked to sing. We sang regardless of where we were, but most times we would be in the bush, in the mountains, and we would sing until one or two o'clock in the morning. Then the comrades would let us return to our homes. Sometimes, after such a night, the soldiers would arrive at dawn and gather us together for their meeting. It was a difficult time, I can tell you.

I remember one morning at sunrise the Zipras came to my home and asked for tea. I said that I had no sugar to make them tea. They asked me how I could say I didn't have sugar when I had a husband. I told them that my husband was not employed and I had no money to buy sugar. They insisted that they wanted tea. They were not joking. Actually I did have a little sugar but I did not want to make them tea and I hoped that they would go away and leave me alone, but they refused to go. So I brewed tea for them.

Then, just after they'd left, the soldiers came. The soldiers had been following the Zipra footprints from the place where they'd spent the night. The soldiers asked me where the

---

* A traditional Zimbabwean home is made up of several separate, usually circular, rooms around an open area or courtyard.

comrades were. I could not deny that they'd been in my house, as the cups hadn't been cleaned and signs of their presence were evident. I pointed the soldiers in the direction the comrades had followed – they could see their footprints clearly – and they went after them, but fortunately they never caught up with them.

That very night the comrades returned and asked why they had been followed by soldiers as soon as they'd left my home. I told them that the soldiers had arrived soon after they'd left and that, even if I'd travelled at the speed of an aeroplane, I could not have gone to the soldiers' base to inform on them, because there'd been no time between the comrades leaving and the soldiers arriving. It was clear that this was true and that is how I survived. I could have been killed.

What also worried me was that while we, in our way, were busy fighting for the country and contributing food and money, we were also required to buy party cards. The card cost fifty cents and having got it we had a regular contribution for being a card-holder. We had no money to feed our children and yet we were required to buy cards. If you had no card you were in trouble. Some people were killed because they were not card-holders. Everyone had to have a card as proof that you were supporting the struggle and fighting for the country. If you had no card it was said that it meant you were not interested in independence and were, therefore, better off dead.

You were as good as a sell-out as far as the party leaders were concerned. I could not understand that. You could not buy a card without paying the contributions, otherwise you would be killed. They said that if you bought a card and did not pay their 'taxes' you were not a sincere party supporter and you had only bought the card for self-protection. It had nothing to do with whether you were interested in politics or not. Anyone and everyone was required to buy these cards, even old women who could not raise a finger to get money for themselves. Where were they supposed to get the money from? So, if there were old people in your family, you had to worry about them. I always wondered why it had to be this way and where the money went and what it was used for.

We asked the leaders to discuss the cards and find a solution that would relieve old people from the burden, but they never entertained our request. Instead one could be called a sell-out for such a suggestion. We tried to explain that we only wanted the contributions restricted to those who could afford them, but such questions could cost people their lives.

I think it is good that we finally got our independence. Of course we were told about it by the authorities and we had even celebrated, but I was not sure that it was true. I could not believe that there really could be peace in the country because so many people had killed one another.

For example, I did not think that a policeman could ever travel safely in the communal areas on a bicycle. One day when I saw two policeman pass by on their bicycles, I was very worried that they might never come back, because I was not sure that all was well after independence. I was surprised to see them returning alive at sunset. It had never happened that a policeman could travel in the countryside so safely. Then I realized that we were free and that there was peace in the country.

But at one time after independence our shops were closed down and we were not allowed to buy anything. I wondered what we were supposed to eat, or whether they just wanted us to drink water? That was the day I was beaten and I will never forget that day. I was pregnant and nearly had a miscarriage. On that occasion it was the soldiers who beat us, not the Zipras.

You see, there was a notorious dissident in the Kafusi area who caused much unhappiness. He did many horrible things, burning down schools, taking property from shops, and so on. As a result, the soldiers closed the shops down. We really suffered because we had no food and we could not buy any anywhere. We had to rely on *mukumbi*, a wild fruit. You can cut it open and mix water in with the pulp, which then forms a juice rather like beer. It also has seeds which look like groundnuts which you can eat. We also ate meat, just meat, when we could get it. Every day the soldiers came to inspect the shops to make sure that nothing had been bought or moved out.

Then the soldiers gathered us together and wanted us to tell them where this dissident was. They wanted us to say we had seen him but we hadn't and we were beaten. But now we can do our work freely and go wherever we like without fear. We can move and travel without ID cards.

Sometimes I travel without an ID and I have no fear because we are free. When one meets a police or a soldiers' truck one has nothing to worry about. They will even give you a lift to your destination, if they are not in a hurry and you can ask for help. During the war one would never wait for a soldiers' truck. As soon as you heard one, you ran away as fast as you could and hid. One would not dare stop a soldiers' truck because it might cost you your life.

So, independence is good and we now have a peaceful life. Our only problem is that the rain does not often fall and, as a result, we do not have food enough to feed our children. Had we enough food I would not complain about anything.

Women played an important role during the struggle because they met with and patiently overcame a lot of hardships. I am not only talking about myself: women worked hard throughout the country. I know men also worked, but sometimes they got tired or fed up, but the women pulled together from the beginning, right until the end of the war – even when it meant going to meetings.

I remember one day we were told to go and attend a meeting at Kafusi dam. This meeting was held during the day because it had been called by soldiers. Kafusi dam is quite a long way from my home but we all went. When we got there we were told to sit apart, women on one side and men on another. When we sat down, in the sun, the soldiers said they were going to kill us. No one, not even one single man answered. We all sat there with our heads lowered, thinking about and fearing for the death that was creeping up on us.

Then a policeman asked why so many people were to be killed and the soldiers said it was because the men were difficult people to work with. They said men had no constructive ideas and their views and were not dependable. One soldier said that if he were to ask any one of the men a question, he was sure it would not be answered satisfactorily.

We sat there for hours, in the sun. The soldiers were angry. After a long time they let us go. I think it was their way of giving us, and particularly the men, a fright.

Women were very important and played an important part in the war. They were dependable. Many things were and are a success because of women. They went to all meetings, they did all the work that had to be done and even now women still do a lot of the work.

In our area I am a member of a farmers' club called *Qubekelaphambili,* which means 'Go forward'. More women belong to it than men. We also have a women's club where we meet to do our sewing. There are no male members although we sometimes invite them to join us, but they don't want to.

My husband has never found employment and I have always had to struggle to provide for my six children. I am thankful for them although it has always been difficult to look after them all and provide all the necessities. I till the land but I usually do not get enough food from my fields because of the drought. Sometimes I only harvest three bags of maize and sometimes there is nothing at all. We try to grow vegetables but often our dam is dry and there is no water to be had.

My wish is for my children to have a better life than mine. I have a problem though, which I think will hinder them from achieving a better life and this is that I will not be able to educate them. I will not be able to give them higher education. I know the key to a better life is education: without education one's life cannot improve.

22 Cheche Maseko

Siphaziphazi, Bulawayo

I WAS BORN in Siphaziphazi. After some years I went to school at St Peter's in Luveve. I was there for three years and I liked it very much. Then I moved to St Patrick's in Bulawayo and remained there until I had completed standard six. My father then died and I stopped going to school.

When my father died my mother, my two sisters and I went to live with my mother's mother and she supported us. She sold her cattle and did her best to provide for us, as my mother had only one brother and he lived with my grandmother.

My early life was very good. I was a very strong, beautiful and proud girl. I had a big body – someone who could be called fat. I did not have any friends outside my family. I played with either my sister or my cousin and I liked doing what I did alone.

I lived with my grandmother until I was fifteen years old. During that time she used to tell us about life: what to do when one married, how to live with a husband, and the proper way of doing things. She taught us good manners and how to prepare samp, how to cook okra, how to grind peanut butter, how to clean maize and other grain using a big round flat basket called an *ukhomane*. I was taught all the proper things about an African way of life.

Then I fell in love with a boy with whom I had gone to school. When he began to visit my home, my uncle sent him away and wouldn't allow him to visit me. So then I sent someone to tell my grandmother and my uncle about him. His parents were called and proper introductions were made. After this formal meeting, he was allowed to visit me. He was called Daniel Nhliziyo and he was from Nyaman-dhlovu.

I think he loved me because he had seen and admired the good manners that my grandmother had taught me and I could see that he too was a good-mannered boy. So when we had agreed to marry, his aunt came to our home to inform my parents of his intentions. After that my uncle and mother called on his father to tell them what they wanted for my lobola. It was a long time ago and in those days lobola was cheap – they only asked for an introductory payment, *kangaziwe*, of twenty pounds. This meant that he would be accepted into the family. After that, they asked them for lobola of thirty pounds.

They paid all this happily because I was a good girl. I loved Daniel Nhliziyo very much and he loved me. I had won him away from four other girls, although he had a child by one of them. After we were married we moved to my husband's home at Tsholotsho. Unfortunately my husband's sisters were jealous of me and so they would not help me. For example, at first I didn't know where to collect firewood, and they would not show me. They also didn't like it if my husband ever sent me anything from town and they would get very angry. In many ways they made my life very unhappy. But when I told my own people what was happening, my grandmother advised me to be patient and say nothing. But, generally, my husband and I lived together very happily and we had seven children.

The only other problem I had was with the elephants which came into the fields, either when the crops were very young and tender or when they were just ready for harvesting. They could demolish a whole crop. We would call our dogs and make a lot of noise with tins to try and frighten them away. During such times we would often sleep in the fields with our dogs, in order to try and keep the elephants out.

I stayed in Tsholotsho for sixteen years and that was where I had all my children. Then my husband suddenly stopped coming home from his employment, as a delivery man, in Bulawayo. Then my life became so difficult that it was almost unbearable. I had just nothing at all. I could not even buy soap. I had a hard time sending my children to school. First, I sold all my chickens to raise money for the fees. Then I went to cut grass to sell in the villages. I went to work in people's fields and did everything I could to raise money to send the children to school.

I wrote many letters to my husband but he never responded. He no longer sent money: he did not care about us any more. I wrote and told him that we had no soap, but he never replied. All my clothes became worn out and torn. My feet began to crack because I had no lotion or Vaseline to put on them and I had no shoes.

So it was for several years, or until I couldn't bear it any more. Then I reported my situation to my father-in-law and the headman, but they told me to stay at home and continue to do what I could. My husband had neither come home, written to us, nor sent us anything for three years; although I knew that he had occasionally visited the district, as I would hear that he had been to see his brother, but he never came to see me or the children. Another year passed and then again I reported my case to the headman and my father-in-law, but again they responded by telling me to go home and continue to do what I could. So I explained how I was suffering and said that I had to return to my own people. But the elders told me to wait as they would write a letter calling my husband back, so that our case could be heard. They wrote their letter but my husband refused to return. After that I was let free and told I could return to my people. They told me to go alone and leave my children behind.

I went home to my people. The day I left I got up very early in the morning and took my four older children to my father-in-law who was, by then, an old man. My daughter cried so much when I left that I also began to cry. But I had to leave her behind. Then, carrying my suitcase, blankets and a mat, I boarded the bus with my three younger children. We were all crying. I felt very sad and worried about being parted from my older children.

I had decided to go through Bulawayo and I had written to my husband telling him when I would arrive. His brother was at the bus terminus waiting for me. My husband had heard that I was going to be set free from his home and he had sent his brother to find out where I was going to stay. I told my brother-in-law that I was going to my mother's and that I knew my husband would not want to see me.

My mother looked after me and my children. I had no clothes, no shoes, nothing.

My mother bought some tennis shoes* for me and some clothes for my children. She obtained a letter from the chief which said that my husband had no claim on me and could not bother me if we met. I stayed with my mother for two months and then I decided that I must look for employment, so that I could support my family.

When I decided to look for a job, I stayed with my sister in Bulawayo. After about three weeks, her husband found me a job as a domestic worker. I stayed with that family for nine years, until they left the country. Before they left, they found me the job that I have now.

Officially my marriage is still considered valid. I have not divorced my husband, although he has now taken four other wives. I am not jealous neither do I have any bad feeling towards his wives. Sometimes I visit my children, the older ones who have been living with him, and his new wife, in what should be my house, in town.

When my daughters married, my husband never gave me so much as a pin, to say thank you for looking after them. He has enjoyed himself while I brought up the children. I suffered, but now he takes everything, all the lobola. He is an unreasonable man who uses all his money on himself. He buys himself suits, beer and whisky, and drinks away his money. He never thinks of others, not even his own children. Even they say that I should demand something from him, but I am not interested in doing this. He should use his common sense to show his appreciation. I tell myself that it does not matter as long as I am alive and getting a little for myself. I do not see why I should punish myself by worrying about this husband of mine. But sometimes I wonder what it means to be a mother, to have children, and then to be forgotten.

---

* Tennis shoes, often called takkies – used to refer generally to canvas shoes which are very much cheaper than any other shoe and, therefore, worn by many people.

I joined ZAPU a long time ago. In those days we used to wear orange T-shirts and black skirts with green stripes round the bottom. I joined during the years when all was well with my husband and he was also a member of the party. I continued to go to party meetings, even when I was living in town and my employers always gave me time off to do so.

During the war two of my sons went to fight for liberation. The older one went first and then his small brother said that he wanted to follow him. I discouraged the younger one but, when he left, I did not feel too bad because I thought it good that our children should fight for our country, if that was a way of bringing about freedom. Many children left the country, even girls who were old enough, they went to fight.

But when my father-in-law wrote and told me that my third and youngest son also wanted to join the struggle, I went to Tsholotsho to see him. I pleaded with him not to go. I promised to buy him a pair of shoes that he wanted very much, and promised him that I would do everything I could for him, if he did not go. In the end he stayed. He really wanted to go, but he was only about ten years old, and as his two brothers had left, I did not want him to go.

The eldest son was fourteen when he left: his brother was twelve. I did not think they would survive but I prayed to God and I also put snuff on the ground to appease our ancestral spirits so that they would keep our children safe. A lot of children died but fortunately mine survived.

It was my daughter who died during the war and that was a very painful experience. She died here at home in Siphaziphazi. She was beaten by a big stick. She was hit hard with a big, big stick as if they were pounding millet. She was hit hard, and at first she was crying and then she was silent but they continued hitting her. She was not the only one who was killed that day. The soldiers came at dawn and took people from different homes and killed them at the same time in one place. We were ordered not to cry or say anything as they were being killed. We just sat there, with the old man Mkandla, singing political songs very low and quietly. They were killed by the soldiers who said they were collaborating with the freedom fighters. They wanted to use them as examples to frighten others. Many people were killed but some managed to run away. Some were badly injured, but survived, after receiving treatment. After the killings, the villagers were ordered to bury the dead within a short time and the elders buried them. I was so pained and so weak that I could not walk to the burial place. Because there was no transport, I had no means of telling her father, and he only heard about the death of our daughter some time later.

After her death, my grandmother wanted to commit suicide but my uncle stopped her, saying that she was not the only person in the country who had lost a child in the war. He told her that she should accept it as it was: what had happened, had happened. He advised her to pray and throw snuff on the ground. But my grandmother was very, very distressed and she could not eat for many days and we had to plead with her to do so. My uncle also grieved, although he knew he had to be strong. He told us that the children had died for us, had died to free Zimbabwe. We salute those that died. They are heroes.

There was another couple in Siphaziphazi who had no children, but they were very rich. They had lots of goats, donkeys and other animals. The wife was killed and her husband committed suicide. Nothing belonging to them remained. All their goats, cattle and donkeys went astray and were eaten by lions as they had no relatives in the district.

Ah, we were very courageous in those days. Very strong. We did not care whether it was a policeman, a soldier on foot or one on horse-back. We were not afraid of guns. We got this courage from talking among ourselves and attending meetings. We told ourselves that we had to be strong since our children were in the struggle. How could we fear when they were out there? If, for instance, it was a women's meeting, we said, "Mothers, be strong. How can we fear for our lives if our children are strong enough to go and fight? We should be as courageous as they are."

Sometimes Smith's soldiers arrived when we were fetching water from the boreholes and they let their horses kick over our tins of water, but we quietly continued, we did not give up. We did not mind what they did because we knew what we were doing. Even if they let their horses drink our water from our tins and afterwards the horses knocked our buckets over, we carried on. We were determined to continue with our political meetings and we refused to care about

Smith's soldiers. Planes constantly flew over our heads but we went on with our chores: going to the fields, collecting firewood and fetching water. Life went on. It seemed pointless to be afraid of dying while our children were out there. What was the point? We did not know where our children were, what they were doing, or whether they were still alive. How could we fear for ourselves?

After the war, when my children returned, I was in town. My brother-in-law sent word to me that my two sons had returned. I was very excited and when I told my employers, they gave me time off. So I went to went to see my children. I was very excited and I bought chicken and rice, beer and fizzy drinks and it was a great day. We danced and gave thanks to the spirits of my ancestors.

Now, I am happy that we are free. You know, I grew up and stayed at home for a long time. I did not know much about my rights. It's only now that I am beginning to open my eyes. My sister helped me to look for employment. That was a first step. Now others have also told me that I have rights and that the authorities will consider the case of my husband and, for me, that is another step.

But I still do not understand how a man and wife can be equal when, in the first place, a woman leaves her parents' home and moves to the one of her husband. How can they be equal when the man paid lobola and took the woman away from her parents to his place? It does not matter whether you are a working wife, the fact remains that a husband should be respected and wives will always remain under their husbands.

One day I met this man, my husband, he greeted me and I replied. He was surprised because he expected me to be miserable. So I told him that I was happy because I knew my children cared for me. He said that he knew this and that he did not think the children loved him at all. So I told him that it was not my fault that the children had nothing to do with him and that, if he felt that I had wronged him, he should report me to the district court!

I am very strong with my children, sometimes even cheeky. I sit down with them and discuss life. I was taught good manners by my grandmother and so now I tell my children about life. I tell them they must learn to be patient; they must respect their husbands; they must behave well in the African custom and kneel to show respect; they must welcome their husbands cheerfully when they come home from work because they will be tired. I am very strong and tough with my children. I have told them that they must make a good life now because I may die at any time, and if they don't listen to me now they won't be able to once I am dead.

I admire my daughter-in-law very much. She is still young but she is well behaved and has good manners. Some people are good at educating their children properly in our customs, I can tell this from my daughter-in-law. She is very kind and she respects me as her own mother. When I go to stay with my son, she gets up early in the morning, to warm some water for me to bath. The next thing I hear is her calling, *maluwazana** you are still asleep. It's time to wake up, the sun is high. Then she gives me water in which to to bathe, and afterwards something to eat, and tea. She jokes with me that I like beer better than tea, and she will send a child to buy me some beer from a home that has some home-brewed beer. I sit on the mat and have my beer, joking and having a nice time with my grandchildren.

Mothers are generally good people. We have children and we have to do our best for our children and teach them to be good citizens. I hope that the Lord will continue to help me to educate my children. If I manage to send them all to school, they will have a better life than I have had. One of my sons who is now working is leading a better life. He has already managed to buy a house and he is trying to help his brothers to find employment. I think life will be better in the end.

I tell you, my friends, a woman is a very strong person. Women are courageous. During the war mothers did a great job. They were committed to helping to liberate the country. Even now women still work very hard. It was they who began to cut the grass with which to re-thatch the schools that had been burnt or damaged during the war. In this way, they made it possible for their children to return to school, even before the schools had been properly repaired. Yes, women are very strong, very courageous.

---

* *Maluwazana* – daughter-in-law (Ndebele). This term is used affectionately to a mother-in-law both to show respect for her age and in recognition that the older person will, one day, be dependent on her grandchildren: thus, loosely, the daughter-in-law to the daughter-in-law.

23 Joannah Nkomo

Pelandaba, Bulawayo

I WAS BORN at Maphaneni in Mbembeswana district, where I grew up and first went to kindergarten. My parents were Catholics so I went to mission schools at St Joseph's and Empandeni Mission. When I had completed standard six, I stayed at home for a year before returning to Empandeni to do a course in homecrafts. When that was over, I went to Bulawayo where I taught for two years in Catholic schools.

In 1948 I met Joshua Nkomo* in Bulawayo. He had just returned from Johannesburg after completing his education. At first, my parents did not want me to marry him because he was of a different tribe and, since I am an Nguni and he is not, my parents considered his tribe to be inferior. However, as my husband was a grown-up, mature man who should have been married a long time before, we decided to get married. And we did, in the Civil Court on October 1st, 1949. But my family were all baptized into the Catholic

---

* Leader of ZAPU during the struggle of independence; now Vice-President of the unified ZANU(PF).

223

Church, so I felt a great loss at not having had a church wedding, because my civil marriage was not accepted by my church.

So we talked to the Bishop of the Cathedral in Bulawayo and he agreed to help us. He said that the church had no objection to our marriage but advised us to discuss the matter again with our parents. I did this and I asked them to allow me to wed in church, although my husband was not of my tribe and not of my church. I told them that the church leaders had said that it was possible to have a mixed marriage.

Eventually my parents agreed as they realized how anxious I was about the matter. So, in 1953, we had a church wedding and a reception at St Joseph's.

At the time we had no children, so the ministers explained that our children would be Catholics. My husband agreed. This was because he never went to church, although his parents were London Missionaries. That is really the reason why I pressed so hard for my children to enter my own church.

When we were first married in 1949, Nkomo had come back home to stay and he was working for the Rhodesia Railways. So I left my job to become a full-time housewife. He worked for the railways for five years and then he entered politics. At first I did not understand what this meant, because I was staying at home with his parents most of the time.

There were three Shona men whom he worked with in this politics business. They were James Chikerema, George Nyandoro and the late Dr Parirenyatwa. He often brought these men home over Easter and Christmas holidays. Then, after some years, my husband left his job on the railways and became a full-time politician. During that time I hardly saw him.

After his father died, I was alone at home as his mother had died many years before. It was then that we decided that I should come and live in Bulawayo as I was lonely at home. I came to Bulawayo in 1955, and he bought me the house in which I still live, at Pelandaba.

It was a very small house with only three rooms. At that time I lived alone because Nkomo was so involved in politics. He was doing a lot of travelling to Ndola, Mutare, Harare . . . all over the place, on this politics business. Even then I did not fully appreciate what he was doing. I think there were many people who did not understand either. Then, as time went on, he started holding meetings in the stadiums and people filled the grounds whenever there was a rally. There would be very large crowds. I did not like going to these meetings and he did not encourage me to do so. I stayed at home looking after my children all the time while he was away.

In 1961 the African National Congress* was banned. At that time, my husband was out of the country. His colleagues were arrested and imprisoned so he was informed and advised not to return home because he would also be imprisoned. They thought that it was better this way and that is why they advised him not to return.

By then I had three children and Nkomo called me to England, so that he could see them. I went and stayed there for two months. I did not like the idea of leaving my people here, in my country. I missed them very much. So I returned to Pelandaba for a month and then I looked for a job. I realized that I had to do something if I was to look after my children and keep the family going. I got a job at Empandeni Mission where I had trained in Domestic Science. I helped the sisters teach the women who were doing homecraft. I stayed there until 1964.

I didn't work together with my husband in politics because I could see that our family would collapse if both of us participated fully in such affairs. At that time, the boers used to imprison politicians without mercy. There was no question of compromise. Moreover, I knew there would be no one to look after the children if we both went to jail as only my mother was alive. We could not take the children to prison with us. So, as I was always anxious about what might happen to them, I decided to remain at home. My husband decided to take on one kind of fight, but I also fought. I fought for the survival of my family.

I left Empadini and my job in 1964. The reason was that my husband, as the leader, was seeing a lot of people being beaten and imprisoned in Bulawayo. So we thought that I should also live in town. We felt that people might otherwise complain that they got into trouble as a result of my husband's activities, while he had hidden his family away safely. So I came to live in Bulawayo where other people were being beaten up. This was during the period before he was arrested and imprisoned for a long time.

* African National Congress (SRANC) – officially the Southern Rhodesian African National Congress.

He was arrested in April of that same year. I was expecting our fourth child. There was no one to look after us. So it was necessary to find some other way of feeding my family. I could not return to the mission since Nkomo had told the missionaries that I was coming to live in Bulawayo.

I had a hard time because I didn't have a house. This one had been destroyed by termites. I was lodging in one room with my children. I realized that it was no way of living, and I decided to use my sewing machine to make and sell clothes. This kept me going.

So, when my husband was in prison, I worked hard and I also gave birth to my fourth child. I called her Sehlule which means 'we have conquered'. She was also baptized Louise. I continued to sew and sell clothes, but it became harder and harder to do this, because a lot of women earned money in the same way.

So I decided to make a lot of clothes at once and then I went down to the mission and left them with a former colleague who had settled in that area. I did not mind what kind of payment I received, chickens or whatever. Indeed, chickens were easy because I could sell them in town. Sometimes I even received goats in payment. So I made a bit of money this way and, after a while, I had saved enough to buy a knitting machine.

I did not know how to use it but someone in Pelandaba agreed to teach me. I took my machine to her house as she had no time to come to mine – she was too busy on her own machine. She taught me but it still took me three weeks to be able to use it well. I managed to make a lot of money with my knitting machine and was able to put my children through primary school.

But when my children had to go to secondary school at Regina Mission, I couldn't afford the fees any longer, because the two elder children had to go at the same time. I tried hard but I could not manage to pay them. I had, however, heard that Smith's government gave assistance to the wives of people detained for political reasons and I applied for such assistance. I did not get it because I was Nkomo's wife. The authorities laughed at me. Fortunately, there was an organization called Christian Care that helped needy families, especially those of detainees. They agreed to help me and they paid my children's school fees while I struggled to keep the house going and feed them.

My husband then came out of detention. But he never stayed in one place. He was always on the move, all over the country, preaching the gospel of freedom. Smith did not like this, as many people now seemed to understand and agree with my husband. So they took my husband into restriction at Gonakudzingwa. They did not take him from home but from somewhere else. One morning the men who had been travelling with my husband arrived to tell me that Nkomo had been taken. He alone; not his companions. The police said they were taking him to Gweru but they were not sure if this was true. I cried because I thought that perhaps they would harm him.

Then, after a little while, the men in Bulawayo gathered together to discuss how they could find out where he was and find a lawyer. The lawyer they chose was Leo Barron and he discovered that my husband had been put in Gonakudzingwa restriction area which is near Chiredzi. We didn't even know what kind of place that was.

I then tried through the lawyer to get permission to visit him. Mr Barron tried his best until eventually I was allowed to do so. The lawyer gave me a letter from the police permitting me to visit him. The first time I went in a truck with some other men and women. It was a very long journey to Gonakudzingwa, which is almost on the border of Mozambique. We arrived and identified ourselves. After I identified myself and showed the permit, the police told me to wait and he would be called. I only saw my husband and we talked in the presence of a policeman who recorded the whole of our conversation. They allowed me to be there for five hours. Then they took him away. I never saw where they took him as the place was a thick forest. They just disappeared with him and we were told to return.

There were five people in restriction then, four men and one woman, Mrs Chinamano. I was the first person to visit them but I did not see them all.

There were women who were deeply involved in politics. They had heard men preaching about liberation and urging the women to pull together with the men. Mrs Chinamano was a leader among the women and that is why she was arrested. They thought that, if they arrested the leaders, there would be no more talk about liberation. That is why they took my husband, Mrs Chinamano and those other four men. Here, in town, there were other women who were leaders in the party and those are the ones who organized certain men to accompany me.

Thereafter I concentrated on working to feed and clothe the children and pay the rent on the house. Later on Christian Care increased the allowances for the detainees' families and this helped me pay my rent.

Food was not such a problem, since I had two children at boarding school. By then I had two knitting machines and had employed two girls to help me with the knitting. I also had a relative who was a factory worker who sold my jerseys to her workmates. And, as with my clothes, I accepted any form of payment for my jerseys. I took the remainder of the garments into the country and, if I returned with goats, I sold them. In this way I managed to earn enough money. My life improved because I was only working for my children's food and clothes. Christian Care used to give the children blankets in winter. My husband's Indian friends were also very kind and helped me a lot with clothes. This was because, although I made them for my children, my girl who was growing up sometimes wanted nice ready-made dresses, and I could not make boys' clothes.

My husband was restricted or imprisoned for eleven years at Gonakudzingwa. At first I was allowed to visit him every three months but since it was very far away, I used to go by train, not by road. The police would meet me and provide accommodation for the night and then, on the following day, they would call him to their quarters where I would meet him. Each time our conversation was recorded and the visits always lasted for five hours. Later they allowed me to visit him for three consecutive days although it was actually two, because on the third day I didn't see him, as I had to return on the train which left early.

As time went on, more people were put into the camp which was separated into different divisions. I do not know how they communicated with each other but, during my visits, I would hear people singing and playing drums. My husband told me that it was their way of welcoming me. The people knew they could not see me but they sent their greetings in that way. In the end we were allowed to visit the detainees for five consecutive days every six months. The authorities recorded the visits as nine days because they included travelling days as visiting days.

Once I was not allowed to visit him for two years, although

other women were allowed to visit their husbands. My application was always turned down. I don't know why. At that time Nkomo, Joseph Msika and the late Lazarus Nkala were separated from the rest of the detainees. They were in their own camp. But, in his third year, permission was again given to me.

I and the other two wives, Mrs Msika and Mrs Nkala, had to go at different times. Then, a bit later, we were informed that our husbands had been moved to a new camp called Buffalo Range which was, in fact, a jail. I was very worried. I did not know whether I would ever see Nkomo again and I did not know what Buffalo Range was like.

So, once again, I struggled to get permission to visit him but it was not given until my lawyer intervened. Even though I didn't know where the prison was, I was determined to get there for, as they say in Ndebele, 'A person with a mouth does not get lost'. The police wrote to say that I could visit him but they did not know how I would get to Buffalo Range as there wasn't a train. So then I asked Mr Sivagu, who had a car and was my husband's friend, if he could take me.

I was lucky! Mrs Msika had also received permission to visit her husband and we went together. Mr Manguni, a friend, also wanted to come with us as he hoped they would allow him to see my husband. When we arrived Mrs Msika and I were taken to see our husbands but the two men who had come with us were told to wait while police decided whether they could see the prisoners.

We then saw our husbands who were dressed in torn clothes. It was really shameful. We asked why they had been moved to this prison. They too did not know. Our visit was supposed to last thirty minutes but we were allowed forty and, as we left, Manguni and Sivangu were permitted to greet them. That was my only visit to Buffalo Range as Smith released them because they were going to hold talks.

My husband then came home, still in his torn clothes. On the day of his return, it was raining heavily. But many people heard about it and they lined the road from the airport. He and his friends were brought to Bulawayo in an airforce plane and men from the party met them and took them to their homes.

I did not go to the airport but waited for him at the house. By then I had managed to buy it and had added a room, so there were now four. But I had nothing in the house, not even a chair, and the little furniture I did possess was old and tattered. I did have a plastic mat which had the look of real tiles and that day it was torn because so many people arrived. The fence I had put round the house also collapsed from the sheer numbers. I had not realized that people could exert so much pressure that property could be destroyed. But it was only because so many people came to welcome my husband. There were people everywhere chanting slogans and giving him a real welcome.

We all wondered what could be happening when they were released. Nkomo said that he was not sure what had influenced Smith to do so, but that talks were to be held. They had the first meeting at Victoria Falls but no agreement was reached and the meeting collapsed. After their return, they organized a congress as Muzorewa had been chosen to lead the party. I am not very clear who did what and what happened, but there must have been a misunderstanding because some members did not come to the congress. I was really not very interested in politics, but I read the papers and my husband sometimes told me what was happening, although at first he never did.

This time he told me that he was going out of the country to fight since things had not worked out. He said that it would be difficult, yes, but he was determined to continue. He asked me what I thought. I said that if he thought this was the best thing to do, it was all right with me, as I had accepted him, as he was, on the day I married him.

He went out of the country just as if he was going to Zambia and would come back. If Smith had known that he was going out to fight and would not return, he would not have allowed him to leave. He left to lead the party from outside. When the war started, I remained here with my children.

My children were at secondary school. My eldest daughter, Thandiwe, had finished form four and had come home, but I wanted her to continue with her education. So I decided to go to Botswana and talk to the leaders, Jane Ngwenya and Dumiso Dabengwa, to see if they could help me place Thandiwe in a school somewhere. Dumiso said I should leave her with him so that he could take her to Zambia where he would arrange for her to study.

When I returned, Smith's people realized that I had

crossed the border into Botswana. So they told me to get off the train at Plumtree and they took me to the police camp and put me in a cell. I had not been to prison before and I was very anxious about my three children whom I had left in Bulawayo.

I thought people would never know where I was: those in Bulawayo would think I was in Botswana, and those in Botswana would think I was in Bulawayo. I was very worried and I cried a lot. In the morning I was given porridge and then taken to the CID for interrogation. They asked me where I had come from, why I had gone there, where my husband was and what he was doing? I said I didn't know and so they put me back in the cell.

Then they asked me if I had met Jane or Dumiso in Botswana and I said that I had not. They probably thought that I had gone to give or take information from them, but there was no evidence of this, even though they searched me thoroughly. When they discovered that I had no information to give them, they let me go.

I don't know how my husband heard that I had been arrested because he had also been imprisoned somewhere. I can't quite remember why, maybe he was trying to come back into the country. Anyway, somehow he heard what had happened to me, and he asked for my release because I was not involved in politics.

Dumiso took my daughter to Zambia but, as my husband was in prison, she was left with Leo Barron who had, by then, left Rhodesia. Leo then sent my daughter to my husband's friends in America and asked them to get her into school.

That was a difficult time because the boers had realized that people were serious and many children were leaving the country to go and train as freedom fighters. The school children at Manama secondary school left the country. As with most of the children who were then leaving, they went of their own free will. Many children left. They knew they might die but that did not stop them.

Then one day a policeman visited one of my relatives and said that he wanted to tell me something important but he couldn't come directly to me, as he was a government worker. It was during the Easter holidays and I was in church. I was called out and I wondered who could want me at such a time. When I went out I saw Dan Ngwenya with a lady. I was frightened, but they told me to get into the car and we went home. When we arrived my relative told me that the policeman, who refused to be identified by name, told her that the government was planning to kidnap my child, Sehlule, to use her as a bargaining counter. The government would tell my husband to return all the Manama children if he wanted his own child back. If he didn't do this, then they would kill her.

I was frightened and I had to act fast. I travelled by night to fetch Sehlule from Regina Mundi. I told the sisters at the mission the truth and they let me take her away and we returned home. Then I kept my child in the house and did not let her out at all for a number of days. She could not understand why all this was happening because she was only ten. At last, I phoned a friend in Harare and told him that I had a problem but that I couldn't say what it was over the telephone. I was afraid that even our phones were bugged.

So Jirira sent someone to talk to me and after I had told him, he explained my difficulty to Jirira. I was very worried because, during that period, I frequently saw strange, unfamiliar people near my house who seemed to be keeping an eye on it. Jirira then phoned and told me that I should bring the child to him in Harare. I was still anxious because I did not know how I could do this safely and with whom. Then my relative came and told me that the same policeman had returned to say that people from the government would soon search my house, because they had gone to Regina Mundi and had not found Sehlule. So people had been watching the house in case she had left.

I had two acquaintances, Mrs Lupepe and Mrs Mazalo, who were very close to me and were also active party members. I confided in them and they offered to take the child in their car to Harare. Then I told my daughter that I was sending her away and she cried for the whole night because she did not understand and she did not know why she had to go away since she was only ten. I was also very worried and could only hope that everything would work out well for her.

The two women, dressed as old ladies to disguise themselves, came to fetch her. They had a safe journey to Harare and were back by nightfall. They had been stopped at road blocks but were fortunate as they were not recognized. Jirira had already organized tickets and, as soon as my child arrived, he took her to Malawi so that he could then go on to Zambia. They had not been able to go straight there because the government people were, by then, really searching for Sehlule and, had she gone directly to Zambia, they might have seen and taken her.

Jirira phoned me from Malawi and told me what they were doing. Then, three days later, lots of CIDs came to my house at night. I do not know how many cars there were, but there were many people. They came and knocked hard on the doors calling, "Open! Open!" while others patrolled right round the house.

I was alone with the girl who was helping me. I opened the door. It was about one o'clock in the morning. They came in and started searching through all the rooms, under the beds, in all the corners: everywhere. They did not say what they were looking for. Unusually, they didn't open the wardrobes and throw the contents all over the place. They just looked in strategic places and seemed to be looking for something in particular, something big which could be easily identified. They left without a word at about seven in the morning.

Two days later, I had a visit from some Regina Mundi sisters asking where the little girl was. They were pleased when I told them that she had left the country. They said the CIDs had come to the school and they had told them that my children had long left. But the CIDs had insisted the child was there and had gone into every classroom in search of her. But all the children also told them that Nkomo's child was no longer with them.

Then I realized that, as they had gone as far as wanting to kidnap my child, they might still plan to do something terrible to me, as I was then the only member of the family in the country. Fortunately, Jirira had then arrived in Zambia and he told my husband what was happening. So my husband sent Chinamano to come and fetch me. Chinamano explained that they were taking the war forward and that, given everything that had happened, they did not think that it was safe for me to remain in Rhodesia. He said that everyone in the party had agreed that it was best for me to leave and go to Zambia.

So I left with Chinamano. We went via England, where I met my husband who suggested that before going to

Zambia, I should visit the children in America. In the meantime, he would try to find me somewhere to live. He did not think that it would be fair for me to stay with him as his colleagues still had to live without their wives. I agreed with him.

So I went to America for three months to see my children and then I went on to stay with friends in England. Nkomo then sent for me. But they were all so busy in Zambia that there was no time for me to be with my husband. So I spent a week with the Kaundas. Then my husband took me to the German Democratic Republic, where I was provided with very good accommodation. The Germans treated me very well. But I was very lonely since I was alone. So Nkomo had a relative's child come and keep me company. The child arrived two months after my husband had left. Sometimes Zimbabwean children who were at school in the GDR visited me during the weekends.

I stayed about three years in Germany. Sometimes I lost hope of ever returning home as time went by so slowly, especially as I was alone, having no children with me. But, after a time, Nkomo arranged for the children to visit me during the holidays and that made things better.

I never knew very much about what was happening in our country, although I read the papers. Most papers were in German and communication wasn't very easy. Even if I watched television, I could not hear what was being said. But I heard rumours and knew things were tough. Sometimes my husband wrote or telephoned me. He told me how and what they were doing and of their progress. He told me that they had formed the Patriotic Front with Mugabe's party and that they were fighting together. Everything seemed to go well as the Zipras fought from the west and the Zanlas fought from the east. There seemed to be no problem at all.

After the Lancaster House conference, my husband said that they had reached an agreement that they should stop fighting and come home to hold elections. The election results were announced on the German television news. They came through slowly and I waited up through the night with some Zimbabwean children who were studying German. When we heard that ZANU had won and would rule the country, we were disappointed: although I was also very relieved that those who had won were blacks. This meant that Smith's government was out. That was really what we had been fighting for. We had been fighting to have a black government. Later, my husband told me that he was going to be the Minister of Home Affairs and he planned that I should return for independence so that I could be together with the others.

I then said farewell to the Germans. They helped me pack all my property and paid for all my fares. I returned during Independence Week and felt at home although I was looking forward to going back to Bulawayo.

Independence Day was a great day. There was great joy and I felt really honoured among others. We were treated well and taken to places we had never been to before, places that had been prohibited like Meikles Hotel and Parliament and it was a great moment to see black people in high places ruling, and it was especially pleasing for me to see my husband among those people. It was also good to meet Robert Mugabe and his wife, because I had not met them before. We all met as one people and that was wonderful.

When I returned home to Bulawayo, I found that all my things were in order and the girl whom I had left in my house was still there. I still have her now. She is a very reliable child who managed to look after everything. There was not even a spoon missing.

24 **Betty Ndlovu**

Tegwane

I AM FROM Bulilimangwe district, in Ndiweni village. I have
six children. The first child was born before I married his
father. But later, when I did marry him, he left me at his
parents' home for two years and never communicated with
me. I did not even know where he was living. So I decided
to go and live with my parents. I stayed with them for four
years and then went to look for employment. I left my child
with my parents.

I found employment and went to live in Cape Town with
my employers. My second child was born there. His father
never helped me to bring up his child, although once he
sent me a little money after I had returned home to
Bulilimangwe.

I have not been lucky with the fathers of my children.
After I had returned home from Cape Town, I went to work
as a domestic worker on a farm in the Plumtree area. There
I met a man who already had a family. I had children with
him, but he was already married and I did not want to
become a second wife. He also could not help me to raise

his children because he was unemployed for many years. I raised all my children on my own and it was a heavy load. My mother helped me because they looked after them at our home when I had a job in Bulawayo. During the sixties, I spent some years working as a domestic on the farm, and some years working in town. It suited me that way. I worked in Bulawayo from 1972 until 1981. Then I returned home to stay.

At every month-end I went to see my children. My father had died a long time before but my mother managed very well alone. She did not worry very much about the war because it affected everybody. What could she do about it? She was committed to the struggle and she just accepted what was going on.

I was mostly in Bulawayo during the years of the war. But I first heard about the liberation struggle when I was still working on the farm near Plumtree in the sixties.

One day, in the morning, after I had made the fire in the coal stove, the old white lady for whom I worked asked me whether I had attended the meeting at the council offices. I said, "How could I have gone? I was on duty." Then she asked if I had not heard that there had been some misunderstanding at the meeting. I said, I hadn't heard that and I didn't think it could be true, because people don't quarrel at meetings. Meetings are held to discuss things that need to be sorted out. It is not necessary to fight at meetings.

After our conversation, her son, Charles, came and asked me the same question.

They seemed worried because the meeting had been about the war and the struggle. It had been at the council offices, so someone like the DC must have called it to warn people. Charles said that I had told his mother that people did not like fighting and I said, "Yes, that is true." Then I had a long discussion with him which ended up in bad taste, as we were not agreeing with each other. He had heard that Sithole's people had burnt down some houses in a township in Gweru, and he said that people should not do this. He said that it showed that people liked fighting.

That was the beginning of the liberation struggle. That is, when people started talking about the war and the first time I heard about it.

Two years later, in 1972, I went to Bulawayo where I

remained throughout the war. There were no incidents that I knew of that year. But it was around that time that I really began to notice that there was a great difference between the blacks and the whites. For instance, when we took buses to the suburbs where I worked, we could never sit on the same seat with a white person. If a black person sat on a seat, then the whole section was left for blacks, the whites sat in the other section. If a black person sat at the front, then all front seats were left, and the whites moved to sit at the back. I wondered why things were like that. I heard that it was due to us blacks, because we had said that we wanted our country and that is why white people shunned us.

In 1975, when I went home I found that almost every young person had left to join the freedom fighters. People were not settled at all. The whole community was full of fear because so many children had left and the ones who left first were returning to take others. People were afraid. I thought of taking my children to live with me in town but I couldn't because it would have been inconvenient to have them in the yard where I was working. Also I wondered what would happen to me after the war if I had taken my children to town. It would be difficult to return home if I once ran away from it.

Once, long long before the war began, I went to fetch firewood and I passed a *muchekesani** tree which was big and dry. Strangely, I had this sudden thought, that if I were to dig under the tree and build a home underground, I would always be safe. I told my children this and they thought it was a very strange idea. But when the war started, they remembered my story and reminded me that we could be safe right under the *muchekesani* tree.

My employer was in the Police Reserve and in 1974 he became a full-time soldier. He often went out of town on duty. My employers helped me a lot in so far as looking after my children was concerned because they used to give me their old clothes and I would sell these to get more money. Sometimes the lady gave me food to send to my children. They were very worried when they heard that my boys had gone to join the liberation struggle. I don't think they were angry or suspicious of me; rather they sympathized

---

* *Muchekesani* tree – Monkey Bread tree/*Piliosdigma Thonningii.*

with and comforted me. The lady told me to pray and be courageous because many children had left and I was not alone.

During this time I did not return home as often as I had done before. Sometimes two months went by. It depended on the situation and what people said. Also, sometimes when you returned home, the freedom fighters would ask you not to go back to work. I thought that was unreasonable because we needed money to buy food, especially me, as I had to look after my family alone.

One weekend when I was visiting my children, I heard that there had been a contact in the area and 49 soldiers had been killed. Only one had remained alive. My children were very frightened and so was I, but I encouraged them to stay at home.

Of my three older sons, the eldest was already working in Johannesburg and the other two were living in Bulawayo. One of the two boys who was with me left to join the liberation war in September 1976. His young brother followed in November the same year.

I had suspected that they might leave because I could see that they were thinking about it. For instance, my elder son, who was a garden boy, told me that he was no longer interested in working for somebody who never appreciated what he did. I advised him that all of us had to learn to do things, just as a baby learns to eat, walk and cope with life. Then he told me that he had heard of others who had gone to fight for the country. I did not like what he was saying and that is why I encouraged him to learn to do, whatever he had to do, better. I said, if he went to fight for the country, and he got it, what would he gain? I told him that the country would not give us anything. All we had to do was work hard for ourselves, because even if we attained independence, we would still not get anything for nothing. We would still have to work for ourselves. Even if one has a lot of money but does not have the proper knowledge to know how to use it, it is useless. I told him that happiness and success come through hard work.

After that, I could not do anything and I said to myself, OK, if the children think it is worth fighting for the country, let them go. I thought about it and realized that the situation was getting worse, even in the way we were treated by our employers. We were now treated like animals, not like people. I thought that perhaps, after the war, the situation would change and people would respect one another, and everyone would be treated equally – like people. We were sometimes called 'monkeys' by our employers. I was very upset when one of my friends told me that her employer had called her 'a monkey that lives in a forest'. I hoped that after the war we would be respected. But, in my heart, I knew that fighting was not the best solution: with understanding and mutual respect one could solve problems.

The following year my oldest son came home from Johannesburg on holiday. When he arrived he asked me where his brothers were. I replied that I did not know. I said they had gone in search of the world and we could therefore say they were lost. He was very disappointed and said, "Do you mean both of them have gone?" I said, "Yes!" He was not satisfied by my reply. He was worried and did not think it was right that he should remain home when his brothers had gone to fight. Since he was the oldest, he felt that it was his responsibility to protect his family, to fight for the rights of the young ones and himself. I understood this because during the discussion, he shook his head and looked very worried. I could see that he felt very depressed and ashamed of himself, as his younger brothers had gone to the war.

That was the last time I saw him. After his holiday he was supposed to return to his work in Johannesburg but I suppose that, instead, he went to join the freedom fighters. I did not hear from him again until after the war.

Several weeks after this, his aunt visited me at my workplace in the suburbs and brought me the bad news that one of my small boys was missing from home. He had been absent for two weeks. I said, "Oh! does it mean that all my children are going to end up living in forests like animals? What can it mean when even a small boy of seven disappears?" She told me not to worry so much, this was something that was happening throughout the country. She said I should pray and trust in the Lord because these things were meant to happen and there was nothing one could do about it.

I told my employer everything I'd heard about my children and then went home. I found that my small boy had returned. What had happened was this. I had sent a parcel of food to my children by bus, after writing a letter to tell them to wait for the parcel at the bus stop. My small boy was the one who was sent to fetch it. But immediately after leaving the parcel in the house, he changed his clothes and went out with friends. He must have talked to them at the bus stop. They told my mother that they were going to a football match. This wasn't the truth because they wanted to go and join the freedom fighters. My son was in the company of bigger boys but when they arrived at a farm where they were to spend the night, the older boys dodged the smaller ones and left them behind. So, the next day, the young ones found themselves on their own and did not know where to go. Then a man who worked on the farm recognized my son and told his employer about the boys. He phoned Plumtree police who collected my son and took him home.

The next day the policeman came to my home and asked my son whether he was going to school, and he said he was. Then they asked about me and he told them what he knew. Then they asked where he had been going and he told them that he and his friends had been going to a football match, but that they got lost and found themselves in the forest. So the boers took him to the Plumtree police station. He spent the day there and they questioned him further. However he did not have to spend the night in a cell because one of the policemen said that he was much too young to do so, and he took him to his own home. Then the police rounded up all the young boys. I do not know what exactly happened, but they were probably beaten.

I was really very troubled by these incidents but there was nothing I could do. I found comfort in going to church. I told myself that whatever happened, happened, and there was nothing I could do to stop it. It was happening to many others throughout the country.

On another occasion I returned home because my daughter had written me a letter saying that certain people wanted to see me. I was very annoyed and said some bad words when I received the letter. But I was also worried because I knew that sometimes the freedom fighters called employed people back to their homes, and then told them they should not return to work.

On the following Friday, I went home. On Saturday there was a party at my neighbours' so I spent the day there. I returned when it was beginning to get dark. There was a dog inside my house. I said, "Get out! *Futseki!"** and then, I remembered the rumours that I had heard about the *vakomana*, so I said to myself, "Oh! heavens, people say that the boys can change their appearances," and I began to worry that I could have told a person, in the form of a dog, to get out. But the dog ran out of the house and away across the yard.

Then I lit a candle and tried not to worry. At that moment there was a knock at the door. I was very frightened but then I cooled myself down and answered the knock with a candle in my hand. Outside the house, I saw a man wearing jeans who was old enough to have left a family at home. He said I should not come out with a light in my hand. I was bothered by this, but I put the candle back in the house and went outside again.

After we had exchanged greetings, he told me that I had brought the bad weather – it was chilly. I was hurt by his comment and I wanted to ask him where he thought I could have brought the cold from, but I decided to remain calm. So I told him that it was usually cold at this time of year, and that the weather would warm up soon.

I invited him into the house, as it really was cold outside. He asked me whether it was safe to do so and I said it was. He went inside and put his rifle down. I felt really pained by his familiarity, particularly as I had already found some man's clothes in my house, and this had puzzled me.

He then asked me when I had arrived home, how the boers were and what they were saying. I said that they had nothing to say because they were living comfortably in their houses in town. Then he asked me what I thought of him. I told him that I could not understand what he was doing in my home, since I knew the freedom fighters lived in the forests and kopjes. "What kind of war is it," I said, "that is being fought in the homes of civilians?"

Then he asked me whether I thought the *vakomana* were late in fulfilling their plan to attack Bulawayo. I said that was so, because the freedom fighters had said that, as soon as they re-entered the country, they would immediately destroy the white men in the city.

He did not like my reply and said he thought I must be a sell-out. I said that if this were so, I would be the first

* *Futseki* – local adaptation of the Afrikaans' expletive, *voetsak*, meaning Push off!

one to die because, if I sold him out, I would have to show the soldiers the way. The leader, I said, is always the first one shot. Moreover, I said, afterwards the freedom fighter would run away (as they usually do) but I and my household would perish. "Is that so, old lady?" he replied, and I said "Yes." I was very angry and troubled and did not want to talk with him.

Then he assured me that everything would be all right and I said, "What will make everything right?" He replied, "When one goes to plough the fields, you first clear the area before ploughing. Then, after removing all the stumps, and buying seeds and tools, you plough." I said, "If that is so, it has taken you a long time."

I wanted to know what kind of preparation he could be referring to. If the soldiers came and there was open fighting, it would be likely that I and my children would die and my home would be destroyed. A freedom fighter could always use his tricks to run away.

Then I went out to the kitchen and put a kettle on the fire. I had not told my children what was happening but they asked me. I said that their 'brother' was in the other house. They all went inside and I heard them laughing and enjoying themselves, but I was worried and annoyed.

After I had brewed tea, I called my daughter and asked whether he ate bread with jam. She said that he did – the only thing he never ate was sadza. I was surprised. My daughter said that he had been told not to eat sadza, or he would get sick. The children took the tea and served him. I sat on my own in the kitchen, asking myself questions: could this be the kind of war that would free us, or did it mean my end . . . and the end of my children and household? After he had finished his tea, I went over and we began our discussion again. He said that I shouldn't be surprised that the boys hadn't destroyed Bulawayo, as there were so many innocent people in the city, including young children. We were fighting a war, he said, but such an action would be unreasonable. I agreed with him.

A little while later, we heard shooting in the Dombodema area. He sent the small boys to watch and listen from outside. It was about eleven o'clock, so I said I was going to bed. I went to sleep with my children in one room and he slept in another. During the night I dreamt that yet another freedom fighter had settled in my home.

The following morning I went to see my sister-in-law because there had been a death in her family. When I returned, I found that there was already yet another comrade in my house. He was holding his rifle and playing with it as if it were a guitar. He seemed to be enjoying himself. I felt very annoyed. When I went to speak to him, he said exactly what the other one had said, that I could be a sell-out. I told him that if he thought so, then he must be one too.

He then told me that when I went back to town, I should buy him some Sting jeans. I told him I would not do so, because I was the father and mother of my children and, if anything happened to me, or if I was imprisoned, there would be no one to take care of them. But he said that women were able to make it through road-blocks because they were not thoroughly searched. So I told him that it was *me* who was doing the travelling, and I knew exactly what happened, and I did not want to take the risk!

He then said that I should bring them beads. So I asked whether they were spirit mediums and I said that if they were, they should get their own beads. I said just what I thought: that they were supposed to be fighting for our liberation but it seemed they were now after many other things.

Then a bit later, he enquired whether I had seen his comrades and I told him that I was not the keeper of his friends and that I would not look for them because they already knew one another. Then he said, "OK, old lady, we shall see you," and he went outside.

I sat down and thought deeply and saw that what was happening at home was unbearable. The comrades were living in people's homes – and there was no man in my home – and our children were having a hard time. I felt it was the end of me and my home. As I sat, busy thinking and worrying, my daughter said I should go outside and see what was happening. I went out. The whole yard was full of people. I did not know exactly what was going to happen next. Some of the boys came to greet me; some just held their big guns in their hands. They said they wanted to teach my little boy Dumisile how to fight.

I stood and wondered. It was Sunday and I was preparing to go back to work. They went into my house and joked with my children. So I told them that I was leaving. They all answered, "OK, old lady, we shall meet again." I just could not believe what was happening. (Later my daughter married one of the freedom fighters, but after she had had a baby, the marriage ended.)

I went back to work. It was not long before the cease-fire. I changed and became very miserable. I told myself that whatever child came back from war, I did not care whose it was, I would talk to him so as to feel that I had talked to my children. I told myself that I would take any child from the war as my own child.

It seemed as if I was lost, but I comforted myself by saying that if only one of my children returned, it would be enough. It is obvious that not everyone comes back alive from war. I just wished for one of my own sons to return.

Then during the cease-fire period, I went to church in Mzilikazi. When I returned, I found a letter from my son Innocent. I told my employer that I had received a letter from one of 'my guerillas' and he said, "Do you mean a terrorist?" and he asked me again who had written the letter. I told him, Innocent, my second son. My employer was very startled and asked me what I wanted to do. I told him that I wanted to go and see Innocent the following weekend at St Paul's. He agreed.

So I went to find him but he was not there and one of the comrades told me that Innocent had gone to Zambezi, so I spent the night there and then returned home. I left my telephone number and a parcel for him with a friend, but I was disappointed. Then, just a few days later, my employer called me to talk to someone on the telephone who sounded as though they were calling from very far away. It was Innocent. I was very excited and I asked if he was well and he said he was and he thanked me for the parcel I had left him. I asked him to come and see me but he said he couldn't as he was very busy and he asked for some money. I agreed to go to St Paul's again and I did. When I saw him he moved very slowly towards me, perhaps he'd been crying, but I was very excited and very courageous. We greeted each other. I even saw my sister's son there on that day. We talked for a while and then we parted.

Then, later in the year, I received a letter from my older son who was at a camp in Gwaai. He said he was going to attend a course in Gweru and so it would not be possible for me to visit him. A while later he visited me at my workplace. I was very pleased to see that he was alive and well.

The third one remained silent for a long time. I finally saw him at the end of that year. All this while I had been very courageous. I comforted myself by saying that I had seen two of my children, so I knew that they were still alive, but I wondered what could have befallen my third son. I knew that in a war it always happened that some survived and some died. But I cried the day I saw him.

When all my children had returned, they told me that I should leave my employment to go and rest at home. But I said that I wouldn't be ready to do that until all my children had settled and had property; only then could I rest. But before I was ready to go home, I had a misunderstanding with my employer. So I left my employment in October 1981.

What happened was that one day she had guests who stayed until it was quite late. Her son was hungry and so I began to prepare supper which was what I normally did, whenever she had visitors. But my employer was very annoyed and started shouting at me. She said that I had started cooking without her permission, because we were now independent, because we were free and planning to send all whites away. She said that she did not care; she would do as she pleased and go where she wanted. I was very annoyed by the way that she spoke to me. It was as if she was speaking to a small child. So, I told her so. I said that I was old enough to be her mother, but that as she was my employer, we were like mothers to each other. I said, at the very least, we should respect each other since I had worked for her faithfully for a long time and had taken care of her child since he was born. I reminded her that sometimes I had taken care of her child all through the night. Those were dangerous days and I had spent sleepless hours thinking where I would hide the baby, or what I would do, if something happened. I told her that, after all that, I was offended that she should talk to me like a small girl. Then she banged through all the doors in the house from the kitchen to her bedroom. I stood stock still in amazement.

Then I left, without even washing the dishes. As far as I was concerned, I had left their employment, even though her husband was more reasonable. I knew he did not want me to leave and he thought things could be solved without fighting.

When I returned home to Bulilimangwe, I didn't have any problems with my neighbours because I had been co-operative in every respect. I contributed towards everything they did. If they had wanted money, I posted it to them. The only problem I had was during the dissident menace. The man I was living with had trouble. His home was destroyed and I had to look after him. People were not very happy about this and they wished that my home would be burnt down too. I was very worried and prayed that I had not done anything wrong and I needed to be protected. Many things happened but I was lucky nothing terrible happened to my home. That man's home is back to normal again now because I protected him by providing him with shelter which was dangerous. But he is doing nothing for me. It's his responsibility that he does not seem to appreciate what I did, but I did my part and that was enough.

Now that we are free, I, personally, am not very happy. My children cannot find employment. Indeed, many children who went to fight – not only my own – cannot find work and it is painful. Sometimes I think it is even worse than the period when the children were fighting. When they were fighting and in the bush, eating wild animals and wild fruits, it seems they were better off. One of my sons is in Plumtree. He just finds any kind of work and all he can get in this way are dirty jobs. This is really very painful. The children are supposed to be free but the situation is not good. I feel betrayed because many children who fought for this country have nothing to do, instead they have turned to stealing and doing all sorts of bad things. Unless I stay at home, I know very well that I will find my things have disappeared, because there are boys who just go about taking other people's things. Many of our children are now in jail for theft. They steal clothes, radios and money from our homes. Parents are very worried. But now groups have been formed who are trying to keep these youth occupied.

I do appreciate my own children because although they are not employed, they are patient and they will do things like cutting firewood or any small job to earn a little money. Also my second son has married and so I am responsible for his family. I have to provide food, soap and all the necessities and there is no freedom at all. But I know things do not always happen as one expects or hopes they will. Things sometimes do turn sour but maybe, in time, things will change and my children will get employment and be able to look after themselves. They were very mature when they returned from the war.

25 Erica Ziumbwa

Madziwa, Mount Darwin

M Y NAME is Erica Ziumbwa. I was born in the Mutoko
district but my parents left for the Murewa area when
I was still a small child. My parents had eight children. I
was the last born. I went to school until I had finished grade
five, but then my father could not afford the fees any longer
and I left. I liked going to school and I wanted to be educated
but there wasn't anything I could do because there was no
money. I tried to help myself by working but I did not earn
enough money to pay my school fees. Soon afterwards all
my sisters and brothers had to leave school because my
father died.

My whole family suffered because we had no one to look
after us. My uncle, who was supposed to assume responsibility for us, could not afford to do so as he had his own
family. But, as you know, some people cannot look after
someone else's child as they would their own. Usually there
is a difference between the way you treat your own children
and the way you treat others. That is another reason why
we had nothing during those years and why my sister

251

married early. We could not make ends meet. We had nothing, no clothes, no blankets. Sometimes we spent the night around the fire without any blankets at all. I went to work for people in their fields and they paid me. I cultivated maize, worked in their gardens and did whatever needed doing but I never got enough money to help myself. I did this for three years and then I went to stay with my sister who was living in Harare with her husband.

During that time I could afford to eat better food, have better clothes and be someone. If I did not have a jersey and I was cold I could wear my sister's and that made a great difference. I was lucky because those of my family who had to remain at home still suffered in the same way. They had nothing, no food, no clothes, none of the necessities of life except for the roof over their heads. I cannot express the suffering I experienced during those years. Even now, when I think of those times, I feel very bad.

I spent two years with my sister and then I met this husband of mine and we married. I married earlier than I wanted or intended to but, because my life was not so good, I decided to get married early. Over the years I have had nine children and each one of them was a difficult birth. In spite of this, I went on having children because I hoped that one of them would look after me when I am old. The doctors often advised me not to have any more children but I was determined to do so because I did not want to live through the experiences of my childhood again. I felt I might deprive myself of the one child who would be kind and responsible and look after me.

In a way, I feel let down because the child who went to join the struggle, and died, is the one whom I thought would be patient enough to look after me in my old age. He was very kind and responsible. I still feel deprived but I cannot do anything about it. It is a source of great unhappiness.

My husband was a gardener in Harare and that is where we lived for some time and where I had my first seven children. During those years my life was even better than it was when I lived with my sister, because I was on my own and I did what I could to help myself. I sold vegetables and sometimes other small things which I had sewn. In this way I managed to get some money to help myself and my children, so I was not a burden to my husband as I helped him support the family.

It was different when we came to live here. We do grow enough food if there is rain and if we have fertilizer, and, even in bad years, we always get something from the fields. But our only source of money or food comes from working hard in the fields. In Harare I could make some money almost every day, although most people earned very little and did not always have enough to look after their families properly.

When we returned to my husband's home, my neighbours looked happy and were helpful. But, after about a year, we went to Madziwa Mine near Shamva because there were misunderstandings in the family and so my husband and I left. The war started when we were living there and after about three years, we were moved from the mine to Pfungwe which is where we stayed until after the war.

What happened was that my uncle, who lived in the Pfungwe district, died. So we went to pay our condolences. My husband took leave in order to come with me. But on the way we met the comrades at several points. Each time they asked where we were going and we told them that we were going to pay our condolences to our relatives following the death of an uncle. The comrades were very informed about everyone and every place. So, when we arrived in Pfungwe, we had to register with the chairman of the area because that was the procedure: anyone from elsewhere was registered as a visitor. The chairman also told us that we should not return because the comrades were planning to destroy the mine. A comrade had died in the Madziwa area and they wanted to retaliate in this way. The comrades in that area confirmed that we were not to go back to the mine until after the war. But my husband wanted to return because we had left our children there. So one night he left, intending to walk to a place where he could get transport to the mine. But he met the comrades who took him to their base and asked him where he was going. Then there was a contact between the comrades and the soldiers, which was very rough and he was lucky to survive. A lot of people were killed. Afterwards my husband was sent back to Pfungwe by the comrades.

We had left our children with my eldest son who was already working and I think it was about three months before they joined us. My sister in Mutoko went to collect them but on her way back she was beaten by the soldiers.

They asked where she was going and how she had managed to leave the mine with the children. She had to make up a story: she said that her family were no longer employed at the mine and so she was taking her children home. It was a long, difficult journey for her because at almost every road-block she was harassed by the soldiers. But, in the end, she made it.

It was just before we left the mine that my son joined the struggle. He went wherever he went and we have never seen him again. It was a time when no one could tell anyone what was on their mind. Also he probably knew that if he had told me what he wanted to do, I would never have agreed to it. It was his own decision to go and fight because he recognized the problems. Perhaps he thought we were not getting enough or what he expected his family to have. There were so many problems then because those were days of hardship. The war was one of the hardships. Everyone was involved, whether you liked it or not. The youth had no rest day and night. They were constantly on patrol to check on the enemy and inform the comrades. Parents sometimes didn't know where their children were for days on end.

The mine employers were very strict and this resulted in many of the youth joining the struggle. Employees were often beaten and their pay was very low. It was even worse during the war because the whites were very rough with everyone. When we went to fetch firewood a white would always question us about where we had gone, who we had met, and so on and they beat us if they felt like it.

One Saturday I noticed that my son had not spent any time at home. At first I thought that he might have gone to a church service because he was a member of the Ayoja church. So I asked his brothers and friends where he was but they did not tell me. When, by Monday, he had still not returned, I asked some of his room-mates at the mine if they had seen him. They told me that he had left with the comrades. I was very hurt and very sad. I could not believe that he had gone. I had always had high hopes of him. I was depending on him to look after me in my old age.

I cried a great deal and mourned his departure. I could not understand what had happened to me. I think I spent a whole month crying and worrying about him. Then, after about a month, the comrades came to a nearby area and my children went to the base with the rest of the youth and they met their brother. He explained what he was doing and he asked for a shirt. I sent one for him, but I do not know whether he got it or not. I wished I could see him or hear news of how he was, but I never saw him again.

Children could not tell parents that they were going to join the struggle. Most of them just left. Often parents were not aware of what their children did. I suppose there were comrades at the mine and they took children to rallies. It was very distressing but we could not do anything about it because it was war. Our children spent nights in the bush and it was really hard for a parent not to know where your child was while such fighting was going on.

At the mine we cooked food for the comrades and the youth carried it to their base, but I never saw them. We contributed cash and bought chickens for them and the youth gave them all these things. We did all this secretly, because if we had been found out, that would have been that.

The mine security was very tight. We were not allowed to go outside the mine boundary and there was a fence around it. That is why it was only the children who saw the comrades: they were able to sneak out.

They had to be very careful so as not to be caught by the security guards. If it was ever discovered that a child had spent the night at a rally, they were beaten hard.

When I met the comrades at Pfungwe I realized that they were just like our own children and they suffered and lived in the bush. Comrades' lives were in the hands of women. At Madziwa we cooked for them and it was the same at Pfungwe. Women had to find food for the comrades. They ate whatever you provided. If there was no mealie-meal, the women prepared sadza from millet or whatever else was available. When there was a drought, there was no food. If there was nothing, everyone, including the comrades, spent the night without food.

But, if we had money, we used to go to Uzumba where we bought or worked for food. There was no transport so we walked and we carried back whatever we had earned on our heads. It was tough but we had to do it.

Uzumba is in the reserves* but people in the area had

---

* Reserves – 'Native reserves': the definition of land allocated to blacks in the Land Apportionment Act of 1930.

food in their fields and so we could work for it. The soldiers would never have allowed us to do this, so we always went at night and by dawn we were there. We had to be careful not to fall into the soldiers' hands. If we heard that they were around, we hid ourselves. Sometimes when you arrived at a home it would be deserted because the family had run away from the soldiers. Some people did not want anyone to work for food but mostly people in the area sympathized with us because they knew there was no food at Pfungwe. You could not go to Uzumba and back in a day: it was far away by foot. So husbands and wives took it in turns. We wanted food and the comrades had to have food in order to carry on fighting. I cannot properly express how hard it was sometimes. It reminded me of my childhood and the period following the death of my parents. I felt I was born to suffer. I had suffered as a child and it seemed to be the same thing all over again.

We had only the few clothes and the few blankets that we had brought with us, thinking that we would only be at Pfungwe for a few days. Moreover, when we arrived at my uncle's home, they had had all their property burnt down, so they also had nothing. Those were hard times. People shared what little they had. We never even had blankets; we slept without anything to cover us.

My uncle was a village headman and the soldiers were told by a sell-out that he was harbouring comrades. So they burnt down his home. My aunt was beaten because the soldiers said she had been feeding comrades. It happened because people sold out on each other during the war. What was said was often not the truth. Fortunately, in this case, one of the soldier's knew my uncle's family and he persuaded the other soldiers not to kill him. So they just burnt down his home and spared his life. Usually the soldiers killed people who harboured the comrades, even if you were caught with some soap or a tin of maize, you could be killed because the soldiers knew the comrades depended on the villagers.

When the comrades came into the area they always asked where the headman lived and then they sent *mujibas* to tell him that they were in the area. This meant they wanted food. The headman then told the people and food was prepared. My uncle was always the first to know about the comrades and, because of his position, the soldiers also asked him for information. Of course, if the comrades heard of sell-outs they beat and sometimes killed them. I don't know whether the person who informed on my uncle was paid by the soldiers. I don't think so, but afterwards he ran away to Harare.

We went to attend rallies at night and returned home as dawn was breaking. Sometimes, before we had eaten anything, the soldiers arrived and the shooting began. We would all run away and everyone would seek their own safe place. We hid ourselves and counted each minute, each hour and each day that we survived. People were dying. It was different from the situation at the mine: at Pfungwe we lived with the comrades.

Sometimes some of the *mujibas* gave me news of my son. During the cease-fire I heard that he was in Dendera camp. So my daughter went to look for him but she was told that he was very busy treating injured comrades and so she never saw him. After the cease-fire we heard that he had gone to Harare and had not returned to his assembly point. It was all rather confused. I cannot really explain it, but I was worried.

Then I heard that the comrades would be returning to their homes for a visit before they were assigned to some duty or other by the government. I was excited at the thought of seeing my son. I bought a blanket for him so that he would have a new blanket after so many nights without one at all. I was going to use the blanket as a kind of 'red carpet' for his home-coming: I wanted him to walk on the blanket into the house. I kept that blanket for a long time, hoping that he would one day return home. When I saw comrades walking in the direction of my home, I hoped he was among them. I attended all the meetings with the comrades – we used to have get-togethers after the war – but I never once saw him.

Then I heard that some injured and disabled comrades were in camps. So I visited all of the camps, including Ruwa*, but I did not find him. I even consulted spirit mediums but I heard nothing of his whereabouts.

A long time afterwards, my daughter, who was going to school at the mine, started behaving as if she was mad. The headmaster took her home to my son and explained

---

* Ruwa – a small town near Harare where a school for people disabled during the war was established after independence.

how she was behaving. She then started to shout and told people not to touch her. Then a voice coming out of her identified itself as her brother who had died during the war and he explained what had happened. He said that he and his nineteen friends had left Dendera camp on their way home, when they were washed away by the Mazowe river as they tried to cross it. They were washed away and ended up in the Zambezi river. He said that if we had time we should go and collect his remains from the place where he was washed ashore. That is when we knew that my son had died. That is what happened to my son and I am still very disturbed about it.

But we did as he said. We appeased his spirits. We bought and killed a goat, brewed beer, killed an ox and called a n'anga. People spent the night drinking and dancing and we dug a grave for my son and did as we were instructed by him, and we had the advice of the n'anga. After that my daughter started eating. She had stopped eating sadza from the time her brother entered into her. Now she is fine, although sometimes she acts as though she was not quite normal, but she does not behave as she did before her brother spoke through her.

This is an experience which I do not like to talk about because it distresses me so much. What makes it worse is that our leaders do not even acknowledge the death of our children. When they have come here, they have never once said 'Thank you' to us, the parents of the children who died for the country. We had gone everywhere looking for our children. The least they could have done is tell those parents whose children died in the war that they are sorry. That was all the consolation we needed. Just an acknowledgement from the leaders that our children had died.

Those comrades who returned with their lives have had some recompense or reward. The parents have their children and that, in itself, is some kind of reward. Even if the child is unemployed or hasn't received any money, at least the parents have their children and they can help their parents in some way in the fields or at home. Those of us who lost our children have not received anything. It is really very painful. Our children bought us the country with their lives. Now the government does not even acknowledge that we exist. If this war was to start again, I would prefer to be killed.

After the war we decided to come and settle at home because it is better for people of our age, and with the size of my family, to have their own home. So we came to build one for ourselves and started ploughing our fields. If and when we work hard in our fields we do get enough food to eat and sell. But I do not know if ever I will have rest and a peaceful life before I die as I am still so unsettled by the death of my son.

26 Dainah Girori

Madziwa, Mount Darwin

I WAS the eldest of eight children and I was a weakling. People thought that I would never grow up and become a woman as I was always sick. I had a problem with my heart but my parents were still alive and they had no other problems. All my brothers went to school but I could not continue with my education because of my health. I was always being taken from place to place in an attempt to find a cure, so I was the only one in our family who received no education.

After a long time I got better and I went to live with my parents for the first time. I had been living with relatives as I was not supposed to live at home until I was well. By then I had passed school-going age and shortly after I returned home, I married. I have ten children and one of them went out to join the struggle.

Before the war life was not too bad. I had problems, of course, but just ordinary family problems. Our lives only really became very difficult once the war had started and we had been moved to the keep. We had nothing to feed our children on. I was in the keep with all my children. Our fields lay outside the area of the keep, cattle ate all our crops and we did not get much from our fields. Some days we went without food.

You see, soldiers would come by asking where the guerillas were. We could not say where they were: we would just point in any direction as long as it was not the right direction. Then the guerillas would come and ask where the soldiers were. We were always caught in between, not knowing what to do or say. That is why we were put in the keeps: the soldiers thought that we harboured guerillas and because the guerillas came and asked for food and killed sell-outs. Life was better before we were put in keeps because we got enough food from our fields but in the keeps there was never enough food.

We had heard about the war before the comrades came into our area. We had heard that they were very troublesome. We wondered what people meant when they said that the comrades were troublesome. We had heard about them for quite a long time before they actually arrived in our area and we were anxious to see these people.

They came and knocked at the door at night. We woke up and they said they wanted food. When they came and asked for food we had to get up and start preparing it for them. We could not ask many questions or refuse to do what they wanted. Usually they went to the headman of the village and as they did not have time to explain anything: they would just say that they were guerillas and they wanted sadza.

All the people from Madziwa district were put into keeps but we were mixed together from different villages. We carried our belongings and our food on our heads as there were no trucks. If you had many things you went back and forth as often as was necessary. We spent the whole day moving our property from our home into the keep. Everyone in the family helped, including my husband. He carried the heavier things. In the keep we built our own huts. Each headman was supposed to have all his people together around him and all the huts were very close together. Had there been a fire all the huts would have burnt down. If you had a large family you could build four huts: a kitchen, a girls' room, a boys' room, and the main bedroom.

We left our homes as they stood. We did not destroy them although later on the security forces instructed us to remove the roofs on all the houses because they thought the comrades might hide in them. After that some of the houses fell down because of rains.

There was a big fence around the keep and there was a gate through which we all had to go. Each time we went through it we were searched by the security guards. They said that they wanted to make sure that when we came into the keep we did not bring any harmful things.They searched everyone, regardless of age. We were told to jump up and down so that if we were carrying anything for the guerillas they would fall out. If ever you were found carrying food you were thoroughly beaten.

We were supposed to be in the keep by four o'clock in the afternoon so if you were late you ran as fast as you could in order not to be shut out, because once that happened it could cost you your life. We were supposed to go out at six in the morning. The children went to a school outside the keep. They came and went every day, but both the school children and the teachers stayed in the keep. Three of my children went to school in this way.

People were beaten in the keeps, but no huts were burnt except those when children caused a fire. In our keep what happened was that, if there was a fire, the security forces came to put the fire out. If your huts got burnt, all your property was burnt and there was nothing to help you. You just had to suffer.

People in other keeps suffered more than we did. What happened was that the comrades would accuse the people of supporting the security forces and then sometimes they cut through the fence and entered the keep. When this happened people ran away. Some injured themselves because they fell into pits and some were cut by wire; some came to hide in our keep and sometimes all their houses in their keep were burnt down. When the comrades arrived, the security forces always hid themselves.

Once the comrades shot at our keep from outside. The soldiers returned fire but, instead of hitting their target, they killed a woman who was in her hut. Our huts were only made of poles and mud so they were not very strong and bullets could easily pierce them. The woman had a child who witnessed her mother's death and she later explained how her mother had been shot at by a soldier's bullet. The child blamed herself terribly because she had woken her mother up when the shooting started. The woman had then tried to keep the child lying flat but as soon she raised her own head she was shot dead.

On this occasion the comrades were angry with the security forces and they hoped that when they opened fire, the security forces would come out and pursue them. They did not intend to shoot into the keep because they knew people would be killed. But the soldiers did not follow them because they were afraid. They shot from inside and that is why the woman was killed.

When the war got really hot in our area, most children ran away from their homes. Some children went to look for work on the farms and some went to stay in Harare with friends and relatives. Children ran away because the soldiers harassed them. All my older children had left.

My son, my fifth born who joined the struggle, was interested in reading and he was going to school and had reached grade seven. He was at home most of the time and so I was surprised when he did not return home to eat the evening meal. I asked where he was but everyone said they didn't know. I began to worry because he was not someone who was a latecomer. When we went to bed he had still not come home. The following morning I went out to look for him in case he had been locked out, but I could not find him. I went to the fields but he was not there. I returned to my home and could not do anything. I could not even cook for the rest of the children because I was so worried and absent-minded. I could not believe that my son had gone and that I might not see him again. I hoped that perhaps he had gone to look for a job in town and that I might just see again.

For a long time I could not eat I was so worried. My friend often came to talk to me and keep me company. She persuaded me to eat and tried to comfort me. When she was there, I tried to act normally but once she'd gone I immediately began to cry. After some time my children also tried to persuade me to eat. I told them that I was eating again, but actually I could not eat. When my children noticed this, they wouldn't eat either. My husband often had to force me to do so. I felt that dying would be preferable to never seeing my child again. I knew that anything could have happened to my son – he could have been killed by the soldiers because they beat and killed people when they did not get the answers they wanted.

I think he decided to go because the security forces were giving the boys such a hard time. Sometimes our children said that they would rather join the struggle than suffer the constant harassment.

Each time I heard what was going on in other areas, I worried that my son might have died. If I heard that so many people, or so many comrades, had been killed, I thought my son was among them. Worry changed me: I lost weight and my skin became chapped and dry. My friend and my family comforted me as best they could, but we had to be so careful because, had the security forces got to know that my son had left, we would have been in hot soup. If ever the soldiers were aware that a child had left, the family suffered. The soldiers told the parents to bring children back, as if they were the ones who had sent them, but mostly parents never knew where their children had gone.

As a man, my husband was strong, and he talked to me kindly, persuading me to eat and saying nice things to me. He also asked his relatives or acquaintances to come and keep me company and persuaded me to relax, but I could see that he was very worried.

After my son had gone, my son-in-law was informed by the comrades who had accompanied him that when they had left him, he was well. So I heard that he had arrived safely and was receiving training, but I worried about him until the war was over. At cease-fire the comrades came into the keep. They were allowed to because the fighting had ended. Everyone was excited, so I too went to see them. I looked and looked, but my son was not among that group. Then I heard that some comrades were in the rest camp so I went to look for him there, but I didn't find him. I checked almost all the places where the comrades had gathered, but I never found my son. Some people said that some comrades had remained in the countries from which they had been operating, so I wondered if he was one of them.

I was in suspense all the time. There was a period when guerillas were being moved from the assembly points and I would go and spend the whole day at the township, so that I could see every truck that went by. I looked closely at each of them, making sure that my son was not on one. Sometimes I thought that perhaps he no longer loved me and I wondered how I had wronged him enough for him to desert me.

When the whole cease-fire exercise was over, I remained in suspense for a long time wondering what could have happened. Then, much later, my son entered into his cousin and talked through her. She had begun to run away from her home and towards ours, but people used to hold her back, thinking that perhaps she was going mad. Then, on one occasion, they could not restrain her because she had become very powerful. She ran to my home. When she arrived she cried a great deal and started to explain the circumstances of my son's death. It was my son who was speaking through her. He told us that he had died in the war at Cabora Bassa*. He said that he had been shot in the leg, could not move and had no help. He managed to crawl and hide himself in a cave, hoping that he might somehow find help, but unfortunately no one came to his aid. If someone had found him, maybe he would still be alive, even if crippled. But he died of hunger in the cave. He said that he wanted us to come and take him, and if we did not, then the girl, his cousin, would also die.

We went and told the authorities about this and we were driven in a government truck to Cabora Bassa with male and female soldiers. It is a long way from here and we had to spend a night on the way at a police station, although his cousin tried to persuade us to go on. She did not want us to stop for the night. We arrived there in the afternoon of the following day. But it was raining heavily, the rivers were overflowing. We went to the home of some elders who knew my son because he had lived in that area for some time and my son had told us where to go. We told them what we had come for. The elders said that the dead boy should have revealed himself to us during the dry season when it would have been easy to fetch him from the little hill where his remains lay, but as it was raining heavily, the hill which he had talked about was surrounded by water which had overflowed from the dam. They said that it was

---

* Cabora Bassa – dam built on the Zambezi river in Mozambique which, at its southernmost point, reaches Zimbabwe's northern border.

impossible to go and everyone who tried would be killed by an *njuzu**.

The elders talked to my son and explained everything that we had done and they told him to rest where he was because there was no way we could fetch him. He listened and complied with what was said, then he told us that we should go and appease his spirit at home. So we returned home and brewed beer, killed an animal, and spent the night drinking and dancing. The following morning we buried him and had a feast. That is when he rested and let the girl alone. He said he was leaving her, because we had done as he had asked and he was going to rest. So he left and the girl is well and has not had that experience again.

By then we had left the keep. After the war we were told to go and rebuild our homes and that we could take our time. Each family did this and, as and when the building was completed, they moved back to their homes. When we moved back to our villages, we did not have to return to the same place as before: we could build a home wherever we chose; so we moved and we are no longer living where we were before.

Our lives returned to normal, except for the painful experience around the loss of my child. It's very difficult, indeed impossible to forget one's loved ones who have died. Even if I enjoy life and have all I would wish for, I still miss my son and that is the sad thing. It is better when one has seen your loved ones die and have buried them. You can comfort yourself in the knowledge that the dead are at rest. But with my son it is different, because I do not really even know where he is.

It is good that we achieved our independence and people are happy and free, but it is very difficult for those of us who had children who died in the war to relax and enjoy our freedom. After independence everyone else is happy but we who had children who died, never got a word of appreciation. It pains me because I suffered to bring up my child, feeding him, bathing him, washing for him, and looking after him alone as everyone else does, but now my child has died in the cause of everyone else and no one knows that. My son died and no one appreciates that he lost his life in the struggle, or at least no one has told me

* *Njuzu* – water spirit.

that they appreciate us, the parents of those children, and no one has paid their respects to them.

It is clear that mothers fought the most as they brought up the children who fired guns, and they got their food, again from the mothers. Women did a great deal. Without them the children would have died of hunger, but the children had been given some supernatural power. But women helped them to win the struggle for liberation.

27   Elsi Chingindi

Zowa

I WAS BORN in Makanga, in Chiweshe district. My father
was a driver in town. My mother worked in the fields at
home. There were seven girls and five boys in the family.
I never went to school because our parents did not believe
that girls should go, but a few of my brothers had some
schooling. I stayed at home and looked after the cattle. We
earned a little money for clothes and other things from
selling groundnuts in Chinhoyi.

I met my husband in Nyamatsanga. To be honest, I don't
know where he originally comes from, but when we went
to Nyamatsanga, the Chingindis were already there. My
husband was employed in Harare. After I had married, I
stayed at our home while he worked in town. Later, when
he left his employment, we both lived on Jim's farm where
he was employed as a farm labourer. Then we left that farm
and went to live in Chirau reserve. After that we moved to
the Zowa farming area.

We left the reserves because we were so poor. We could
not produce enough on the land we had. The first thing we

had to do when we arrived in Zowa was to clear the land for ploughing. My husband and I had to do this alone. Our children – we had ten by then – were small and they could not help us. In addition, I did all the housework.

It was very hard work. We cut down trees, removed the stumps, ploughed and cultivated. We used our cattle and ploughs. When we ploughed I walked in front leading the cattle while my husband held the plough. I dug contour ridges. It was the most difficult task: the women did it on their own. But our hard work was worth it because we grew more crops and managed to look after our family better. When our children were older, they were also able to help us.

All my children went to school. My husband provided the money for this. He sold his cattle and some crops to find money for their schooling. We lived like this in Zowa for a long time.

Then, one day, when Everest, my eldest son (who was by then 21 years old), was helping us in the fields, he met the comrades. They came and told him that they were fighting a war, fighting to free our country. My son brought them home and took them to his room. We then went to greet them and they introduced themselves as guerillas, though to us they were just seven boys who were wearing jeans and carried guns. We were afraid of the guns. They told us not to be afraid because they were our children, fighting for our country and they asked for food. They said they had come from Zambia and that they were members of ZANU. Some of them were old, but several of them looked very young. My husband and Everest sat and talked with them, but I did not.

They told us to keep their visit a secret and not to tell anyone anything about them. We cooked for them and we also gave them food during the time that they lived on the mountain just behind our home.

You see, using stones, they had built themselves a place up there and they asked for food about twice a day. They bathed themselves in the Msengezi river but we gave them drinking water. They had no blankets but they had a radio and their own pots. We gave them raw foods and they cooked for themselves.

They were just like normal people and quite friendly although we were afraid of them because of their clothes and their weapons. They preferred to live in the mountains so that they could easily take cover.

My son spent a lot of time with the comrades. Sometimes he stayed a whole day with them. We did not know that he was planning to join them until he came to bid us farewell.

What happened was that the comrades came to the field where we were shelling maize and told us that they were leaving, because some of their friends had been killed in Chinhoyi*. Then my son told us that he would be going with them. They left and spent some days in another area where they killed a white man who was very rough with his employees. Then they returned. My son was still with them and he came to see us alone and told us that he would continue with the comrades to Mupfure.

We refused him permission to leave. But he said he must go, otherwise we would all be killed. He thought that there would be retaliation for the white man's death. My husband pleaded with him not to go, but he insisted that he must: "Otherwise," he said, "we will all die." We could not do anything but cry. My son said that it was better for one person to die than for the whole family to do so.

Then the comrades, together with my son, left early the next morning. He bade us farewell saying, "Perhaps we will meet again, but it is not likely." He did not take anything with him, not even his clothes. He did not have a gun of his own but he was given one while they were in the bush.

After they had gone, the soldiers came to our home – some by helicopter and some by road. There were a lot of them and they arrested my sons and other boys who had been helping in the fields. They were loaded on to a truck and taken to Nhapata camp at Murombedzi. The soldiers said that my sons must have seen the comrades, because they had found empty bully-beef tins on the mountain, so they knew the guerillas had been in the area. You see, they had already been to the farm where the white man had been killed.

The soldiers who took our sons did not beat us, but they hit our younger children hard with their guns and slapped them across their faces. I just watched, crying, but we could not do anything. It was very painful. They did not beat us

* The 'Battle of Chinhoyi' in April 1966 marked the beginning of Zanla's armed struggle.

then – we were beaten by the second group of soldiers that came.

When the soldiers came back for us, they called us over to the trucks, saying, "Come here! We have already taken your guerillas." My husband and I went over to them.

Mr Chingindi*: There were three black CIDs and they wanted to take our children, the ones that were going to school, to prison. We said that the children were not guilty and should be allowed to continue with their education. However they insisted that they should come with us. This angered my wife. She slapped one of the CIDs three times and our boys ran away.

The CIDs remained quite calm and just told us to get into the truck. We were taken to Nhapata camp which was where they had already taken our other children. They said they were arresting us because we had harboured guerillas. We denied this.

We were afraid. When they asked us about our son Everest, we told them that he had gone with the guerillas. Then they said that we had sent him to be a guerilla and so we were also guerillas and they beat us.

Mrs Chingindi: Yes, I remember now, that is what happened. My husband, the four small children and I were at home. The CIDs said that they wanted to take us all away – even the children who were still going to school. I said they should not take our children as they would miss school. I suggested that they take me and my husband, but leave my children behind. They refused.

So I stood up and slapped one of them.

I was so pained, so angry by what they were doing, wanting to take away my small children who were still going to school that I did not think of myself. I felt ready to take the consequences, whatever they were. I felt that if they were going to shoot me, then I was prepared to die. After I had slapped this CID, my children ran away, so they did not come with us to Nhapata.

When we arrived there, we found that many people had been arrested. Our children who had been taken from the field were there. My sons had been badly beaten by the soldiers. They mistook my second born for Everest and they

---

* Mrs Chingindi requested that her husband and a younger son help her from time to time, as she did not feel that her memory would serve her well.

thrashed him. All the children from our area were there too, except for the comrades who had run away. There were also people from Zvimba and Makonde. Everyone was arrested because the authorities said that we had supported the guerillas.

A few days later, the police returned to my home for another two of my sons.

We were all put in one big tobacco shed. Children were in one section, men in another and women in a third. We were given food but there were no blankets. Life was difficult. We could not even wash properly because there was nowhere to do so. It was all trouble in that place. That is where we were each asked questions and beaten. We were there for a whole month. I was only beaten once, but my husband was beaten several times.

Our relatives were afraid the soldiers would give them a hard time and so no one visited us. Even when we returned home, people were afraid to visit us, because they thought they would be harassed, if they met soldiers.

After we had been asked questions and beaten then we were just left to sit day after day. They said we had to remain there, because if we returned to our homes, we would cook for the guerillas again. They said that we had to stay in the shed until the people who had been found guilty were taken to prison. My husband was among those who were sent to prison.

My husband's second wife cooked for the two children who were left at home. She was not taken by the police, I don't know why. She came to visit us during the month that we were at Nhapata. Then we were released.

Mr Chingindi: They questioned us and said that we harboured guerillas therefore we were also guerillas. They asked why my son had gone and I said I did not know. We were beaten very hard and we did not get enough food. I was beaten twice a day. They cut big sticks from the trees and used those for beating us. On the first day I was beaten by a white policemen and two black policemen and the next day I was beaten by black CIDs.

There were only a few women in the shed, but there were a lot of men. They called each person out one at a time and took them into the forest which is where they questioned and beat us. They wanted to know why we had not told them that the guerillas were in the area, and why we had given them food.

The children were very afraid and so they told the police all about the guerillas and about my son who had left with them. I was then beaten again because I had told them that I did not know anything. Then I was arrested and taken to Kadoma prison where I was detained for eleven months. After that I was moved to Sikombela for two years.

Mrs Chingindi: After a month, I was sent home but my children stayed at the camp. No one told me that my husband had been sent to prison. For seven whole months I did not know where my husband was and I was very worried. We thought he might have been killed by a beating. I did not try to find out about my husband because I did not know where to start. Also the soldiers often came to our home to see if I was here and to ask questions about the guerillas, and so I did not have the opportunity to go anywhere.

I regretted that my son had left with the freedom fighters because I could see that his father had suffered and I knew that his brothers had been tortured. I felt that if he had not gone, we would have not suffered so much.

When I returned home I, and my husband's second wife, did all the work. We ploughed the fields alone because the children who had been left at home were still small. Then, after some time, the children were released and came home. On the day of their release the soldiers said, "You can go! Your guerilla has been shot." And so, although I was relieved that my sons had been released from the camp, I mourned my son as I thought he had been killed.

Then, seven months later, my husband wrote and told me that he had been detained in Kadoma prison and so I knew that he was still alive. My children often asked me about their father and all I could tell them was that life was like this and things did not always go smoothly. Also our neighbours did not like us. They called us guerillas and wanted us to be moved from the farm so they could buy it for themselves.

Once I went to visit my husband in detention. We were allowed to see him for three days. He was no longer being beaten but he was worrying about his children. We told him about the problems of sending children to school and he told us to go and talk to organizations such as Christian

Care to see if they could help us. After that visit, I and my husband's second wife took it in turns to go and see him, first in Kadoma prison and then in Sikombela. After two years he was released. He just came home. I was not expecting him. We were very happy that day. For a person who had been in prison he did not look too bad.

Then we heard from the police that my eldest son was not dead but that he had been sentenced to death after being arrested in Bulawayo. He was taken to Harare. We went to see him and we talked with him. I was very worried and my heart was troubled. My son said that I should not worry too much.

Mr Chingindi (junior son): When the police told us that my brother had been sentenced to death, we decided to go and see him. We talked to him through a window in the prison. We were in the presence of a policeman and so we just talked about things generally. He told us that we would be informed when he was to be killed. He asked us to look after his family and not send his wife away, home to her family. That was all we could talk about. We could not ask him what had happened or what they did in the bush. My mother was with us and so she also talked to my brother. He told us that he was not being mistreated. The prisoners just sat and ate and waited, that was all.

Visitors were allowed once a month but it was usually only for one person at a time and so, sometimes, I did not see him for three or four months. We were very worried that our brother was going to be killed.

After his arrest the soldiers continued to visit our home regularly. They always asked questions about the *vakomana*. They did not believe that they did not come to our home. Later, as time went on, there were very many guerillas, from both ZANU and ZAPU, in the area. We said we could not look after them because we were afraid.

They did not bother us. They just asked for what they wanted and went away. These comrades did not stay in our homes: they just asked for food and left. There was only a problem if soldiers came from Chinhoyi or Chegutu soon after the comrades had left. If that happened, there could be trouble. Sometimes the Selous Scouts came disguised as Zanlas or Zipras. We all knew who they were from the colour of their eyes.

Mrs Chingindi: I thought of my son and I was afraid that something else might happen to us. We were really afraid to cook for the comrades but they pleaded with us and we did so. They came with their guns and just asked for food. They said that they were not interested in staying with us because they had heard the history of our home.

One day the soldiers came just after the comrades had left. They beat us because they said we had lied to them about the comrades, when we said that they never came to our home. They did not take me away but they took my daughter-in-law. They took her away for three days but she said that all they did was ask her why she cooked for the comrades.

My son was not killed. He came back in 1980. I did not know that he was coming. I just saw him when he arrived. I killed an ox for him as I was so pleased. Later he went to work in Gweru. He studied while he was in prison but they were not allowed to sit any exams.

My son is not a rough person; he is a happy one. Prison did not change him. My life is good now but because our bodies got tired of being beaten, I am not strong. But my son is helping me. He has hired people to work for me. Sometimes he visits me three times a year. I am very pleased about the fact that my son was released and came back home. So I want to encourage other women to be strong and patient.

Helen Karemba

Chitomborwizi, Chinhoyi

I WAS BORN in Goromonzi district in the Chikwaka area in 1935. I was one of six girls. I went to school at Kadyamadare, St. Paul's Musami and Murewa Mission. But after I had completed standard five, I left because my parents could no longer afford the school fees. I stayed at home for about a year and then, in 1948, I got married.

My husband whom I had known since I was a child, was from the same district but employed in Harare. After the birth of our first two children, we bought a farm and moved to this area, Chitomborwizi. We now have eight children, my ninth child died during the war.

Life was very difficult when we first settled here because we had to start from scratch. We worked hard to cut down trees and stump the fields. After a few years, we began to do quite well. We grew a lot of food and tobacco and we became successful. We managed to send all our children to school and even the last born completed form four.

My husband and I worked on the farm together but we had two employees; later we employed a third, and they helped us until my children were old enough to do so. My husband and I share all the tasks that have to be done on the farm.

I get up before six o'clock and prepare breakfast for my family. Then at around seven we go to the fields, returning at about ten for our mid-morning tea. After that we go back to the fields, returning at about one o'clock for lunch. During that break I start preparing the afternoon meal and then we have a rest until about four o'clock, when we go again to the fields. I come home a little earlier than everyone else in order to have the water for bathing ready and to see about supper. By eight we will have eaten and be very ready to go to sleep.

Before the comrades came to this area, we had heard that people were fighting a war to liberate us, so that we, the blacks, could rule ourselves. ZANU also held political meetings when we were informed about what was happening in the country. The comrades had been in surrounding areas such Msengezi and Zvimba before they came here, and they also held *pungwes* to teach people about the war.

At first I did not really understand what war meant: I saw that some children were leaving the country and others were living in the bush, even my sister's children left, and I wondered why they were doing so. They did not tell their parents they were going, they just disappeared from school.

My eldest son was the organizing secretary of ZANU in Mwenje. But after some people had been killed in an incident in Karoi, he was arrested and imprisoned for a long time without trial. The authorities said that he mobilized boys and brought them here, to Chitomborwizi, so that they could be sent to Mozambique. He was sentenced to death but his case was referred to the high court. He was in prison when the freedom fighters first came into our area.

This was towards the end of the war and they, the comrades, came first to our house. Although it was at about ten o'clock in the morning, I was frightened because I had never seen them before. There were about ten of them and they were all young men. They told us that they were freedom fighters and said they wanted food. I called my husband who was very excited and happy as he had been helping to send the *vakomana* out to fight for a long time.

What happened was that children were encouraged to go and join the liberation fighters at political meetings. Then, afterwards, my husband and a certain man from Chinhoyi did the organization and helped the children to leave. My husband had a car and so he transported the young people from Chitomborwizi to Chinhoyi. They were collected from there and taken to Mozambique in lorries.

I never knew very much about the work my husband did because I was not involved and, you know what men are like, there are always certain things they do that they never talk to their wives about.

But I think the reason that the first group of freedom fighters in the area came to my home was because they all knew our name, Karemba. It was towards the end of the war, during the time of Muzorewa's government and Zimbabwe-Rhodesia.

So, on the first occasion that I saw the comrades, my husband welcomed them and told me to prepare some food. I killed two chickens and cooked sadza. Then they told us that there was going to be a *pungwe* here at our house and they spent the whole day sitting under those mango trees – that is, all but two of them who went to the school. There they told the children to inform their parents that there would be a *pungwe* at Karemba's place that evening. In the meantime I informed other women – my neighbours – and they helped me to prepare more food.

We were going to hold the *pungwe* after supper. So, after our meal, a lot of people, about a hundred or so, gathered under the grapefruit trees. We sang songs and the comrades told us about the war, their objectives and their wishes. Then at about eleven o'clock, I told my child that I was feeling funny. I do not know what it was but I suddenly felt odd. The soldiers, who had never been to Chitomborwizi before, had surrounded my home without anyone realizing it. They started firing from one side of the yard, so they were shooting at very close range.

When the soldiers, some of whom were black, and some of whom were white with their faces painted black, began to fire at us, the comrades ran away but no one realized that they had gone. Everyone lay down after a boy shouted *lalapansi**. The firing continued until seven o'clock in the morning and we lay flat on the ground all that time. Two children, both from the same family, were shot dead, although

---

* *Lalapansi* – lie down.

they had been involved in previous contacts and knew what to do. They rolled across the ground during the shooting to get away, but they didn't realize they were rolling towards the soldiers. That is why they were killed. Their parents were here at the time.

Bullets riddled a tractor which was parked in the yard and the house was full of holes but fortunately, apart from the two boys, no one else was killed. In the morning the soldiers threatened to kill all the men. They told all the women who were of a nervous disposition to go away while they did this. The men were told to lie down and black soldiers walked up and down on top of them. Everyone was there – the women and the children – we were all there. Then a soldier said, "Where is the father of guerillas?" My husband stood up and said "I am here," and he was taken away to Gangarahwe. I did not do anything except cry and all the women in the community cried with me. After everyone else had been told to get up, they left.

The soldiers then arrested my husband and a few older boys from other families who they said were *mujibas* but later they were returned home.

When my husband had been taken away by the soldiers, I remained at home with my children feeling quite helpless. But, on this occasion, we were lucky as they only kept him in prison for a week.

After that contact, not all the soldiers left, some remained behind because they said we would feed the guerillas again. They asked me how many chickens I had killed and I replied, two. Then they asked why I had done this and I said it was difficult to refuse if someone had a gun. I said that if the soldiers pointed a gun at me and demanded something, I would give it to them and that was why I had fed the guerillas. I was afraid of guns. After I had said this, neither I nor any of the other women were beaten.

Later we heard that the soldiers had got to hear about that *pungwe* because there had been an auxiliary belonging to Muzorewa's party at the school and he had informed the soldiers.

Some time later when my husband had gone to the trial of my eldest son in Harare, I went to Chinhoyi to sell my vegetables. My children were alone at home. The soldiers came to our house and saw two of my sons and my daughter. They shot my sons. I do not know why. The soldiers never talked to them or asked any questions, they just shot them – perhaps they thought they were the comrades, I don't know. Perhaps they had heard that the *vakomana* sometimes stayed with me, I don't know. But, by then, nearly all the comrades had gone to the assembly points. A few had remained behind, but none of them had been to see us that day. Anyway, whatever the reason, the soldiers arrived shooting.

My daughter hid under my bed, the boys hid behind the sofa but it made no difference. My youngest son was shot in the head and he died. The soldiers shot from the door, they stood right at the door, the boy's head was blown to nothing. Then his older brother raised his hand and his arm was ripped by a bullet. Next the soldiers went into the bedroom and started shooting there. They shot at random and some of the wall fell into the room. They even shot under the bed but fortunately they missed my daughter. She then climbed out from under the bed and raised her hands. The soldiers did not kill her but they beat her very hard saying she was a wife of the comrades. She still has a big ugly black scar that was caused by the beating they gave her.

The soldiers instructed my daughter to carry her dead brother to the truck and they told the injured boy to get in as well. Then they drove a few kilometres down the road and stopped. They told my daughter to get out and carry the dead boy home. She could not do that so she just stood by the side of the road crying. Our neighbours saw her there and they carried the body home.

The soldiers took my injured son to Chinhoyi hospital where he contacted my son-in-law. He knew I was in Chinhoyi and came to find me at the market place. It was a terrible time. When I heard what had happened I felt so weak that I had to be helped home.

The soldiers said that my son should not be buried because he had died a comrade. Then police officers came from Gangarahwe to make enquiries. I showed them his birth certificate and they permitted us to bury him. My husband returned from Harare for the funeral and, as my eldest son's trial was over, and he had been released, he came home. But somehow I could not celebrate his return. My heart was too heavy.

Two weeks later, when people were still coming to pay us their condolences, the soldiers came again and this time they beat my husband. White soldiers came and called out from behind the gum trees, "Upi lo Karemba*, the father of guerillas?" Then they hit my husband several times and he collapsed. I knew there was no life in him since he was already weak from his previous imprisonment. I went over to him, his nose and one ear were bleeding badly. Then they pushed him into their truck.

Before they left, two soldiers came and asked me where the guerillas were. I told them I did not know. My daughter-in-law was with me and they said that they would shoot her because she must the wife of a guerila. I grabbed the gun they were pointing at her and told them that they should kill me instead. They just laughed and drove away in their truck with my husband.

It was terrible, terrible. I could not do anything: I had just lost a son and the other one was in hospital. They just took my husband and put him in prison. They said that he had helped the comrades. They said the *vakomana* travelled all the way from Mozambique and then my husband took them wherever they wanted to go. His wounds healed whilst he was in prison, but, since then, I have never been well.

Some time later I heard that my husband had been moved from Gangarahwe to Chinhoyi so I went to try and see him. When I arrived the policemen said that I should also be imprisoned with my husband because I had fed the guerillas. I did not reply as I thought of my children, knowing that if both my husband and I were in prison, there would be no one to look after them. However, after waiting there a long time, they allowed me a glimpse of my husband. I was not allowed to speak to him. He had been badly beaten. After that I was permitted to return home.

It was the harvest season, so my children and I did the harvesting. My second eldest son was already at the university studying agriculture. I stopped him from visiting us, because the security forces did not like university students. They said that they were politically motivated.

It was very difficult for me to find out about my husband. We were very frightened of the soldiers. But then the comrades returned and said that they would protect us and that my husband would be released in due course. Some of them stayed with me, on and off, for a long time, as part

* Upi lo Karemba – where is Karemba?

of my family – sometimes we even went to the fields together. My child, I suffered. After three to four months, I felt I could no longer afford to send my children to school and one of them had actually been given a place at St Peter's. So I made a request to the church and they helped me with money and clothes and my child was able to go to school. They also wanted to see my husband and they did. Both his jaws had been broken. He was powerless. He could not lift anything. He could not hear properly.

When my husband was in prison I often visited him. He sympathized with me knowing that I was having a hard time managing the family alone. He remained in prison until the 1980 elections. He even voted from prison. I had gone to Chinhoyi hoping that he would be released to cast his vote but he wasn't. He was let out a week after that.

By the time my husband was released, things at the farm had slowed down. Working there on my own, looking after the children and worrying about my husband had slowed everything down. There was war to fight so we were not harvesting as much as we had been before. But unfortunately when my husband returned, he was different: he was sort of stupid and he did not have a well balanced mind. His brains had been damaged by the beating he had been given. So there was still no one to help me in the fields. Those were tough times and everyone had their own problems, so no one could afford to assist me.

We parents were required to buy clothes for those boys, the comrades. Some of them had none at all, so we bought clothing for them – usually jeans. We spent a lot of money on the *vakomana*. They also came to our homes and women cooked for them, because they were often very hungry when they arrived. Some of them were very thin, so it was easy to see how hungry they were. We killed chickens for them and, if we had goats, we killed them too and served the meat with sadza. Anything that we could afford to give them, we gave them. We served them food at home but they did not come inside the houses. They sat outside. The girls and the *mujibas* washed their clothes.

Those boys had good manners. When they arrived I would send a child to inform the neighbours and they would help me prepare food. Everyone worked together and even if the comrades went to the homes of PF ZAPU supporters, they were treated well. Sometimes the Zipras came into the area but only to buy from our shop. They never interfered with us. Sometimes we gave them food and then they returned to their own zone. When the comrades from both parties first came into our area, they worked well together. But later they divided the area, using the road as the boundary: one side became the Zanla ward and the other the Zipra ward. But there was no division amongst ourselves over helping the comrades.

I had a big family but I never felt that feeding the comrades was a burden. We all liked them and so we tried to do our best. I think everyone understood what was happening and why the *vakomana* were fighting. If there was a *pungwe* everyone attended regardless of whether they had babies or little children, they simply carried them to the meetings.

The comrades moved about in groups and they would move from here into other areas and then come back. We were not inquisitive, we knew they had a purpose for going wherever they went, and whatever they did was not our concern. The comrades did not like the white people and sometimes there was a contact on a commercial farm.

Our land is adjacent to the European commercial farms and the solders patrolled and protected those farms but they hardly ever came into this area because they were afraid of the comrades. Sometimes they would drive by and then we would inform the *vakomana* who protected us. Everyone appreciated what they were doing, and they rarely had contacts with the soldiers.

However, towards the end of the war, when the *vakomana* had already gone to the assembly points, the soldiers became bothersome.

Generally I was not afraid of the soldiers because I knew they would only confront someone, if someone else had given them information; and that sort of thing did not happen in our area. I do not know how or what the soldiers knew. I have never heard my husband say anything about it.

You see my husband had been a politician for a long time. He joined the NDP when it was first formed – that was shortly after we were married when he was working in Harare. Later when the party was banned, he joined ZAPU and then the PCC*. Later still he became a member of ZANU. I think it

* PCC – People's Caretaker Council formed by Nkomo in 1963 to act for ZAPU which had been banned.

was some time in the sixties, when all the other parties had been banned. He once met President Mugabe during the struggle at Matoranjera when the party officials were planning how to send young people out of the country. Only children who wanted to go, left.

I do not think my children knew that my husband helped other children to leave the country. At that time, my eldest son was at school and only the small children were with us. I don't think they ever assisted girls to leave the country, I never heard that they had done so.

I joined the party in the early days because of my husband. I attended meetings and participated just like everyone else. I was not afraid. I remember that once – perhaps it was in the fifties – we lifted Comrade Nkomo's car right up, calling out that we wanted our country to be free, but we did not understand politics. Some men were imprisoned during those early years but I am not aware that any women were imprisoned.

During the war I had many difficult days. I was often very unhappy. I lost a son, my husband was beaten and imprisoned, I could not find enough money to send my children to school and my home was damaged, but the Lord opened a way for me and I did manage somehow. When I asked for money I was helped and my younger son completed form four. The church helped to pay his fees for two years and then I paid for the other two.

A lot of our property was destroyed during the war especially on the day the soldiers killed my son. They were very cruel, they would sometimes just smash a dish without reason: it was destruction for the sake of destruction. I have managed to replace a few things, at least I now have the essentials. If my husband was in better health, I think we would have managed to replace everything but because he is not well, and neither am I, we are not getting as much as we could from our farm.

All my children are working except for the last boy, so the help we receive is given by our labourer. We pay him ourselves and give him food as well. I have a girl who helps me with the housework and I pay her. I also raise and sell chickens and so I earn a little cash to help myself.

Today I can say that we are happy. After the war we began a new life. We have bought a new tractor and we have managed to re-open our grocery. The shop had been destroyed, the doors and windows were nothing but holes. We have now managed to replace nearly everything except the door, but the old one still functions. I think we are once again leading a good life.

Looking back over my life I would urge women to be courageous: to have courage and work hard. We should not depend on men on the farm, we should be able to work on our own.

29 Feresia Mashayamombe

Zvimba

I WAS BORN in Mhondoro but I'm not sure when. My father's name is Godha Nyere. He was a communal farmer. I was one of ten children – five girls and five boys. I never went to school because my parents were not aware that education was very important for children. Even if they had known about schools, I would not have gone as they had very little money. As children we just stayed at home, worked in the fields and did all the various home work that has to be done, ordinary day to day chores.

My husband came from Zvimba but we met in Mhondoro. He was employed in Harare as a clerk in a factory which manufactured towels. Later he went to work for Swift Transport. We married two years after we had met and we had a wedding reception at Chibero after being married by the DC and in church.

Then I went to live with my husband's people and my husband continued to work in Harare. I had four children but the youngest died while he was still a baby. I worked in the fields with my in-laws and, as the children got older,

I occasionally visited my husband in Harare during the school holidays and he used to visit us once a month at home.

Living with others is always difficult. My husband's younger brothers helped me plough but only after they had ploughed all their own fields. I handled the plough and my brother-in-law controlled the oxen. These belonged to my husband. I used the money I got from selling our crops, to buy clothes and things for our home. My husband always bought the farm implements and so on.

Before the war my husband was a member of a political party and so I joined it as well. I became a chairwoman of the women's section. Our duty was to organize meetings to mobilize members. We told people that we should all join political parties so that when the country was free we would rule ourselves. The white man did not want us to hold such meetings and so at times we were chased and beaten by the police. But we continued to hold them. At that time my husband was still in Harare.

The day my husband was arrested, I was in Harare. My husband's colleagues returned my husband's jersey to a cousin and told him that he had been arrested and then I was informed. I was very worried. I did not do anything, I did not know what I could do, I just sat and cried. But my husband's younger brothers were staying with him at his house in Harare and they comforted me by saying that politics was just like that.

The next day my husband's brothers went to enquire about my husband and they were put in a cell for twenty-four hours. So then I and my husband's sister went in search of him at the Harare Central Prison but I was told that I had to go and see the chief officer of the Special Branch who was a man called Beans. The people at the CID offices were very hush-hush. Mr Beans said that he did not want to hear of anyone enquiring for Mashayamombe. We spent the whole day at the prison hoping that we might be given a chance to talk to him. At sunset we were told that he had been moved from the Special Branch offices to the remand section of the prison.

I realized that my husband was 'under fire' and he would not be released because he had been dealing with people who wanted to fight the government. Two days later, we went to the prison and were allowed to see him, but we had to talk across a distance with a glass partition between us. He had on a vest but no shirt and his whole body was black and bruised because he had been badly beaten. His arm was so swollen he could not lift it. He said that he was not going to be released and, if I decided to go home, I should go. One of his brothers came and helped me pack up all his belongings and I took them home.

When my husband was transferred to Goromonzi I went with a brother to visit him. We were allowed to meet him in a little office. Then he wrote and told me that he had been transferred to Gweru and I went to the prison there. We saw each other through a glass window and talked to each other over a telephone.

One needs the assistance of a husband, even with ploughing. He may not actually be there to help till the field, but it helps to plan things together. After my husband's arrest, I started to run short of food, clothes, blankets, ploughing implements and so on. But I ploughed and I grew groundnuts which I made into peanut butter, a bucket at a time, and took it to my sister in Norton who sold it for me. I did this once a month. Occasionally I sold an ox.

My children were still quite young: the oldest was only in grade three, and I worried about how I would manage to send them to school. But later on Christian Care helped me with three dollars a month. I do not know how they heard of me but their money was helpful and I used it for food and various school things that the children needed.

I was very worried and upset by my husband's arrest, but I was not afraid. His relatives wanted me to move away from our home because they said my husband would never be released. It was even suggested that I should take one of his brothers as my husband, but I refused to allow this. They said there was no point in me remaining, because his house would not turn into money. I told them that I was not staying for money: I was staying because I had made a vow to remain true to my husband, no matter what happened and, even though he was in prison, he was still alive. I said I would not go unless he died or was killed. I explained that I wanted my children to go to school and, were I to return to my own home, my father could never afford to look after us all. I knew it would be better for me to stay in my husband's home, ploughing my fields, using my husband's oxen and working for my children.

You see, my husband was the oldest son and so he had a lot of property: in fact, everything at home belonged to him – the cattle, ploughs, farm tools and so on. His brothers, all young unmarried men, wanted me to leave, because then they would take over all the property. They actually plotted against me so that I would be persuaded to leave and they could do as they pleased.

My husband's parents could not help me either as they were old people and, anyway, my father-in-law was living at Makunde with his second wife. So there was no one in his family to help me. My parents agreed that I should stay – in fact, they said that I had no right to leave – but they could not provide me with any material assistance. I did sometimes discuss my problems with some other women and some felt that I should return home, but others comforted me by saying that there would always be people, like my husband's relatives, who liked creating problems. I really only found comfort in going to church.

Once a month I went to visit my husband. The visits always distressed me a great deal. As soon as I began to make preparations to go, I began feeling very hurt and dejected. I would try to console myself by committing everything to God. When I got to the prison, I was allowed to see my husband for fifteen minutes. He always complained about the food they were given which, he said, was only fit for pigs.

I would discuss some of my problems but I never told him that some of his relatives had wanted to make me their wife. I did not want to worry him too much, so I decided not to tell him. I did, however, tell him about the other things they had said: that I should return home, that he was never going to be released, that I should remarry and have more children, and so on. He advised me not to worry about what people said and comforted me by saying that everyone was given certain blessings and I had my children, so I should not worry about what I did not have.

But, you know, there are people who will say anything to upset you if they really do not want you. Here people even went to the extent of calling me a witch and said that I had killed many others. I was so worried by this accusation that at one point I wanted to commit suicide. I only decided against doing so as I know that God does not approve of a person who takes her own life. I managed just to go on.

What happened was that a neighbour's two children had died from measles in hospital. I helped with the funeral arrangements and contributed a goat to feed those who came to mourn. Nonetheless, it was still said that I had killed them. The neighbours were my husband's brothers. I was told point-blank that I was a witch and that I had killed the children. I did not do anything because there was no one I could tell who could help solve the problem. My husband's relatives knew that I was being called a witch because they were directly involved, but there were others who also said that I was a witch.

I told my brother-in-law that it was not true. I did not get angry and shout at him but I denied his allegations. Nonetheless, he continued to spread rumours – even his other younger brother said I was a witch and on that occasion we scolded each other.

After the children had died, people went to a n'anga, as is usually done, to find out who had killed the children. The n'anga said the reason was that the children's father had not paid the ox he owed to his mother-in-law. No one was thought to have killed the children. But, despite the n'anga's statement, my brother-in-law continued to insist I had killed his children.

He also said that I had tied my aunt's child and his children up with wire and beaten them. Yet I had gone to the grinding mill when the episode was supposed to have taken place. It was my brother-in-law himself who beat my aunt's child and my children. You see, when I returned from the mill, I found them at home having been beaten because some cattle had gone astray, cattle that belonged to my husband. My brothers-in-law do not have cattle of their own: they use my husband's because he is the oldest and like a father to them.

My brother-in-law had tied the children up with wire and then beaten them very hard. The children had by then fallen into a nearby donga* and were quite helpless, but he continued to hit them. My mother-in-law eventually stopped him and she set the children free. They were so badly bruised that they could not go to school.

All his accusations were part of a plan to try and drive me away from here. From that time we became enemies and we stopped ploughing together.

* Donga – a gully or ditch – often created as a result of erosion.

There was even another story that I had given my aunt some *muti** to put in his children's food. They said the poisoned food had been cooked in my mother-in-law's kitchen.

My children often asked where their father was and I always said that he would return after he had been released but I didn't know when that would be. The children missed his visits as he used always to come home bringing them nice things like sweets and biscuits.

He finally came home having been in prison for twelve years and just before the war began in this area. He had written to tell me that he was going to be released and he said that he would go to Harare before coming home. When he arrived, he went past our home on the bus, because the area had changed so much he did not recognize it. Large areas of land had been cleared either for fields or new homes. When I saw the bus go past, I shouted to my mother-in-law that her son had come at last and we went to meet him. We were very excited, and crying and dancing we came home together.

We had heard of the war before it arrived here. It was said to be in the Mutare area. We heard that people were dying and being burnt. We could hardly believe it. We thought perhaps it was just a story. It was a long time afterwards that the war reached us. The Zanlas came from Zowa and through Msengezi and based themselves at Chikumba. Then the *mujibas* came and told us to prepare food. They wanted relish, eggs, chickens and goats.

Sometimes the comrades came and asked – they just gave orders – for clothes which they wanted us to buy for them; but we did not have the money to do so. The Zipra fighters once came and asked us for clothes but we were excused, because my husband had been in prison for such a long time and we had nothing. The comrades saw that this was true and my husband really did have no clothes to give them. What I did for the comrades was prepare food and wash and iron their clothes. It was a dangerous time and I was always afraid of the soldiers. I could not have hidden the comrades because they came in large groups. Sometimes they just came to play the radio in our house.

The Zipras did not have any base: they just spent the night

* *Muti* – medicine (Shona).

in the bush somewhere. Sometimes they spent the day sleeping in a house, resting and hiding at the same time. They were constantly on the move and sometimes they passed our home on their way to the beerhall. Once they spent the night here and slept on the bed. I was away visiting my mother so my husband looked after them. In the morning they opened the wardrobe to look for clothes and my husband had to explain that only my clothes were inside.

What hindered the progress of the war in Zvimba was that there are no trees. The comrades had nowhere to hide. After there had been a contact, they usually had to run away and hide on nearby farms. The *madzkutsaku*, Zipras, Zanlas and the soldiers were in the area during that time but it was really right at the end of the war, just before cease-fire.

I went to the base when we were called to go there. Comrades danced, and they beat and killed people who were called sell-outs. Some people were beaten so hard that they had to be carried back to their homes because they could not move. Sometimes people were beaten as a punishment for having children who were police officers, but others who had children in the police force were asked to pay with cattle which were killed for the comrades. Such people were the lucky ones. If by any chance the child was present, he was beaten to death.

Once, some of my neighbours went to the Zanla base and told them that I was a witch and that I should be killed. Other people told me that I had been sold-out as a witch and that I should run away or I would be killed. I refused to do this because I knew I had not bewitched anyone; my hands were clean. I said that if it was the Lord's will that I should die, let it be so, but I was not going to run away.

Then the Zanlas left and the Zipras arrived. Again people said that I should leave because the Zipras were more ruthless than the Zanlas. They said that my husband should also leave because he was the leader of the UANC*. This was not true: he was only a member of that party. At the time everyone was told by the Zanlas that they must join a party or they would be considered sell-outs. Anyway, we refused to run away because the allegations were false. My husband said that if the comrades wanted to kill us they would do so wherever we were.

* UANC – United African National Congress formed by Bishop Abel Muzorewa in 1977.

I do not know why people felt we were sell-outs but one thing which was said was that everyone who had a house with a corrugated roof was a sell-out. There were not many people who sold out on others and when it happened it was just due to hatred. Some people hated me so much that they planned to go and ask the Zipras for grenades so that they could use them on my home. Their plan was to go away and spend the night somewhere else having asked others to plant the grenades for them. They thought they would return after the explosion, so no one would know who was responsible.

The people responsible were my brother-in-law and his friends. They had not liked me having cattle when they had none but, at the same time, they used my husband's cattle whenever they wanted to. Had I left after my husband's arrest when they wanted me to go, all our property would have been taken and my home destroyed. My brothers-in-law also did not like the fact that even when my husband was in prison, we had no misunderstandings.

After his release we – my husband and his relatives – decided to go and consult a n'anga to see if we could find a solution to the witchcraft story. We went to a n'anga in Manhambara. He said that I was not a witch and he said that my husband's family should return their grandmother's cattle to their rightful owners. The n'anga also said that if we wanted to, we could drink *mutewo*. If a witch drinks this medicine they will not vomit, but if an ordinary person does so, they will. So it is a way of finding out if someone is or is not a witch.

My husband and I drank the *mutewo* and we vomited but my husband's brothers and his wife, who also drank it, did not. This n'anga was not the only one we consulted. Another had also said that I was not a witch, but my husband's relatives do not want to listen.

After it had been categorically confirmed that I was not a witch, the headman decided that my brother-in-law should pay us damages of an ox. He agreed to do so at the time and even showed us the ox, but then he refused to abide by the agreement and he has now left the area.

Even today very few people seem to believe that I am not a witch although I am not, and every n'anga we have consulted has proved this to be the case. People still tell their children not to visit my home as I am a witch and will eat them because witches eat people. Yes, even today, people mock me. I am not at all happy here. If I had to make the final decision, I would leave. I am so tired, so fed up with this allegation. It is a constant source of worry.

Otherwise, I am now very happy to have my husband back in the family. I am happy because now we can work and plan things together. We have ploughed and produced a lot of crops which I would never have been able to do on my own. My husband is fit and well. He was not permanently affected by his ill-treatment in prison. We are even thinking of opening a store.

If I think back on my life, I would urge other women to be patient because if you are long-suffering, big problems diminish in their importance. I also think it is important to remain in the church because it can help you to have patience and bear your suffering well. It is also important to work hard: you must be able to plough and harvest your own crops. Laziness does not feed anyone. I am pleased because I managed to educate all my children and now the eldest is a nurse, my second-born is a clerk and my last-born is married.

Commentary from Mr Mashayamombe explaining his early involvement in the struggle:

I joined ANC in 1959 after Stonehouse had come out from Britain and addressed us at a rally in Highfield. When the party was banned during Federation our leaders formed the National Democratic Party and tried to communicate with the government of the time, but they refused to compromise. Then the NDP was banned and we formed ZAPU. By that stage many people – indeed the whole country – had become politically aware. People wanted to have their own government. ZAPU did all it could to put across our point of view to the white government, but the white man did not want to co-operate. We talked, we went on strike, we demonstrated, but the white man did not move an inch. So we started damaging their property, we went on to commercial farms and destroyed their tobacco and cattle, but they did not want to discuss anything with us. Then ZAPU was banned and we went underground and ZANU was formed in 1963. I was arrested on the 9th September, 1966 when I was working for Swift in Harare. My work-mates disclosed that I had received a consignment of weapons from Zambia.

You see, Swift Transport goes as far as Zambia and the drivers were given weapons – usually firearms and grenades – to bring into the country. Other drivers who knew I was involved in politics brought their weapons to me, after they had transported them from Zambia. I distributed them to different branches of the movement in Harare and they distributed them to different areas of the country. I also helped people who wanted to leave the country. I organized transport for them in the trucks, but I myself never met them.

On the occasion of my arrest, I had received a consignment of weapons and had hidden it in a forest near Ford Motors, but some of my colleagues betrayed me and informed the authorities. I refused to disclose the names of the drivers who had brought in the weapons. I could not have done so, even had they killed me. I was taken to the headquarters of the Special Branch and we were interrogated. My colleagues admitted their guilt but I refused to say anything. I was in Harare prison for five weeks and then I was transferred to Goromonzi. There I was confined in a dark room without any light: there was darkness all day and all night, and the room was too small for its occupants.

I was beaten hard both at Harare and at Goromonzi as they tried to get me to admit my guilt. They beat me whenever they felt like it. They would even fetch me from the cell at night to take me for a beating. Once the Special Branch beat me so hard that the spears hanging on the walls of their office fell down and, because of the violence, windows broke.

I was transferred from Goromonzi to Gweru prison in 1967 and then, in 1972, I was transferred to Wha Wha. I refused to stay there because they wanted to rehabilitate me and so they took me back to Gweru. After the Pearce Commission in 1972, I was moved from Gweru to Gonakudzingwa. But when Mozambique became independent, they moved us all to Harare because they thought that we might escape into Mozambique. In 1976 I was again transferred to Wha Wha and released from there on 27th August 1978 by the government of Zimbabwe-Rhodesia.

Before my arrest, no one knew that I had been involved in such things. Those were difficult days, I could not even tell my wife about it when I went home. I felt the only way we could free our country was to fight and to do this we needed weapons. That is why I decided to involve myself. I was not paid because the fight for liberation was voluntary, and you did not expect payment for it.

30 Emma Munemo

Gurupa Village, Buhera

I WAS BORN in Buhera. I was the second child in a family of four girls and two boys. Three other children died. I'm not sure when I was born but my mother said it was in the year of the grasshoppers and I think that was 1937.

We all went to school. My parents were poor and didn't have enough money to send us, but we worked in people's fields for money. The school fees were two shillings and sixpence a term. All of us went to school in this way. I completed standard one, only the last born went as far as grade seven, the rest of us left after we had had two or three years at school. We did not think so much of education in those days.

I married in 1958, as soon as I had stopped going to school, and I stayed with my husband's parents while he went to work in Kwekwe for two years. Towards the end of the second year I went to live with him and, in the third, we both came back home.

My husband comes from Range, which is a very poor area. There are not enough fields and life is difficult. It was better in my own home. My husband had no father and he had to look after his mother and his whole family. So we decided to settle in Buhera, even though it was a backward place. We moved in 1965 with our three children. Now I have ten children; two others died.

When we first came to the area we were given oxen to plough by my father. Later he moved to Masocha which is in the same district. But because he hadn't ploughed that year and had no food, he offered to exchange a cow for meal. The cow had a calf which was eaten by a leopard. But the cow produced other calves and we managed to raise cattle. But for some years the chiefs and headmen took all our calves, our implements and our grain. This was because we were strangers who had come from another area. It was a problem and we suffered. We also bought a field and we brewed beer to raise money to send our children to school. But, after harvesting our crops, the person who had sold the field to us always demanded a part – the larger part – of it for himself. Once Chief Chiweshe took away our yoke and chains and we had to wait until everyone else had finished ploughing before we could borrow others to use. This situation went on for a long time, about five years, and we depended on brewing and selling beer for our income. It was very hard – we had to live on scraps like ants.

Then my husband was arrested because the people in Buhera said that he was not supposed to have a field as he came from Range. But the authorities at the district offices said that he should be released because Buhera and Range fell into the same district. The person who had sold his field to us was instructed to return everything we had paid him; and the headman was told to allocate a field to us as we were his people by right.

After that my husband returned to work as a builder in Kwekwe and I stayed at home, working in the fields. As we had by then been allocated fields by the headman, we could now grow enough food for our children. My husband also sent money and clothes from Kwekwe. But a year or two later, there was a great famine in the district. My husband sent us food but again we had to depend on the beer we made to send the children to school. After the famine, we moved to Gurupa, where we are now and we were allocated fields.

The elder boy had completed grade seven when the war

started. That was in 1974. By then I had heard of the war
– that there were 'terrorists': people who turned into tree
stumps, stones or anything in order to disguise themselves.
But the war really only got hot in this area in 1976 and
that is when my son went to join the struggle. By then he
had been a year at home, as he had offered to leave home,
because he knew his father could not afford to educate him
as well as all the other children. He went to look for a job
in Harare, but he returned three months later as he had
not been able to find one. Then he stayed with us for about
a month before he was taken by the comrades.

When they first came, we were told to bring blankets and
come to a meeting because the *vakomana* had arrived. We
asked who they were and whether they were the same people
as the 'terrorists' and were told that they were, and that
they were fighting for the country. We were afraid and
wondered how we would behave when we saw them.

Everyone had to go to the meeting. That year I had given
birth to twins and I was expecting again, but I went with
everybody else. When I arrived, the comrades said that I
could return home because carrying a child in the womb
was a great war. They said that I need not attend the
meetings because it was too risky for a pregnant woman
to be there, if there was a contact. After that I stayed at
home and did not go to the *pungwes*.

But at that meeting the *vakomana* introduced themselves
and said that they were the people about whom we had
heard and that they were just like us. Once we realized that
this was true, we liked them. The only problem was that
the soldiers often came into the area and this frightened
us all very much.

At that time my son was selected to become a *mujiba*.
It was only later that he went to join the comrades. When
that happened I was not at home, I was visiting my mother.
He told his father. He said he would have not told me,
because I would have refused to let him go. He told my
husband because he was a man, and my husband told me.
He said that I shouldn't complain because our son had gone
and talking would not bring him back.

The women used to cook for the comrades and I helped.
At first we used to cook in our homes but later we cooked
at a home near their mountain base. Then the owner of the
home was beaten by the soldiers and we moved on to the

next village. At the time the soldiers constantly used to search the homes in the area, and so we kept moving from home to home.

Both men and women worked equally hard. Everyone was supposed to do their share: if two ladies were chosen to cook, they did so regardless of how many comrades they had to feed. If you were on duty you had to provide food for the whole day, for example, a goat for the morning meal, a goat for the afternoon meal, and another one for the evening meal. If only two women were responsible for that day's food, they had to provide everything: even if it meant three goats. The system of everyone contributing food was what we did at first, but later we took it in turns. As soon as the comrades left the area, there was a committee which allocated the next round of duties, so that everyone was always prepared.

In a way mothers worked harder than the men because they had to provide food, fetch water and do all the other housework, while the men went on patrol and kept a look out and were sometimes sent here or there. Even today ZANU acknowledges this as did the comrades then when they used to say, *"Pamberi nemugoti,"* meaning, 'Forward with a cooking spoon'. Actually they said that women should be assisted so as to make life a bit easier for them, but nothing tangible ever happened.

Every mother who had a sick child was referred to me. The comrades would tell them to go to *Mbuya* Mandere. That is the name I am known by here. I am a herbalist and I am able to treat various ailments. You see, there were no clinics around and I helped a lot of people, especially children. Sometimes comrades also treated the children. They had certain medicines and could give injections. At other times, the comrades referred people to me, because they could not help them.

We also contributed money to buy uniforms for the *chimbwidos* and *mujibas*. We bought them greyish clothes which they used as uniforms. We also bought beer for the *vakomana*. We found the money somehow and we borrowed from one another because it was a matter of life and death. Later, towards the end of the war, the comrades sent their girlfriends, the *chimbwidos*, for beer or cigarettes and some even went shopping with them. They would also go to a home where beer was brewed and take it from there.

There were no buses but people went on foot to Dorowa where there was still a shop: many were closed down. The school was closed, but not by the comrades. The children were afraid to go to school and there were rumours that children were being taken away by the soldiers and so everyone was afraid. Older children were forced to join the security forces without the knowledge of their parents. Sometimes they simply heard that their children were in the main camp at Dorowa and sometimes a child returned after being beaten by soldiers. Children were beaten as the soldiers tried to force them to provide information about the comrades. However, they could not say anything as they would then be branded as sell-outs. Towards the end of the war, the comrades told us that we could give the soldiers information about them as long as it was false and we pointed them in the wrong direction.

There was a time when we saw helicopters flying above my home and we locked ourselves in our houses until they had gone away. The security forces had heard that the *vakomana* were being given shelter in our homes and they were searching for them. But the comrades never did this: they always stayed at their base. Sometimes they held *pungwes* in the villages and sometimes they ate there, but they always spent the night at their base camp.

The soldiers usually came with questions about the comrades, usually just after they had left. But no one was ever seen with soldiers although, of course, some people were suspected of being sell-outs. Only one woman that I know of was killed for being a sell-out because she had reported a man who was later beaten by the soldiers. So, he reported her to the comrades and she was killed.

We liked looking after the comrades. We did not complain at all. After cease-fire a lot of people, especially the young, visited them at the assembly points. I did for them as I would have done for my own children. They were fighting for everyone.

At cease-fire the soldiers came to my home. I was there with my child, a girl who had just come back from school and was still in uniform. My husband was asleep outside. One of the soldiers pointed a gun at my husband. I was very frightened and pleaded with my ancestral spirits not to allow such a thing to happen. At first I thought there were a whole lot of soldiers but there were only two white ones and two black ones. They woke up my husband and demanded that he show them the way to St Alban's school. So he did this and later returned home.

Shortly afterwards we were told that we need not worry any more because the war was over and all the comrades were moving into the assembly points. I did not believe that soldiers and comrades could be in the same place together without fighting, but that is what happened. You see, the peace-keeping forces were already in the country.

As time passed, I realized that the situation had changed. People could move freely, parents and sisters travelled to look for their children and brothers, and the country was quiet.

My son came back from the war. He travelled via Harare where he met his brother and my uncle and they travelled home together. My son went straight to our home. I was at my parents and we had a celebration and carried out all the rituals. You see, people had asked my grandfather – that is, my grandfather's spirit which appears through me – what had happened to my son. The *Sekuru* had said that my son was on his way home. The following day, my brother arrived and told us that my son had returned home. People could not believe it, but we all were very happy and started ululating. Then we all left for home. It was late and by the time we arrived, my son was already asleep. We woke him up. He was very strong and healthy. I wanted to cry but the *Sekuru* came again and welcomed my son home. He said that we should kill a chicken so that he would see blood before he slept. Then the *Sekuru* left me and we did as he said, and all was well.

The following day I killed a goat for my son. I was not pleased by his clothes, so I offered him my shirt. At first he refused because he did not want to put on a lady's shirt, but I insisted because it was a nice one and, once he had tried it on, he liked it. It looked a lot better than the clothes he had been wearing. I insisted he do this because I knew a lot of people would be coming to see him. I felt very proud and happy that he had come home and had brought independence with him.

After a day at home he was free and relaxed. He went round the village talking to the *mujibas* and they spent many nights at my home with him.

He is now working with the communications department

in the army. Since then he has given me many things to use at home like a scotch cart and a radio. Now he is doing a good job. I think he is a chef* of some sort because last time I went to see him, the soldiers put down their guns, some went to prepare food for me, some carried my baggage and everyone made me feel at home. I then realized that my son was a somebody.

After the war I helped some of the comrades who came for cleansing. You see, everyone who had fought had to be cleansed of the death they had witnessed. There was a particular comrade who came from Masvingo, because people there were afraid of him, as he had not been cleansed by a n'anga, and still had blood on his hands. His own people ran away from him. So he came to me and the *Sekuru* told him that he should not return home, without being cleansed, or else he would meet with misfortune. But he must have forgotten what the *Sekuru* told him, because he left here to go and meet his girlfriend. He was killed by a car while he was on his way to see her.

Now I am leading a much better life. A long time ago I had to struggle to clothe my children and they often went around without clothes. At times, we shared our blankets with the children. Sometimes they were too old to share a blanket with us, but there was no alternative. I could not leave them to die of cold.

There is a great difference in our lives today. We can sell our grain at the Grain Marketing Board. People from the agricultural extension unit have come to teach us and the government has encouraged us all to work for ourselves. Everyone must do so, because nothing comes by itself.

Now we realize that everyone has a part to play. The war opened our eyes and life has changed. Once it was rare to find a family which had tea and bread every morning, but now it is common: almost everyone can afford something for themselves. People learn from others.

When the war came, we did not like it, we thought our children were mad. They told us they were fighting to liberate us but we did not understand what they meant. Before the war the ordinary man was nothing; his home was just nothing. Only teachers, demonstrators, and so on had nice houses, but now everyone can improve their

---

* Chef – commonly used in Zimbabwe today to mean an important person.

homes, and some ordinary people have better homes than those who are employed. This is the result of the war that we fought, cooked sadza for and spent sleepless nights thinking about.

If the women had not helped, the comrades would have starved and perished. You can't walk carrying weapons for such long distances as those boys did, without eating. It is impossible. So the women who provided the food worked as hard as the comrades themselves did.

In the future, only those children who are educated will be able to lead a better life. If a child is not interested in learning, there is no future for that child. Zimbabwe is now free and life is good for those who are educated.